Journal of Semitic Studies Supplement 5

ANCIENT YEMEN

Some General Trends of Evolution of the Sabaic Language and Sabaean Culture

by

Andrey Korotayev

Published by Oxford University Press
on behalf of the University of Manchester

1995

Oxford University Press, Walton Street, Oxford OX2 6DP
Oxford New York
Athens Auckland Bangkok Bombay
Calcutta Cape Town Dar es Salaam Delhi
Florence Hong Kong Istanbul Karachi
Kuala Lumpur Madras Madrid Melbourne
Mexico City Nairobi Paris Singapore
Taipei Toronto Tokyo

and associated companies in
Berlin Ibadan

Oxford is a trade mark of Oxford University Press

Published in the United States
by Oxford University Press Inc., New York

A catalogue for this book is available from the British Library

Library of Congress Cataloguing in Publication Data
(Data available)

ISSN 0022-4480
ISBN 0-19-922237-1

Subscription information for the *Journal of Semitic Studies* is available from

Journals Customer Services
Oxford University Press
Walton Street
Oxford OX2 6DP
UK

Journals Marketing Department
Oxford University Press
2001 Evans Road
Cary, NC 27513
USA

Printed by the Charlesworth Group, Huddersfield, UK, 01484 517077

CONTENTS

LIST OF TABLES

ACKNOWLEDGEMENTS

My deepest gratitude goes to Dr G.M. Bauer (Moscow), Professor A.G. Lundin (St. Petersburg), Professor G.Rex Smith (Manchester), Dr John Healey (Manchester), Dr D.V. Deopik (Moscow), Mrs Tatyana Korotayev (Moscow), Mrs Judith Willson (Manchester) and Mrs Olga Vasylchenko (Kiev) for their help in the preparation of this book.

Some parts of this book have already appeared separately. I am grateful to the editors of these publications for their kind cooperation in granting permission to publish here the revised and modified versions of their texts. The following parts originally appeared in:

1. Part a.3. of the Introduction - *Bulletin of the School of Oriental and African Studies*. 57 (1994);
2. Chapter II - *New Arabian Studies*. 2 (1994);
3. Chapter IV - *Journal of the Economic and Social History of the Orient*. 38 (1995).

NOTES ON TRANSLITERATION AND TRANSCRIPTION SYSTEMS

The following transcription and transliteration symbols have been used to represent Epigraphic South Arabian and Arabic graphemes:

Epigraphic South Arabian Graphemes	**Arabic Graphemes**	**Transcription Symbols**	**Transliteration Symbols**
𐩱	ء	’	’
𐩨	ب	b	b
𐩩	ت	t	t
𐩻	ث	ṯ	th
𐩴		g	g
	ج	ǧ	j
𐩢	ح	ḥ	ḥ
𐩭	خ	ḫ	kh
𐩵	د	d	d
𐩸	ذ	ḏ	dh
𐩧	ر	r	r
𐩹	ز	z	z
𐩪	س	$s = s^1$	s

𐩦		s²	sh
	ش	š	sh
𐩮	ص	ṣ	ṣ
𐩳	ض	ḍ	ḍ
𐩷	ط	ṭ	ṭ
𐩼	ظ	ẓ	ẓ
𐩲	ع	ᶜ	ᶜ
𐩶	غ	ġ	ġh
𐩰	ف	f	f
𐩤	ق	q	q
𐩫	ك	k	k
𐩡	ل	l	l
𐩣	م	m	m
𐩬	ن	n	n
𐩠	ه	h	h
𐩥	و	w	w
𐩺	ي	y	y
𐩯		s³	s³

ā - long a; ū - long u; ī - long i.

Transliteration is confined to proper names, terms, book titles and article headings.

In this book the ancient South Arabian consonants are rendered outside the direct quotations from the inscriptions as if they occurred in Modern Arabic words; the ancient pronunciation of the sibilants, however, seems to have been different from the modern one (see e.g. Bauer 1966, 38-40; Beeston 1962 a; 1962 b, 13-14; 1984 b, 8-9; Robin 1991 g, 92 &c).

To Tanya and Sonya

GENERAL INTRODUCTION

a. Some terms and notions

a.1. The periods of the ancient South Arabian history

In this book the history of ancient South Arabia is divided in three main periods:

a. the Ancient Period (roughly speaking, the 1st millennium BC). The Ancient Period can be subdivided into two sub-periods: Ancient Sub-Period I (the Most Ancient Sub-Period, the Sub-Period of the *Mukarrib*s of Saba', roughly speaking the first half of the 1st millennium BC) and Ancient Sub-Period II (roughly speaking the Sub-Period of the Traditional Kings of Saba', the second half of the 1st millennium BC).

b. The Middle Period (the 1st century BC - 4th century AD, roughly speaking the Period of the Kings of Saba' and dhū-Raydān).

c. The Late ("Monotheistic") Period (the end of the 4th century - the 6th century AD, roughly speaking the Period of the Kings with Long Royal Titles).[1]

---

[1] While using the Period names derived from the respective monarchical titles it is necessary to take into consideration the following points:

a. the *mukarrib*s of Saba' seem to have been the kings of Saba' in the same time (the title of *mukarrib* was much more important than the "royal" one in the Ancient Period, and those with the former title would not usually mention the latter).

b. "The Sub-Period of the Traditional Kings of Saba'" is not relevant for South Arabian history as a whole, because in this Sub-Period the Sabaean kings (who seem to have lost the *mukarrib* title by that time) were not dominant in South Arabia.

c. During the Period of the Kings of Saba' and dhū-Raydān a considerable number of Mārib kings had the title "king of Saba'" (without "and dhū-Raydān"); yet the 1st - 3rd centuries AD of Sabaean (and Himyarite) history could be called in this way because during this period there was usually at least one king (if not two) with this title: the Sabaean monarch in Mārib could be "the king of Saba'", yet the Himyarite ruler in Ẓafār would always be "the king of Saba' and dhū-Raydān".

d. "The Period of the Kings with the Long Titles" starts almost a century before the

a.2. The notion of *sha^{c}b*

In ancient South Arabia an important socio-political role was played by entities called *'s^{2c}b* (sing.: *s^{2c}b*), *sha^{c}b*s, and their institutions. In most of the Ancient Period *sha^{c}b* was usually a politically autonomous or even independent territorial community, occupying an area of several dozen square kilometres. Such a community would usually have a distinct central settlement, *hagar* (*hgr*), a communal religious cult of the tutelary deity of the *sha^{c}b*, a more or less unified irrigation system and so on. The political leader of such a community would be very often called *mlk*, "king"[2] (though he might have had another title, like *bkr*, "first-born").[3]

In the Yemeni Highlands of the Middle Period we find a much more complicated situation. As has been demonstrated by Robin, the Middle Sabaic notion of *sha^{c}b* designated in different contexts quite different types of collectivities which constituted a certain structural hierarchy (Robin 1979, 2-3; 1982 a, I, 71-77; 1982 b, 22-25).

*Sha^{c}b*s of the first order (= *sha^{c}b*s1) were quite amorphous ethno-cultural entities lacking any political centralization.[4] Each of such communities cohered because of its common tribal name, common tribal deity, and some other common cultural features like "tribal" calendar, eponym &c. Such ethno-cultural entities occupied territories of several thousand square kilometres each. Robin denotes these formations as "confédérations" (Robin 1979, 2-3; 1982 a, I, 71-72; 1982 b, 22-23), but it is also quite possible to speak here about the tribe as an ethnic unit (Malinowski's "tribe-nation" [1947, 252-258]).

*Sha^{c}b*1 may include 2-3 *sha^{c}b*s2 which were considerably more politically centralized entities, occupying territories of several hundred square kilometres and headed by *'qwl*, "*qayl*s" (Robin 1979, 2-3; 1982 a, I, 71-93; 1982 b, 22-24). *Sha^{c}b*s2 are most often denoted as "tribes" (*tribu, Stamm, plemya*: Rhodokanakis 1927, 119; Hartmann 1909 [1978], 216-217; Lundin 1971, 205, 221, 232, 236; Beeston 1972 a,

---

Monotheistic Period.

[2] See for example R 3945, 7, 15, 17, 18; Beeston 1972 a, 260; 1975 c, 191; Lundin 1971, 217; 1973 a, 166; 1979 b, 152; Bāfaqīh 1988, 27 &c.

[3] R 3946,8.

[4] If they were not identical with *sha^{c}b*s of the second order (= *sha^{c}b*s2).

258; Robin 1982 a, I, 71-77; &c). This designation seems to be correct if one considers the tribe a political, rather than an ethnic unit, i.e. "tribe-state" as distinct from "tribe-nation" according to Malinowski (1947, 259-261). Robin provides serious counter-arguments against the understanding of the political leaders of *sha*^{c}*b*s2, *qayl*s, as something like *shaykh*s, "chiefs" of the modern Yemeni tribes, and on this basis argues against rendering of *'qwl* (pl. for *qwl/qyl*) as "chiefs of tribes" (Robin 1982 a, I, 83-84). However, it should be kept in mind that the *sha*^{c}*b*2 conforms completely to the definition of chiefdom understood as "an intermediate form of political structure that already has a centralized administration and a hereditary hierarchy of rulers and nobility, where social and property inequality is present, but that still lacks a formal and certainly a legalized apparatus of coercion" (Vasilyev 1980, 182; for the general theory of chiefdom see for example Earle 1987; 1991). I would stress that within the context of this theory the rendering of *qayl* as "chief" seems to be quite acceptable.

It was the *sha*^{c}*b*2 that played an extremely important role in the political system of the Middle Sabaean cultural-political area.

Finally, each *sha*^{c}*b*2 usually included several *sha*^{c}*b*s of the third, lowest, order (= *sha*^{c}*b*3) occupying territories of several dozen square kilometres. *Sha*^{c}*b*s of this order were quite compact autonomous territorial entities with a marked central settlement, *hagar* (which usually gave its name to a whole *sha*^{c}*b*3), a communal religious cult (see for example Robin/al-Mashamayn 1) and so on. *Sha*^{c}*b*3 could be designated as "local community", but it may be also considered as "section" of tribe (cp. for example: Evans-Pritchard 1940 [1967], 139-147). As one can see, *sha*^{c}*b*s3 of the Middle Period closely resemble in some respects the Ancient *sha*^{c}*b*s. However, the difference is also significant. The *sha*^{c}*b*s3 of the Middle Period were considerably less autonomous, they usually had no formal political leaders, and it is completely unthinkable to find a *mlk*, "king", at the head of such a community.

a.3. Sabaic, Sabaean, "Sabaean"

As is evident from the title of this book, I accept Beeston's proposal to refer "to linguistic data as Minaic, Sabaic, Qatabanic and Hadramitic, leaving Minaean etc. for non-linguistic contexts" (Beeston 1987 b, 13). His argument (at least with respect to the distinction between "Sabaean" and the "Sabaic") looks entirely convincing:

> "The Sabaeans were the inhabitants of the area around Ma'rib. But they shared a common language (no doubt with dialectal varieties) with the peoples of the desert fringes between Ma'rib and Wadi al-Jawf, of a considerable part of Wadi al-Jawf itself, and of the high plateaux lying in the angle of those two areas - Arḥab, Qāᶜ al-Bawn, Qāᶜ Ṣanᶜā' etc. It is dubious whether these other peoples would have called themselves Sabaeans,[5] and it might be preferable therefore to term the language Sabaic rather than Sabaean" (Beeston 1979 a, 115).

However, though Beeston's proposal is very reasonable, it does not solve the whole problem; and the problem is that, in addition to the common language, the above-mentioned peoples (*shaᶜb*s) shared some common cultural features and common politics with the Sabaeans. So the question remains how to refer to the non-linguistic phenomena related to those peoples. Before answering this question a few words must be said about the circumstances which led to the appearance of the "Sabaeans" beside the Sabaeans proper. A few words are also necessary to argue for the term "Sabaean cultural-political area" rather than terms such as "Saba'" or "the Sabaean kingdom".

The fact is, that from the point of view of the inhabitants of this area (as far as we can reconstruct it), Saba' (*SB'*) is neither a state or a kingdom, nor indeed a country, but rather a collective of people, a *shaᶜb*;[6] and this collective ("the Sabaeans") included only a part of the members of the political formation lead by "the king of Saba'"[7] (who would also have the title "*mukarrib* of Saba'" in the first half of the Ancient Period - Beeston 1972 a, 264-265 &c).

Saba' (="the Sabaeans") are likely to have been one of the *shaᶜb*s, "communities", of the edge of Ṣayhad desert. There is some evidence that very early,

---

[5] I myself do not see any serious grounds for such caution as that of Beeston. I would prefer to say that in all the known ancient South Arabian texts those peoples are **never** called Sabaeans.

[6] As has already been repeatedly stated by Beeston. For example he has drawn attention to the fact that "the Greek text of an inscription (*Deutsche Aksum-Expedition*. Berlin, 1913. Bd. 4, Nr. 4) of the 4th century A.D. Aksumite king ᶜEzānā, who claimed suzerainty over part of South Arabia, distinguishes him as king 'of the Sabaeans' in the plural", hence, "the Greek version shows that Saba is visualized as a group, not as a territory" (Beeston 1972 a, 260, incidentally the same could be said about ᶜEzānā's inscription discovered in 1969, where on lines 6-8 we have practically identical Greek version of the "South Arabian" part of ᶜEzānā's title [Caquot, Nautin 1970]; see also Beeston 1976 b, 3; 1979 a, 115; 1987 c, 5-7 &c). The fact that Saba' **were** a certain group (and not something like a kingdom, state, or a country) is also well confirmed by such expressions of the Sabaean inscriptions as *SB' w-'s²ᶜb-hmw*, "Saba' and **their** tribes" (C 601,9 &c), where Saba', the Sabaeans, are evidently considered as "they", as a certain group of people very often explicitly denoted as a *shaᶜb*, "community, tribe" (C 397,7; Er 24 §2; 31; 32; Ja 647, 23; 660, 14; 662, 3-4, 13-14; 690, 10-11; 703, 8; 735, 8; 740 A, 7, 13-14; NaNAG 12, 22; R 3910, 2; 4624, 5; 4775, 4; Sh 7/1; 8/3; 32 &c).

[7] Beeston 1972 a; 1976 b, 3-4; 1979 a, 115; Bāfaqīh 1990, 71-80 &c.

at the beginning of the 1st millennium BC,[8] the political leaders (*'mlk*?) of this tribal community managed to create a huge "commonwealth"[9] of *sha*^{c}*b*s occupying most of the South Arabian territory[10], and took the title *mkrb SB'*, "*mukarrib* of the Sabaeans". That time this title was quite logical, because these rulers were more important than the ordinary "kings"(*'mlk*) of the ordinary autonomous communities, "tribes" (*'s*^{2c}*b*), and the Sabaeans constituted the core of the Commonwealth. When it was necessary to mention "the Sabaean Commonwealth" as a whole, very reasonable notions were applied - *SB' w-gwm*, "the Sabaeans and every (other) community" in the Most Ancient Sub-Period,[11] or later *SB' w-'s*^{2c}*bn*[12] "the Sabaeans and the communities", and not just *SB'*; to my mind it shows that the Sabaeans (*SB'*) were only an element (though the central one) of the system of the Commonwealth.

The vast early Sabaean Commonwealth turned out to be a relatively short-lived entity. By the second half of the Ancient Period it had almost disappeared. The area under the control (direct or indirect) of the Sabaean kings drastically (by a dozen times) reduced. One of the results of this process seems to have been that the Sabaean kings had lost the title *mukarrib*. What remained, however, from the early Sabaean Commonwealth turned out to be considerably more long-lived and stable than that Commonwealth itself. In the area described above by Beeston, for several centuries after the end of the early Commonwealth of the Sabaean *mukarrib*s (during the second

---

[8] This is supported by the radiocarbon datings obtained by the Italian, Russian, American and French archaeologists (Sauer *et al.* 1988, 91, 100; de Maigret, Robin 1989, 278-291; Breton 1991; Sedov 1992) as well as by the data of Suhu texts (Liverani 1991), the Assirian royal inscriptions (Pritchard 1950, 284-286; Lundin 1971, 99; Eph^{c}al 1982; Knauf 1989, 85-86; Liverani 1991, 1, 4-5 &c), the Old Testament (I Kings 10, 1-13; II Chronicles 9, 1-12; Jeremiah 6, 20; Ezekiel 27, 22-24; 38, 13; Isaiah 45, 14; 60, 6) &c. See also v. Wissmann 1982.

[9] The term is proposed by Beeston (1972 a, 259).

[10] Bauer 1989, 155; Beeston 1972 a, 259; Breton 1988, 11,114; 1989, 152; Drewes 1980; de Maigret, Robin 1989, 278-291; Pirenne 1979, 49; 1990, 35-42, 46-49, 128-129; Robin 1987 b; Ja 2892-2896 &c.

[11] See e.g. Ja 2848.

[12] See for example Qatabanic R 3858,4, Sabaic C 375 = Ja 550,2 or an analogous formula in Minaic R 2980 bis (= M 203),7 &c; see also Rhodokanakis 1922, 41-95; Beeston 1972 a, 259. The use of the indefinite *gwm* in the Most Ancient Sub-Period might have reflected the idea that the Sabaean "Commonwealth" included every *gw*, i.e. all the Southern Arabian communities, it might be a reflection of the Most Ancient Sabaeans' claim to dominate over the whole of the South Arabia; whereas the more recent formula with the determinate *'s*^{2c}*bn* must reflect the more recent situation of the second half of the 1st mil. BC, when the Sabaeans lost their authority over most of the South Arabia retaining their suzerainty over a very restricted number of the Yemeni *sha*^{c}*b*s. On the Sabaean side it seems to be an unconscious recognition of the existence of the other powers (with their "commonwealths") in Southern Arabia.

half of the first millennium BC and at least till the end of the 4th century AD) we find a group of *sha*^{c}*b*s which not only shared with the Sabaeans the common epigraphic "Sabaic" language and some common cultural features, but also more or less stably and consistently recognized the terrestrial authority of the Mārib kings and the celestial authority of the Sabaean "national" deity Almaqah.

This system consisted of more than a dozen different *sha*^{c}*b*s and Saba' was only one of them, though the most important one. However, even the political leaders of this entity, the "kings of Saba'", would not usually be the Sabaeans in the Middle Period. So there would seem to be no serious grounds for denoting this entity as Saba', or even "the Sabaean kingdom". In addition to what is stated above, the last notion does not seem to be completely acceptable, because it has strong implications of a "regular state". This was not true with respect to the entity under consideration, at least during the Middle Period, when it was more like a system consisting of a weak state in the centre and strong autonomous chiefdoms on its periphery (see Chapter 4 for details). In addition, the notion of "the Sabaean kingdom" neglects the cultural dimension of the entity under consideration, which was as important as the political one. Hence it might be preferable to denote this entity as "the Sabaean cultural-political area".

The other problem of terminology is how to denote the inhabitants of this area. To call them just Sabaeans is evidently mistaken, simply because the majority of them were **not** Sabaeans (*SB', 'SB'N*). So to distinguish the "Sabaeans" (the inhabitants of the area most of whom were not Sabaeans and who would never have been denoted as such in the inscriptions) and the Sabaeans proper (the members of *sha*^{c}*b* Saba', who would be denoted as Sabaeans, *SB', 'SB'N* in the inscriptions) I shall designate the former as "Sabaeans" (in inverted commas) and the latter as Sabaeans (without inverted commas). Hence, for example "the Sabaean clans" in this book will mean "clans affiliated to *sha*^{c}*b* Saba'", like ḤZFRM, GDNM, ^{c}T̲KLN, MQRM &c; whereas "the "Sabaean" clans" will denote all the clans of this area including the non-Sabaean clans of Ḥumlān, Ḥāshid, Ṣirwāḥ, Ghaymān &c. "The Sabaean Lowlands" (with respect to the Middle Period) means the part of the interior Yemeni Lowlands mainly populated by the Sabaeans (areas of Mārib, Nashq and Nashān), whereas "the "Sabaean" Highlands" denote the region of the Yemeni Highlands mainly populated by non-Sabaeans, but constituting an integral part of the Sabaean cultural-political area.

a.4. "The Middle Sabaean cultural-political area"

In general, the area described above by Beeston is identical with the Sabaean cultural-political area in the Middle Period. During this Period, in addition to the land of Saba', this area also included the lands of the following main *sha^{c}b*s2 (see map 2): Ṣirwāḥ-and-H̲awlān (*ṢRWḤ-w-H̲WLN*) to the west of Mārib, Tan^{c}īm-and-Tan^{c}īmat (*TN^{c}MM-w-TN^{c}MT*) and Ghaymān (*ĠYMN*) to the east and south-east of Ṣan^{c}ā', and Ma'dhin (*M'D̲NM*) to the north and north-west of this city. Further north, we would find *sha^{c}b*1 Sum^{c}ay (*SM^{c}Y*) consisting of three *sha^{c}b*s2, Ḥāshid (*ḤS^{2}DM*), Ḥumlān (*ḤMLN*) and Yarsum (*YRSM*). To the west of Sum^{c}ay we would find *sha^{c}b*1 Bakīl (*BKLM*) also consisting of three *sha^{c}b*s2, dhū-Raydah (*s^{2c}bn BKLM rb^{c}n d̲-RYDT*), dhū-^{c}Amrān (*s^{2c}bn BKLM rb^{c}n d̲-^{c}MRN*, with a rather special status) and dhū-Shibām (*s^{2c}bn BKLM rb^{c}n d̲-S^{2}BMM*). To the west and south-west of Ma'dhin we find two other *sha^{c}b*s2, Sihmān (*SHMN*) and Yaqna^{c} (*YQN^{c}M*). In the third century AD the southernmost "Sabaean" *sha^{c}b* of the Highlands was Samhar (*SMHRM*) with the centre in Na^{c}ḍ. At that time the border with the southern neighbour, the Himyarite-Radmanite cultural-political area ran roughly along the parallel of latitude 15° north, and the distinct point on this border was Naqīl Yiṣliḥ[13] (for a detailed description of the ancient tribal geography of this area see von Wissmann 1964 a; Robin 1982 a, vol.1; 1987 a; Bāfaqīh 1990, 156-174).

The Middle Sabaean cultural-political area seems to have also included *sha^{c}b* Amīr (*'MRM*) in the Lowlands.[14] This *sha^{c}b* appears to have differed greatly from the other "Sabaean" tribes (see for example von Wissmann 1964 a, 81-158). For most of the Middle Period the Sabaean kings execised their suzerainty over a vast area around Ṣa^{c}dah (the land of *H̲WLN GDDM*) and the territories of some Arab nomadic tribes (Ja 561 bis, 12-14 &c). However, these regions do not seem to have been an integral part of the Middle Sabaean cultural-political area. It might be more reasonable

[13] Quite strikingly, at present the line between the tribal North and non-tribal South is often drawn precisely at the same place (e.g. Dresch 1989, 14). In general the territory of the Middle Sabaean cultural-political area appears to be almost identical with the modern area of the tribal confederations Ḥāshid and Bākil (see Dresch 1989, 4, fig. 1.2).

[14] As well as some other smaller non-Sabaean communities in this region.

to consider them as the periphery of this system.

The Middle Sabaic inscriptions were composed in considerable numbers, not only in the Middle Sabaean cultural-political area but also in the southern, Himyarite-Radmanite area. That is why in this book the former is often denoted as "the Northern part of the area of the Middle Sabaic epigraphy" (or simply "the Middle North"), whereas the Himyarite-Radmanite cultural-political area is often denoted as "the Southern part of the area of the Middle Sabaic epigraphy" (or simply "the Middle South").

a.5. "The kings of Saba'"

It might look slightly strange that the political leader of the system consisting of more than dozen *sha^{c}b*s in addition to *s^{2c}bn SB'* could call himself (and be called by the others) simply *mlk SB'*, "the king of the Sabaeans".[15] Would it not have been more appropriate to call oneself something like *mlk kl 's^{2c}bn*, "the king of all the *sha^{c}b*s", as was done by the famous Yūsuf As'ar Yath'ar (Dhū Nuwās) in the 6th century AD (Ja 1028,1; Ry 507,[1]) ? However, there is nothing really surprising in this phenomenon. Since the origins of the Sabaean civilization, the kings of Saba' were the suzerains not only of the Sabaean community but also of some other *sha^{c}b*s (though the number of such *sha^{c}b*s differed considerably in the different periods of Sabaean history). Thus the title *mlk SB'* would inevitably imply *mlk SB' w-'s^{2c}bn*, "the king of the Sabaeans and the *sha^{c}b*s" (i.e. the other communities affiliated with the Sabaean one). It would automatically mean "the supreme political leader of the Sabaean cultural-political area", and in such circumstances to add something like *w-'s^{2c}bn* would have been redundant.

The situation would change if someone claimed his suzerainty over another cultural-political area. For example *mlk SB'* did not imply the suzerainty over the Himyarite-Radmanite cultural-political area, so to claim such a suzerainty it was necessary to add *w-d̲-RYDN* to *mlk SB'* (where *d̲-RYDN* denoted the central element of the Himyarite-Radmanite cultural-political system - for details see Korotayev 1994 c, 214).

[15] No doubt this phenomenon is in the basis of the misleading tradition in South Arabian studies of denoting the whole entity headed by the kings of Saba' simply as "Saba'".

On the other hand *'mlk SB'*, "the kings of Saba'" created the earliest (and the largest, before the 4th century AD) "empire" in South Arabia, so it is not surprising that this title acquired very high prestige. Thus even Abraha, or the late Himyarite kings, who were not Sabaeans in any sense, whose realm considerably exceeded even the territory of the earliest Sabaean "Commonwealth" and included the land of Saba' neither as its central nor as its most important part, would place *SB'* in their royal titles immediately after *mlk*, before the denomination of all the other parts of their realms.

This phenomenon is not without some analogies in the other parts of the ancient world. For example, in ancient Mesopotamia the earliest[16] "commonwealth" (whose organization seems to have been surprisingly similar to that of the Sabaean one, notwithstanding the great distance both in space and in time between the two) was created by the Kish community. This "commonwealth" appears to have been even more short-lived than the Sabaean one. However, centuries after the end of the hegemony of Kish in Mesopotamia, when this city became relatively unimportant, the Mesopotamian kings claiming their suzerainty over the whole country would call themselves "the kings of Kish" (Oppenheim 1964, 397; Roux 1964, 118-119; Diakonoff 1969, 186-189; 1983, 168; Saggs 1984, 18-19; Yakobson 1987, 8; 1989, 22). The other aspect of this phenomenon is that to denote oneself *mlk SB'* in ancient South Arabia must have meant to denote one's loyalty to the ancient Sabaean (and South Arabian) cultural-political tradition; and that is why the decision of Dhū Nuwās (seeking to break the ancient South Arabian cultural-political tradition) to omit *SB'* (as well as all the other traditional elements) from his royal title seems to have been really logical.

a.6. "The Himyarite-Radmanite cultural-political area" ("the Middle South")

In the third century AD this area included the following main *sha*^{c}*b*s (see map 2): the central tribe, Himyar (*ḤMYRM*), seems to have occupied the territory around Ẓafār, the capital of the area; in the North along the border with the Sabaean cultural-political area we find two *sha*^{c}*b*s, Muha'nif (*MH'NFM*, more to the west) and Qasham

[16] The first half of the third millennium BC.

(*QS²MM*[17],more to the east). To the east from Muha'nif might have been situated Alhān (*'LHN*). To the south, in the area of modern Dhamār one would find the *shaᶜb* Muqra' (*MHQR'M*); to the west from Dhamār, in the area of Baynūn - al-Aqmār, Shadad (*S²DDM*) was situated. The area also included vast territories to the south from Ẓafār (see for example Robin - Bron/Banī Bakr 1 = BF-BT 5,4) as well as to the south-east from it where the important tribes Maḏḥā (*MḎḤYM*), (Southern) Ḫawlān (*ḪWLN*) and Radman (*RDMN* - in the region of modern Radāᶜ - al-Bayḍā') were situated (for a detailed description of the ancient tribal geography of this area see von Wissmann 1968; Robin 1987 a; Bāfaqīh 1990, 175-220).

The Himyarite cultural-political area included the main parts of the more ancient Qatabanian cultural-political area (von Wissmann 1964 b; 1968), and at least the Sabaeans seem to have considered the Himyarites as the Qatabanian "heirs", as they explicitly denoted the main inhabitants of this area as *wld ᶜM* "children of (the deity) ᶜM" (see for example Ja 589, 10: *'s²ᶜb w-msyrt ḤMYRM wld-ᶜM* "tribes and armies of the Himyarites, the children-of-ᶜM", or: Ja 577, 2: *'s²ᶜb ḤMYRM wld-ᶜM* "tribes of the Himyarites, the children-of-ᶜM"; see also: Ja 576, 16; 578, 7, 18), just as the inhabitants of the Ancient Qatabanian political area denoted themselves - see for example R 3550, 1-2: *YDᶜ'B ḎBYN bn S²HR mkrb QTBN w-kl(2.)wld-ᶜM*, "YDᶜ'B ḎBYN son of S²HR, *mukarrib* of Qatabān and all the children-of-ᶜM"; see also: R 3675; 3858, 4; 3880, 1-2; 3881 (+ TSb [CIAS I 47.11/b2]), 1a; 3946, 2; 4328, 1-3; 4337A, 5; &c. As we shall see below, the Qatabanian legacy might indeed have played an important role in the formation of the Himyarite-Radmanite cultural-political area. However, the Himyarites themselves seem to have been much more interested in the Sabaean legacy than the Qatabanian one. The Himyarite kings consistently called themselves (and were as consistently called by their subjects[18]) *'mlk SB' w-ḏ-RYDN*, "the kings of Saba' and dhū-Raydān" (incidentally always placing Saba' before dhū-Raydān), thus claiming (sometimes not without success) their suzerainty over the

---

[17] Qasham (*QS²MM*) was in fact the southern part of *shaᶜb*1 Dhimrī (*ḎMRY*) which northern part (Samhar) belonged to the Sabaean cultural-political area (Robin 1987 a).

[18] But naturally not by the "Sabaeans" when they were independent from Ẓafār (with only one exception [Ja 631, 26-27] which can be easily explained by the exceptional circumstances described on lines 17-36 of this inscription).

Sabaean cultural-political area.[19] Sabaic[20] (sometimes with the evident Qatabanic influence) was used in the Himyarite-Radmanite cultural-political area much more widely than Qatabanic &c.

a.7. Sabaic "titles"

The word "title" is used in this book in a conventional way; here it designates any piece of information given by the authors of an inscription in the initial formulae of the official self-identification, in addition to their personal names, patronymics and clan names. For example, in this book "*nisbah*" (the designation of tribal affiliation) is considered to be a "title".

a.8. "Epigraphic activity"

"Epigraphic activity"[21] is the number of inscriptions created in a certain area during a certain unit of time (for example a century). An area producing a large number of inscriptions (or a period when a large number of inscriptions are produced) will be called epigraphically active.

a.9. "Barbarism" and "civilization"

In this book I apply these notions within the Fergusonian tradition (Ferguson [1767] 1966; 1792; Morgan [1877] 1963 &c) where "barbarism"[22] and "civilisation"[23] are considered as a certain stages of cultural evolution.

I would not accept Fergusson and Morgan's theory without serious reservations, not least because both scholars tend to consider "barbarism" and

[19] Those Sabaean kings who claimed their suzerainty over the Himyarite-Radmanite cultural-political area would also naturally call themselves (and be called by their subjects) as *'mlk SB' w-ḏ-RYDN*.

[20] That does not seem to be the vernacular of the "Himyarites" at all (see for example Beeston 1982).

[21] The term is proposed by Deopik (1986, 81).

[22] Very often considered to be based on clan-tribal organization.

[23] Usually characterized by such features as the existence of a system of writing, regular administration, artificial territorial division, private property, &c.

"civilization" as too rigid stages. This seems to be an oversimplification, as it is quite evident that a "civilized" society is not necessarily more developed than every "barbaric" one.[24] Certain "barbaric" societies managed to reach quite a high level of development in many dimensions (some aspects of material production and exchange, political organization &c) comparable with or even exceeding that of the early civilizations. Within certain limits, the same level in some dimensions could be achieved both through the transition to early civilization and through the transformation of the late "barbaric" society. Hence, the second process may be considered as a certain alternative to the first one (see for example: Korotayev, Obolonkov 1989; 1990). However, the Fergusonian set of notions still appears to be useful, and from my point of view no adequate substitute for it has been proposed yet.

When Fergusson or Morgan call any community "barbaric", there is nothing pejorative in it at all.[25] Yet the pejorative associations almost inevitably accompany this word. That is why in this book, in most cases, I prefer to use more neutral "archaic" or "archaization" instead of "barbaric" or "barbarization".[26]

b. Information output of historical sources

The majority of the studies recently published on Ancient South Arabia are publications of new inscriptions and their analysis. Until now this has been the main way of increasing our knowledge of Ancient Yemen, for epigraphy is the most important source for the main part of its history. However, this does not seem to be the only possible way.

---

[24] For example, it would be an evident oversimplification to say that the "civilized" societies of Mesopotamia or Egypt in the 3rd millennium BC were simply more developed than any "barbaric" communities of the European Iron Age.

[25] What is more, the most prominent followers of the Fergusonian tradition appear to "idealize" barbarians significantly. See for example Morgan [1877] 1963, especially pp.561-562, or Engels [1884] 1990, especially the well-known passage beginning with the words "*Und es ist eine wunderbare Verfassung in alle ihrer Kindlichkeit und Einfachheit, diese Gentilverfassung!*" (p.51).

[26] At least in Russia, "archaic" (*arhaicheskiy*) is quite often used to designate post-primitive pre-civilized (or non-civilized) societies. Perhaps it might be reasonable to apply the even more neutral "tribal" for this purpose, yet at least the fact that the term "tribe" is very often used in South Arabian studies to render epigraphic *$s^{2c}b$* (whereas *sha*ᶜ*b*s universally existed both on the barbaric periphery and civilization centres of ancient Yemen) makes it inexpedient. Yet I would definitely prefer *qabalī* for the rendering of "barbaric" (or "archaic") in Arabic.

> "Progress in historical cognition ... cannot be confined to finding and introducing into scientific circulation new groups of historical sources which were unknown to scholars before; not less important is that new generations of scholars get from the previously known sources the data which were inaccessible to historians before" (Danilov 1963, 11).
>
> "...The demand for data which are not directly expressed in the sources ... can be satisfied firstly through drawing into scientific circulation new sources which were not used before, and secondly, through the increase in the information output of the previously known sources. The first way (as any extensive approach) is limited in the end. That is why the working out of new principles, ways and methods of raising the information output of sources becomes a more and more urgent task of the Study of Sources[27]" (Kovalchenko 1987, 108; see also: Schmidt 1969, 44; Pronshtein 1971, 22; Kovalchenko 1984, 9; 1987, 125).

The most important way of increasing the information output seems to be to reveal the "structural" information latent in historical sources.

b.1. Overt and latent information

> "... The contradiction between what is directly, patently reflected by the sources and the information which an historian needs is not insoluble. In addition to directly expressed data the sources contain latent information. This characterizes the multifarious relations immanent in the phenomena of historical reality. These relations are not expressed directly. That is why the information about them is called latent. To reveal it one needs special processing and analysis of the data directly represented in the sources" (Kovalchenko 1984, 9).

The notion of "structural (sometimes termed latent or potential) information" was proposed while working out the general theory of information. The specialists in this field have noticed that any structure represents "information in itself ... in potential, 'accumulated' information" (Vedenov, Kremyanskiy 1965, 85). This conclusion was applied with respect to "social information". Here it has been proposed "to discern two types of information: firstly, the structural information, contained in any products of the human culture ... which ... have an information aspect, as information is a property of material objects; secondly, the free information that takes part in social processes..." (Ursul 1973, 113). It has been stated that "the social systems contain information which does not go through consciousness. A human being either does not know about this type of information, or he has no sufficient scientific and technical means of extracting it ..." (Afanasyev 1975, 56-57).

It is necessary to stress that historians came to similar conclusions quite

---

[27] In Russia, "Study of Sources" (*istochnikovedeniye*) is considered as a special institutionalized branch of historical science (for example you would find separate departments of the Study of Sources in all the major Russian Universities), and that is why I have to apply this term while translating *istochnikovedeniye* into English - A.K.

independently from the specialists in the theory of information. For example, in 1964 Medushevskaya noticed that "information which the original authors intentionally included in sources ... represents only part of the information" contained by the historical sources (Medushevskaya 1964, 15-16). In 1968 she explicitly proposed to distinguish "intentional" and "unintentional" information of historical sources (Medushevskaya 1968, 120; see also: Gromyko 1968, 86). Later the thesis of the presence in the sources of the latent (structural, unintentional, potential, implicit) information in addition to the patent (intentional, actual, explicit, free) information found wide recognition and further development (Kovalchenko 1979, 35, 37-38; 1982, 132-133; 1984, 9; 1987, 81, 110; Kovalchenko *et al.* 1981, 9; Deopik 1986, 95; Kuzishchin 1984, 8; Mironov 1984, 96-97; Pronshtein 1971, 264-265; &c.).

b.2. Information inexhaustibility of the sources

One of the important conclusions of research in this direction is that latent information "constitutes the overwhelming part of social information" (Kovalchenko *et al.* 1981, 9; see also: Kovalchenko 1979, 37; 1982, 133-134; 1987, 110). "That is caused by the fact that the relations of certain objects, phenomena and processes are always more numerous than their direct characteristics; and what is more, as the quantity of the extracted information increases, the quantity of the latent information grows faster than that of the overt information" (Kovalchenko 1987, 110).

Some scholars maintain that the structural information has some advantages over the overt data.

> "Structural information is less vulnerable to subjective influences at the moment of its fixation. It reflects the objective reality more adequately" (Kovalchenko *et al.* 1981, 9; see also: Kovalchenko 1979, 38; Mironov 1984, 97).

The other conclusion is the thesis of the inexhaustibility of the information contained in the sources.

> "The multiformity and boundlessness of the relations which exist between the phenomena of the objective world cause the fact that historical sources contain essentially a boundless quantity of the latent information about the interrelations of the phenomena. The analysis of these interrelations on the basis of directly expressed information lets reveal the latent information. That creates the possibilities for the boundless increase in the information output of the sources..." (Kovalchenko 1982, 140; see also Kovalchenko *et al.* 1981, 10; Mironov 1984, 97).

b.3. Quantitative methods for the extraction of structural information

It has been stated many times that the most promising way of extracting structural information is that based on quantitative methods (Kovalchenko 1979, 42-43, 46; 1984, 9; Kovalchenko, Borodkin 1987, 8; Litvak 1969, 105). They are especially useful in the study of mass sources, for "any attempt to systematize the facts taken from mass sources leads to the application of statistical methods" (Litvak 1969, 105). On the other hand, most ancient South Arabian epigraphy (the main part of dedicatory, construction, commemorative and funerary inscriptions) can be considered as mass sources. However, the quantitative methods of extracting the latent information have not yet been widely applied here. At the same time, the first attempts to apply the simplest quantitative methods to the study of the ancient South Arabian inscriptions have brought very promising results (Ryckmans 1964 a, 9-10; Lundin 1971, 42-46, 107, 123-125; Beeston 1978 c, 15).

b.4. Perspectives on the application of quantitative methods of extracting structural information to South Arabian epigraphic studies

For several reasons South Arabian (and especially Sabaic) epigraphy represents a kind of source fairly well fitted for the application of quantitative methods.

For example, from the point of view of many scholars one of the main obstacles to the application of quantitative methods to historical studies is the difficulty of the formalization of the historical information (Borodkin 1986, 138; Kovalchenko 1969, 133; 1987, 325-335; Kovalchenko, Borodkin 1987, 11; Tatarova, Tolstova 1987, 53; Tolstova 1987, 7). But in the case of South Arabian epigraphy it is necessary to stress that a significant part of the work to formalize the contents of the inscriptions was done by the ancient Yemenis themselves. Indeed, the contents of the South Arabian epigraphic corpus are significantly formalized simply because most of the inscriptions consist first of all of stereotypical formulae. It looks like a disadvantage if one treats an inscription as a unique historical source (see e.g. Beeston 1959, 17), but it turns out to be an obvious merit if one takes the inscriptions as mass sources and tries to analyze them quantitatively. On the other hand, to extract a significant amount of information from such formulae seems to be possible only by using quantitative methods. Thus, their application in this case appears to be a real necessity and not just a tribute to scientific vogue.

I would add that it is not difficult to find the indicators for the identification of such formulae in the text (it is another serious problem for scholars applying the quantitative methods - Borodkin 1986, 138). For example, in the part of the Middle Sabaic dedicatory inscriptions which deals with the authors' requests to the deity, the "protection formula" can usually be identified through the words *nḍ*^{c} and *s*^{2}*sy*, which were not practically used outside this formula &c.

As a result, the corpus of the Middle Sabaic dedicatory inscriptions after entry into the computer in standard Latin transliteration, with the addition of a very limited set of subsidiary signs and the necessary indications of time, place, dimensions, &c, can immediately be considered as a machine-readable data base.

CHAPTER I
QUANTITATIVE ANALYSIS OF SABAIC TITLES

a. Introduction

The Middle Sabaic inscriptions have a remarkable feature: the plural is often used where the singular or dual are expected. For example the Middle Sabaean title *'b^{c}l bytn* ***X*** "lords of the house **X**" (where "house" denotes some kind of a "castle" - prestigious fortified building, a symbol of power) is always used in the plural, irrespective of number of authors (see table 1 below). If an inscription has one author, it looks as follows: ***X*** *bn* ***Y*** *'b^{c}l bytn* ***Z*** "**X** son of (the clan of) **Y**, lords of the house **Z**".

In general several explanations seem to be possible here.

1) One may suppose that in this case we have a title with only one (plural) grammatical form; it might have not had any other (singular or dual) forms.

The counter-arguments against this supposition are as follows:

a) the singular form of *'b^{c}l (b^{c}l)* is quite well attested in other contexts.[1]

b) The other titles used in the plural with one author could be also used in the singular. For example, the title *qyl(qwl)/'qwl* ,"*qayl*/s, chief/s (of the *sha^{c}b*, tribe)" is employed in the plural in 21 of 41 qaylite inscriptions belonging to one author; yet in 18 inscriptions it is used in singular (see table 6 below).[2] The title *^{c}bd/'dm*, "client/s", is used in the plural with one author in 15 cases; but in the other 52 inscriptions it is employed in the singular (see table 12 below). Finally, "*nisbah*" forms are also used with one author both in the plural and singular (see table 21 below). Hence, the convincing explanation of this phenomenon is more likely to be

---

[1] For example C 565, 2 mentions *b^{c}l byt-hmw* "the lord of their house" (i.e. the tutelary deity of the respective clan community); see also: C 567, 2; R 4578; Na NNSQ 22, 2-3; Na NAG 18, 3 (*b^{c}l-bytm*); C 189 = DJE 9 = Gr 25, 2 (*b^{c}l bytm*); &c.; see also Jamme 1947, 122-123; &c.

[2] There are even two curious cases of its use in the dual with only one author (MAFRAY/ d̲ī-Ḥadīd 1, 1-3; 2, 1-2).

social than purely linguistic.

2) Another probable interpretation could be based on the supposition that in such cases we are dealing with a *pluralis majestatis*.

The counter arguments against this supposition will be as follows:

a) such a "title" as *'dm*, "clients", is also quite often used in the plural with only one author,[3] whereas this category of the ancient Yemeni population seems to have constituted the lowest known stratum.[4]

b) In several cases a single author uses one title in the plural and another in the singular (Er 13 §1; Ja 649, 1-4; 650, 1-2; 651, 1-4 &c), or two authors employ one title in the plural and another in the dual (Er 26 §1; Ja 578, 1-2 &c). This fact shows that the phenomenon under consideration is more likely to reflect the character of social relations standing behind respective titles than the status of the authors.

On the other hand, long ago quite a convincing explanation of this phenomenon was proposed: in such cases the title characterizes the clan of the respective person and not the individual person himself (*Répertoire* 1950, 154; Ryckmans 1959, 173; Jamme 1962, 40; &c.). In these cases we are dealing with the clan, collective, and not individual, titles.

b. Titles *'bᶜl bytn X* and *mqtwy*

The most evident clan title is the above mentioned *'bᶜl bytn X*, "lords of the house **X**". That is most explicit if we compare its usage with that of the only[5] frequently employed completely individual (not clan) Middle "Sabaean" title, *mqtwy/mqtt*, "personal assistant/s, steward/s":

---

[3] See for example C 410: (1.) *LḤYᶜṮT ḏ-ḤṮ[Ṯ](2.)'dm ḏ-ḤḌNN*--- "LḤYᶜṮT (of the clan) ḏ-ḤṮ[Ṯ], clients (of the clan) ḏ-ḤḌNN", or R 4229: *(1.) 'LRS^{2}D bn S^{2}L'L(2.)'dm ḏ-'NWYN*--- "'LRS^{2}D son of (the clan) S^{2}L'L, clients (of the clan) ḏ-'NWYN"; see also C 397; 531; 534; Fa 102 = 8; Ja 689; 696 ≈ 697; 725; 726; 2111 (CIAS II 39.11/o7 N2); 2112 (CIAS II 39.11/o2 N7); Na NAG 2; 3.

[4] A clear indication of this is the fact that when the different strata of a certain community are listed, *'dm*, "clients", are always mentioned in the last place - Gl 1573 a; Ja 2856; Robin/al-Mašamayn 1; Madrid 1; &c. However, to be exact it is necessary to say that real slaves (extremely rarely mentioned in the inscriptions - Gl 1376; R 3910) must have occupied a position below "clients"; but it is quite symptomatic that in R 3910,3 real slaves are denoted through *ᶜbdm* (i.e. the absolute singular form of *'dm*).

[5] Excluding the royal title.

Table 1. USE OF THE TITLE *'BL BYTN X*,"LORDS OF THE HOUSE X"[6]

	1 AUTHOR	2 AUTHORS	3 OR MORE
Singular	0	0	0
Dual	0	0	0
Plural	7 **100%**	4 **100%**	7 **100%**
TOTAL	7 **100%**	4 **100%**	7 **100%**

Table 2. USE OF THE TITLE *MQTWY*, "PERSONAL ASSISTANT, STEWARD"

	1 AUTHOR	2 AUTHORS	3 OR MORE
Singular	54 **100%**	0	2 **15%**
Dual	0	14 **93%**	2 **15%**
Plural	0	1 **7%**	9 **69%**
TOTAL	54 **100%**	15 **100%**	13 **100%**

To facilitate the comparison I present these tables below in the following form:

Table 3. USE OF THE TITLES *'BᶜL BYTN X* AND *MQTWY* BY SINGLE AUTHORS

	'bᶜl bytn **X**	*mqtwy*
Singular	0 **0%**	54 **100%**
Plural	7 **100%**	0 **0%**
TOTAL	7 **100%**	54 **100%**

[6] The detailed description of the sources for the tables of Chapter 1 is presented in the notes to these tables at the end of this chapter.

Table 4. USE OF THE TITLES *'B^cL BYTN* ***X*** AND *MQTWY* IN 2-AUTHOR INSCRIPTIONS

	'b^cl bytn ***X***		*mqtwy*	
Dual	0	**0%**	14	**93%**
Plural	4	**100%**	1	**7%**
TOTAL	4	**100%**	15	**100%**

Table 5. USE OF THE TITLES *'B^cL BYTN* ***X*** AND *MQTWY* IN 3-OR-MORE-AUTHOR INSCRIPTIONS

	'b^cl bytn ***X***		*mqtwy*	
Sing. and Dual	0	**0%**	4	**31%**
Plural	7	**100%**	9	**69%**
TOTAL	7	**100%**	13	**100%**

c. "Positive" and "negative" deviation

As one can see, singular, dual and plural forms of *mqtwy* are used in strict accordance with the number of the authors who bear this title. The only significant deviation takes place here in the direction which is completely contrary to that observed with respect to the usage of the title *'b^cl bytn* ***X***; i.e. in 4 cases with 3 or more authors the title is used in the singular or dual. Such a deviation from the expected plural to the dual or singular can be denoted as a "negative deviation".[7] The negative deviation is not at all surprising in this case if we interpret this title as

[7] It is evident that the negative deviation can be considered as a certain indicator of the level of "individualization" of a certain title: the higher it is, the better grounds we have to maintain that the respective title characterizes the status of certain individuals, and not their clan groups, for if an inscription is installed by several clansmen but the title is used in the singular (or dual), it shows explicitly that the title denotes the status of one (or two) of the authors, and not the collective status of his (or their) clan.

strictly individual.[8] Indeed, there is nothing surprising in the fact that only one or two of the clansmen who install an inscription (and not all of them) would bear an individual (and not clan) title.

The usage of the title *'b^{c}l bytn* **X** shows the completely contrary deviation, i.e. from the singular and dual to the plural. Such a deviation will be denoted as "positive".[9] In this case it has its maximum value (100%) both for the singular and dual. Hence, we have quite firm grounds to maintain that these "house-castles" were considered to be the property of whole clans (and not individual nobles).

d. The title *qayl*

Quite clearly expressed "clan" characteristics can be found with respect to such an important Middle Sabaean title as *qyl(qwl)/'qwl s^{2c}bn* **X**, "*qayl*/s of the tribe **X**".

The general picture of its usage is presented in table 6:

Table 6. USE OF THE TITLE *'QWL S^{2c}BN X*, "CHIEFS OF THE TRIBE **X**", (on the basis of all the accessible Sabaic inscriptions)

	1 AUTHOR		2 AUTHORS		3 OR MORE	
Singular	18	**44%**	1	**5%**	1	**4%**
Dual	2	**5%**	1	**5%**	0	
Plural	21	**51%**	20	**90%**	25	**96%**
TOTAL	41	**100%**	22	**100%**	26	**100%**

[8] The only "positively deviant" case here is Ry 515, where two authors employ the title in the plural (and not dual). Yet it is necessary to take into consideration the fact that this text is very late (AD 518 or 523); i.e. it is written at the time when the well-known trend towards the supplanting of the dual by the plural in Middle Sabaic (see for example: Beeston 1954, 315; 1978 c, 21, 25; Robin 1991 a, 175) must have brought the most remarkable results. The general context of the inscription (lines 1-4: *M^{c}WYT bn WL^{c}T N^{c}MT bn MLKM mqtt S^{2}RḤ'L ḏ-YZ'N* "M^{c}WYT son of (the clan) WL^{c}T, N^{c}MT son of (the clan) MLKM, *maqtawīs* of S^{2}RḤ'L dhū-YZ'N") clearly shows that here we are dealing with a purely linguistic and not social phenomenon. Indeed the authors come from **different** clans; hence, here the title is most unlikely to denote the clan status.

[9] In general for Sabaic epigraphy the positive deviation can be considered a certain indicator of the collective, clan character of a certain title; and what is more, the very absence of the positive deviation can be considered here as a sufficient indicator of the individual character of a certain title (even in the absence of any negative deviation).

As one can see the positive deviation here is quite high: **+51%**[10] for the singular and **+90%** for the dual. On the other hand there is a significant proportion of cases when the title is used in the singular (**44%** of the single-author inscriptions), and certainly this fact must be also taken into consideration. For the adequate interpretation of this fact it seems useful to consider separately the usage of the title in the Northern (the "Sabaean" proper) and the Southern (the "Himyarite-Radmanite") parts of the area of Middle Sabaic epigraphy.

As a result we get the following picture:

Table 7. USE OF THE TITLE *QAYL* IN THE **NORTHERN** PART OF THE AREA OF MIDDLE SABAIC EPIGRAPHY[11]

	1 AUTHOR		2 AUTHORS		3 OR MORE	
Singular	1	**6%**	1	**5%**	0	
Dual	0		0		0	
Plural	16	**94%**	19	**95%**	20	**100%**
TOTAL	17	**100%**	20	**100%**	20	**100%**

Table 8. USE OF THE TITLE *QAYL* IN THE **SOUTHERN** PART OF THE AREA OF MIDDLE SABAIC EPIGRAPHY

	1 AUTHOR		2 AUTHORS		3 OR MORE	
Singular	13	**72%**	0		1	**(20%)**
Dual	2	**11%**	1	**(50%)**	0	
Plural	3	**17%**	1	**(50%)**	4	**80%**
TOTAL	18	**100%**	2	**100%**	5	**100%**

These tables could be also presented in the following form:

10 + 56% if we also count 2 cases of the dual in 1 author inscriptions.

11 Tables 7 and 8 take into account inscriptions of the *Middle* Period only.

Table 9. USE OF THE TITLE *QAYL* IN "THE NORTH" AND "THE SOUTH" BY SINGLE AUTHORS

	"THE NORTH"		"THE SOUTH"	
Singular	1	**6%**	13	**72%**
Dual	0		2	**11%**
Plural	16	**94%**	3	**17%**
TOTAL	17	**100%**	18	**100%**

As we see, the use of the title in the South (i.e. in the Himyarite-Radmanite area most of which was under the Qatabanian cultural-political influence in the Ancient Period) differed significantly from that in the North (i.e. in the Sabaean cultural-political area proper).[12] In the North it has almost completely a clan character (there are only two exceptions). However, there are four more "Northern", "Sabaean" inscriptions whose authors designate their status using the singular form of the title (*qwl* - C 317, 1; 642, 1-2; R 4231, 1-2; 4638, 1; see also 4624, 6-7). However, all these four inscriptions come from the Ancient Period (and incidentally I do not know any other Ancient "Sabaean" inscriptions authored by *qayl*s, except, perhaps, Na NAG 16, from the very end of the Ancient Period, authored by a member of Banū Bata^{c}, the qaylite clan which played very important role in the Middle Period). This leads one to the supposition that this title was more individualized in the North in the Ancient Period. Certainly an epigraphic "corpus" of 4-5 inscriptions isnot sufficient for making any decisive conclusion. Nevertheless, as we shall see below, the picture we have found (the title which was used to designate the individual status in the Ancient Period becomes a collective, clan one with the transition to the Middle Period) is not fortuitous, and it correlates quite well with a number of similar transformations which took place in the North at the end of the Ancient Period.

In the South in the Middle Period the title is used as a mainly individual one.

It is also necessary to take into consideration the following. All the positive deviation to the plural in the South is created by only four inscriptions. Yet in one of them (Ja 2862 [= MAFRAY/al-Mi^{c}sāl 7]), from Radmān, the title is used in the plural by a single author, but it is put **before** the clan name. Hence, it cannot characterize the status of the author's clan, but rather it identifies the status of his concrete ancestors mentioned by their names just before the indication

[12] This phenomenon has already been noticed by Robin (1982 a, I, 79) and Avanzini (1985, 86-87).

of the title.[13] Three other inscriptions contain purely collective, clan usage of the title but they come from the area of the tribes MH'NFM and QS²MM, which were situated on the border with the Sabaean cultural-political area, and what is more important, since the Ancient Period they were under the strong Northern influence.[14] Taking into consideration these details, the individual character of the application of the qaylite title in the South in contrast with the collective one in the North looks even clearer.

Hence we have sufficient grounds to suppose that in the Middle "Sabaean" North whole clans were usually considered to be *qayl*s of respective tribes;[15] in the Middle "Himyarite-Radmanite" South certain individuals were considered in this capacity. All that leads one to the supposition that in the Middle Period social relations in the South were more "individualized" than in the North. As we shall see below this supposition is well corroborated by other data.

e. Numbers of authors and forms of titles

Incidentally, the epigraphic material which has been already analyzed above allows one to establish a remarkably regular pattern: persons using the clan titles tended to act together, persons bearing individual titles tended to act individually.

---

13 See also 2 Southern single author inscriptions where *qyl* is used in the dual (the Sabaic form *qyly* in MAFRAY/ ḏī-Ḥadīd 2, 2 and the Qatabanic *qylw* in MAFRAY/ ḏī-Ḥadīd 2, 1, 2-3) and characterizes the status of concrete persons: the author's "father" and "grandfather" in # 2, and both the author and his "father" in # 1 - and not their clan as a whole. Hence, the title here should not be regarded as "collective"; though such a usage, of course, can be considered as "intermediate" between purely individual and purely collective versions.

14 The whole area between the Yiṣliḥ pass and Dhamār seems to have been a part of the Sabaean cultural-political area in the Ancient Period (the territory to the south of Dhamār seems to have been a far periphery of the Qatabanian area in that Period). For example in the Ancient Ja 555,3 a Sabaean official (royal *qayn*) mentions *'byt-hw w-ᶜbrt-hw w-'rḍt-hw w-'ġyl-hw b-bdᶜ s²ᶜbnhn MH'NFM w-YBRN*, "his houses and his terraced fields and his *ghayl*-irrigated lands in the area of the two tribes MH'NFM and YBRN" . Just before that he also mentions *byt-hw ḤRWR b-hgrn GHRN* "his house ḤRWR in the town GHRN", which seems to have been situated in Qāᶜ Jahrān, just in that area. In any case this fact shows a perfect political control exercised by the Sabaeans over the area under consideraton during at least some part of Ancient Sub-period II. See also e.g. C 42 and 43 from Ḍāf with the Sabaean invocation &c. The fact that ḎT BᶜDNM was considered as one of two tutelary deities of QS²MM (Er 40) is itself quite strong evidence of the Sabaean cultural influence. Since the affiliation to one cultural-political area seems to be a necessary condition of the emergence of any tribal unity, the very existence in the Middle Period of ḎMRY supertribe consisting of "Sabaean" SMHRM and "Himyarite" QS²MM (Robin 1987 a) shows that sometimes those two tribes belonged to one political area; and this area (due to what was already stated above) is most likely to have been the Sabaean one.

15 In some respects it seems possible to compare this with the situation in some tribal areas of modern Yemen (whereas the territory of the "tribal zone" of Yemen is more or less identical with that of the Middle Sabaean cultural-political area - see e.g. Dresch 1989, 4-14), where "although there is usually one leader of a tribe (the Shaykh), the shaykhly clan is in fact regarded as a leading group with Shaykhs being interchangeable or inter-replaceable..." (Weir 1994, 1; see also Weir 1995).

Indeed, in the "individualized" South in 18 (72%) out of 25 inscriptions with a precisely known number of authors *qayl*s act[16] alone. In the "clan" North of the Middle Period the *qayl*s act alone only in 17 (30%) of 57 cases. The bearers of the "clan" tittle ***'bˁl bytn X*** act in a similar way - 7 (39%) of 18 cases. On the other hand, the bearers of the most individual[17] Sabaic title *mqtwy* act in a very "individualistic" way: in 54 (66%) of 82 cases they act alone.

These data were arrived at on the basis of tables 1, 2, 7 and 8. The number of the inscriptions with two or more authors was calculated by simply adding the numbers of the inscriptions with two and three or more authors. But in these cases a significant group of inscriptions is not taken into consideration, i.e. those inscriptions which are known to have **either** two **or** three or more authors, due to some lacunae in the beginning of those inscriptions, &c. It is evident that those inscriptions should be also taken into account to provide a fuller overall picture. The summary table of this kind (taking into consideration the above mentioned group of inscriptions) looks as follows:

Table 10. NUMBER OF AUTHORS OF INSCRIPTIONS BY *QAYLS*, *MAQTAWĪ*S AND "LORDS OF THE HOUSES"

	Clan	**titles**	**Personal**	**titles**	
	"LORDS OF THE HOUSES"[18]	"NOR-THERN *QAYLS*"	*MAQTAWĪ*S (MIDDLE PERIOD)	"SOU-THERN *QAYLS*"	"ANCIENT *QAYLS*"
1 AUTHOR	7 **37%**	17 **28%**	45 **64%**	18 **72%**	5 **100%**
2 OR MORE	12 **63%**	43 **72%**	25 **36%**	7 **28%**	0 **0%**

By adding the figures in the both halves of the table above we obtain a

16 In the context of this book "to act" means to undertake the action which is considered as the main subject of a certain inscription, i.e. usually either "to dedicate" or "to build" (with variants).

17 Excluding the royal title.

18 It is remarkable that if we exclude from the sample the "Southern" inscriptions (Er 40; Ja 1819 [= VL 23 = Doe/ W.Shirjān 19] and 2867), we shall get for the "Northern lords of houses" the proportion which will be even closer to that of the "Northern *qayls*" - 5 single authors **(31%)** to 11 group authors **(69%)**.

summary table which is presented below:

Table 11. BEARERS OF COLLECTIVE AND INDIVIDUAL TITLES (Summary)

	Collective titles		**Individual titles**	
1 AUTHOR	24	**30%**	68	**68%**
2 OR MORE	55	**70%**	32	**32%**
TOTAL	79	**100%**	100	**100%**

The tables show an evident difference in the behaviour of the bearers of individual and collective titles: the former more often act alone, the latter seem to feel "uncomfortable" alone and tend to author an inscription together with some of their clansmen (the number of inscriptions authored by members of different clans is really insignificant).

f. The title *ᶜbd/'dm*

As has been already stated above, the use of "the title" *ᶜbd/'dm*, "client/s", shows certain "clan" features. The general picture is as follows:

Table 12. USE OF "THE TITLE" *ᶜBD/'DM* (on the basis of all the accessible inscriptions)

	1 AUTHOR		2 AUTHORS		3 OR MORE	
Singular	54	**78%**	6	**33%**	2	**5%**
Dual	0		2	**11%**	0	
Plural	15	**22%**	10	**56%**	36	**95%**
TOTAL	69	**100%**	18	**100%**	38	**100%**

At first sight it is quite difficult to interpret this picture precisely. Indeed, in a noticeable number of cases (15 of 69 - **22%**) individual authors use the title in the plural, but in the overwhelming majority of cases (52 of 67 - **78%**) it is used in the singular; and what is more, there is a small but quite visible negative deviation (**-5%** for the plural and **-30%** for the dual). That is why the only possible conclusion here seems to be simply that this title was usually applied as an individual one and only sometimes was it used as a collective designation.

The separate consideration of this title in the North and the South is not valid here, as the overwhelming majority of the cases refer to the North, and the number of the "Southern" cases is too insignificant to make any statistical conclusion on such a dubious basis. Yet another method clearly bears fruit, i.e. to consider separately the use of the title in the Ancient and Middle Periods.

Table 13. USE OF THE TITLE *ʿBD/ʾDM* IN THE ANCIENT PERIOD[19]

	1 AUTHOR		2 AUTHORS		3 OR MORE	
Singular	26	**100%**	5	**71%**	2	**67%**
Dual	0		2	**29%**	0	
Plural	0		0		1	**33%**
TOTAL	26	**100%**	7	**100%**	3	**100%**

Table 14. USE OF THE TITLE *ʿBD/ʾDM* IN THE MIDDLE PERIOD IN THE NORTH

	1 AUTHOR		2 AUTHORS		3 OR MORE	
Singular	19	**56%**	0		0	
Dual	0		0		0	
Plural	15	**44%**	12	**100%**	37	**100%**
TOTAL	34	**100%**	12	**100%**	37	**100%**

To facilitate the comparison, these tables can be set out below in the following form:

[19] The overwhelming majority of the Ancient Sabaic inscriptions comes from the North.

Table 15. USE OF THE TITLE *ʿBD/'DM* BY INDIVIDUAL AUTHORS

	ANCIENT PERIOD		"MIDDLE NORTH"	
Singular	26	**100%**	19	**56%**
Plural	0		15	**44%**
TOTAL	26	**100%**	34	**100%**

Table 16. USE OF THE TITLE *ʿBD/'DM* IN 2-AUTHOR INSCRIPTIONS

	ANCIENT PERIOD		"MIDDLE NORTH"	
Singular	5	**71%**	0	
Dual	2	**29%**	0	
Plural	0		12	**100%**
TOTAL	7	**100%**	12	**100%**

Table 17. USE OF THE TITLE *ʿBD/'DM* IN 3-OR-MORE-AUTHOR INSCRIPTIONS

	ANCIENT PERIOD		"MIDDLE NORTH"	
Singular	2	**67%**	0	**0%**
Plural	1	**33%**	37	**100%**
TOTAL	3	**100%**	37	**100%**

It is not difficult to see that the use of the title under consideration in the Ancient and Middle Period differs significantly. For the Ancient Period one notices the complete absence of the positive deviation and the presence of the strong negative one. In the "Middle North" the negative deviation is absent and the strong positive one (**+44%** from singular and **+100%** from dual) is present. It leads one to the supposition that in the Ancient Period the title "client" was individual, i.e. individual persons (and not whole clans) were considered to be in this type of dependence. With the transition to the Middle Period we observe a marked trend to the transformation of this title into the collective one, i.e. whole clans instead of individual persons began to be considered to be in this type of dependence. The dependent relationships of this type became less individualized.[20]

The remains of the above-mentioned collective type of personal dependence in Early Islamic Yemen seem to have been described by Hamdānī in *Al-Iklīl* when he mentions that the only remaining member of the ancient noble clan Sufyān b. ᶜAbd Kulāl had in Wadi Ḍahr[21] *ṯamānūn^a mamlūk^an min [wuld^i] rajul^in wāḥid^in wa-awlād^i awlādi-hi*, "eighty *mamlūk*s from [the offspring of] one man and the children of his children" (al-Hamdānī 1980, 328), i.e. *mamlūk*s forming a certain clan (or lineage);[22] "the last of the Sufyanids" turns out to have had a whole clan of *mamlūks*. It is very important that al-Hamdānī calls these *mamlūk*s *dumam* (sing. *dummī*): *yuqāl^u li-l-rajul^i al-mamlūk^i dummī wa-hum al-dumam* (al-Hamdānī 1980, 328), because as it has been already noticed (al-Ḥadīṯī 1978, 78; Piotrovskiy 1985, 73) al-Hamdānī's *dumam* is most likely to descend from the Sabaic *'dm*.

g. "Positive deviation from the dual": social or linguistic phenomenon?

As the use of the "title" *ᶜbd/'dm* by dual authors shows the most significant difference between the Ancient and the Middle Period, it is necessary to try to answer this question now.

---

[20] In this respect the Middle "Sabaean" clientage appears rather different from Early Islamic *walā'* which "always bound two individuals, both known as *mawālī*, but never groups" (Crone 1980, 49; see also Crone 1991); though it strongly resembles the Pre-Islamic Central and Northern Arabian clientage which normally "was a relationship between groups" (Crone 1991, 875). There are also evident parallels with Central and Northern Arabia of the 19th and early 20th centuries: "The freedmen (and indeed slaves) of modern Arabia formed lineages of their own, and it was through them, not through their manumitters, that they acquired their rights and duties in respect of marriage, succession and vengeance; and it was to the manumitters' tribe as a political entity that they stood in a relationship of dependence, paying it military assistance and/or *khuwwa*" (Crone 1991, 875; references to Burckhardt 1830, I, 181f.; Jaussen 1948, 125f and Musil 1928, 276).

[21] I.e. practically in the centre of what was the Sabaean cultural-political area in the pre-Islamic epoch.

[22] And the organization of this clan of *mamlūk*s appeared to be so strong and effective that in the end they managed to seize the main part of their patrons' possessions (*jall^u amwāli-him*) in Ḍahr (al-Hamdānī 1980, 328).

Generally speaking, it must be stressed that for the Middle Period the positive deviation from the dual is less significative than that from the singular, because in Middle Sabaic epigraphy a marked trend to the supplanting of the dual by the plural can be observed (see for example Beeston 1954, 315; 1978 c, 21, 25; Robin 1991 a, 175).

However, when the positive deviation from the plural reaches considerable values, convincing interpretation of such a phenomenon can hardly be purely linguistic. It could hardly be fortuitous that the more "collective" Middle "Sabaean" titles are **always** used in the plural with two authors (4 out of 4 cases for the "lords of houses", 19 out of 20 cases for the *qayls*[23] and 12 out of 12 cases for the clients). On the other hand the most individualistic (after the royal) Middle "Sabaean" title, *maqtawī* is **always** used in the dual with two authors (14 out of 14 cases);[24] incidentally the same can be said of the most individualistic, royal, title: when two co-regent kings are mentioned in the Middle "Sabaean" inscriptions, their title is practically always employed in the dual (*mlky SB'l w-ḏ-RYDN*: see for example C 172 + 241, 4-5; 314+954, 3-4, 15-17, 20-21, 26-27; 408, 7-9; Er 5 §1, 3, 5; 6 §2; 10 §2; 19; 20 §1; 21 §1; 22 §2; 23 §1, 2; 24 §2; 26 §1, 2; Fa 3, 1; 76, 1; Ja 877,2-3; Na NAG 8, 21-23; Na NNSQ 24, 5; NAM 2659 [CIAS II 39.11/o6 N6], 13-14; R 3929, 2-3; 4139, 1; 4190, 13-14; 4191 + Ja 624, 3-4; 4962, 11-13, 19-21; Ry 404, 2-3; 538, 7-8, 13-14, 41-42; 548, 9-11; &c.; see also Jamme 1962, 406, 407, 409, 410, 412 where several dozen of such cases occurring in Jamme's collection from Maḥram Bilqīs are indicated). I know only two cases when two co-regents' royal title is used in the plural (*'mlk*: Ja 648, 7-9; 664, 12-15). Both of these inscriptions come from the end of the Middle Period and mention Himyarite kings who by that time had conquered the Sabaean cultural-political area and became the "Sabaeans'" suzerains, and I am inclined to consider these two cases as a result of the above-mentioned linguistic trend.[25] Yet even at the end of the Middle Period, the majority of the

---

23 The only apparent exception is C 314 + 954. It should be taken into consideration, however, that the second author of this inscription does not belong to a qaylite clan and the title is used in the singular, not in the dual. As far as I know, till now the dual of *qwl/qyl* has not been attested in the Middle "Sabaean" inscriptions at all.

24 See note to table 26.

25 One may also take into consideration the Himyarite (but not "Sabaean") tradition of the use of the "royal plural" by the kings.

"Sabaean" inscriptions employ the royal title of two co-regents in the dual (see for example Jamme 1962, 407, 409, 412).

All that leads to the supposition that the most significant difference in the application of the "title" *ᶜbd/'dm* by dual authors in the Ancient and Middle Periods must reflect quite a significant difference in the character of social relations hidden behind this title between those two periods. It cannot be considered as a purely linguistic phenomenon. The above mentioned linguistic trend can explain only a small part of the positive deviation from the dual.

h. Changes in the numbers of authors of the inscriptions installed by the "clients"

It is necessary to state that for this title a phenomenon similar to that analyzed above can be observed: the trend towards the transformation of the cliental "title" from an individual into a collective one is accompanied by a significant trend towards the growth in the average number of the authors of the respective inscriptions. Indeed, 26 (**68%**) out of 38 Ancient inscriptions are installed by individual authors. On the other hand only 34 (**33%**) of 102 Middle Sabaic "cliental" inscriptions belong to individual authors.

Table 18. NUMBER OF AUTHORS OF THE INSCRIPTIONS INSTALLED BY CLIENTS

	ANCIENT PERIOD		"MIDDLE NORTH"	
1 AUTHOR	26	**68%**	34	**33%**
2 AND MORE	12	**32%**	68	**67%**
TOTAL	38	**100%**	102	**100%**

As one can see, there is a significant difference between the Ancient and the Middle Period according to this variable. The ancient bearers of the then individual cliental title tended to act individually as well; in the Middle Period the bearers of titles which were transforming into collective titles tended to act "collectively", together with their clansmen.

i. Patrons of clients

Remarkable results were found when I tried to study who were the patrons of clients in the Ancient and Middle Periods.

Table 19. PATRONS OF CLIENTS

	Clans	Royal power	Individual monarchs	Persons	TOTAL
ANCIENT PERIOD	12 **32%**	0 **0%**	20 **54%**	5 **14%**	37 **100%**
"MIDDLE NORTH"	87 **78%**	22 **20%**	1 **1%**	1 **1%**	111 **100%**

The significant difference between the Ancient and Middle Periods is evident here. It was not infrequent in the Ancient Period for individual persons to act as the patrons; in the Middle Period their proportion among the patrons falls considerably. In only one Middle "Sabaean" inscription do clients name an individual person as their protector in the initial formula of the official self-identification (C 581, 1-3). On the other hand, with the transition from the Ancient to the Middle Period the proportion of clan-patrons increases steeply (from **32%** to **78%**). And another remarkable transformation takes place: in the Ancient Period clients of the rulers indicate specific, named monarchs as their patrons; in the Middle Period they almost always indicate the king in general, without mentioning his personal name. Now they depend not on a certain NS^{2}'KRB Y'MN YHRḤB, but on the king (*mlkn*),[26] not on a specific monarch, but on the Royal Power in general. This transformation seems to be essentially similar to that of the transition from naming an individual person to indicating a certain clan as someone's patron.[27]

Thus, with the transition from the Ancient to the Middle Period the following evidently interdependent social changes seem to have taken place: **a)** clans (instead

[26] As has been already shown by J.Ryckmans, "*le terme* ***'dm mlkn*** *était une expression consacrée, mise en relation non avec la personne d'un souveraine déterminé, mais avec le pouvoir royal en général*" (J.Ryckmans 1951, 198).

[27] *'dm mlkn* seems to be parallel to *'dm bn X* (see e.g. J.Ryckmans 1951, 198).

of individual persons) began being considered as objects of client dependence and **b)** as patrons of the clients;[28] **c)** the average number of the authors of the inscriptions installed by the clients increased. It looks as if individual persons had begun feeling "uncomfortable" when they acted alone, and started trying to act with their kinsmen.

j. "*Nisbah*"

Similar changes (though somehow less strong) can be found with respect to the use of the designation of the tribal affiliation ("*nisbah*"). The general picture of its use looks as follows:

Table 21. USE OF *NISBAH* (on the basis of all the accessible Sabaic inscriptions)

	1 AUTHOR		2 AUTHORS		3 OR MORE	
Singular	44	**85%**	1	**6%**	3	**15%**
Dual	0		3	**18%**	2	**10%**
Plural	8	**15%**	13	**76%**	15	**75%**
TOTAL	52	**100%**	17	**100%**	20	**100%**

[28] The situation differs greatly with respect to the *maqtawīs* of the Middle Period. Their patrons are even more individualized than those of the Ancient clients (see table 20); that correlates well with the emphatically individual character of this title. It stresses again the special position of the *maqtawīs* in the social system of the Middle Sabaean cultural-political area (see in more detail below, part **d**.3 of Chapter IV). Generally speaking a certain regularity can be found here as well: the bearers of more individual titles have more individualized patrons. On the other hand, the bearers of the collective clan titles name more often clans and their certain analogy (the Royal Power) in this capacity.

Table 20. PATRONS OF CLIENTS AND *MAQTAWĪS*

	Clans	**Royal power**	**Individual monarchs**	**Persons**	TOTAL
MAQTAWĪS, MID.NORTH	5 **7%**	3 **4%**	35 **51%**	25 **37%**	68 **100%**
CLIENTS, ANC.PER.	12 **32%**	0 **0%**	20 **54%**	5 **14%**	37 **100%**
CLIENTS, MID.NORTH	87 **78%**	22 **20%**	1 **1%**	1 **1%**	111 **100%**

This time again one has an impression that we are dealing with a mainly individual title which was rarely used as a collective one, and it is difficult to add to that. Yet again, we can get a considerable amount of new information if we study separately the application of the title in the Ancient and the Middle Period. In this case the distribution looks as follows.

Table 22. USE OF *NISBAH* IN THE ANCIENT PERIOD

	1 AUTHOR		2 AUTHORS		3 OR MORE	
Singular	18	**100%**	0		0	
Dual	0		1	**(100%)**	2	**(100%)**
Plural	0		0		0	
TOTAL	18	**100%**	1	**100%**	2	**100%**

Table 23. USE OF *NISBAH* IN THE MIDDLE PERIOD IN THE "NORTH"

	1 AUTHOR		2 AUTHORS		3 OR MORE	
Singular	15	**68%**	1	**6%**	2	**12.5%**
Dual	0		2	**13%**	0	
Plural	7	**32%**	13	**81%**	14	**87.5%**
TOTAL	22	**100%**	16	**100%**	16	**100%**

These tables could be also presented in the following form:

Table 24. USE OF *NISBAH* BY SINGLE AUTHORS (comparative table)

	ANCIENT PERIOD		"MIDDLE NORTH"	
Singular	18	**100%**	15	**68%**
Plural	0		7	**32%**
TOTAL	18	**100%**	22	**100%**

The sample for the Ancient Period is certainly very small, yet the difference between the Ancient and the Middle Period is too large to be considered purely fortuitous (or to be more exact, the probability of it being fortuitous is not significant). What is more, it is very difficult to imagine that the similarity between the changes in the use of the title "client" and *nisbah* is completely fortuitous. Indeed, the trend of this change is similar in the both cases: in the Ancient Period both the title "client" and *nisbah* characterized only individual persons. In the Middle Period a marked trend towards the transformation of these "titles" into collective ones can be observed (though this trend never came to its completion).

It seems that the following changes in the "Sabaean" conception of social relations might be hidden behind the above transformation of the application of those two titles: in the Ancient Period only individual persons were considered as clients of other persons, clans and rulers; in the Middle Period whole clan groups began being considered in this capacity. An individual person in this Period is quite often regarded as a client through his affiliation to a certain clan. His clan is a client of another clan or the royal power and the individual turns out to be a client through his affiliation to his clan. His clan affiliation makes him a client. It seems to be the same with respect to *nisbah* (and the institution of *qayl*s ?).

k. Preliminary conclusions

According to the mode of their application the Sabaic titles can be subdivided into three groups:

Table 25. VALUES OF DEVIATION FOR THE SABAIC TITLES (Summary table)

ANCIENT PERIOD

	Clients	***Nisbah***	***Qayls***
1 AUTHOR	**+0%**	**+0%**	**+20%**[29]
2 AU-	**+0%**	**+0%**	-
THORS	**-71%**	**-0%**	-
3 OR MORE	**-67%**	**-100%**[30]	-

MIDDLE PERIOD

	N	O	R	T	H	SOUTH
	Clients	***Nisbah***	***Qayls***	***’b^{c}l bytn* X**	***mqtwy***	***Qayls***
1 AUTHOR	**+44%**	**+32%**	**+94%**	**+100%**	**+0%**	**+17/28%**[31]
2 AU-	**+100%**	**+81%**	**+95%**	**+100%**	**+0%**	**+50%**[32]
THORS	**-0%**	**-6%**	**-5%**	**-0%**	**-0%**	**-0%**
3 OR MORE	**-0%**	**-12.5%**	**-0%**	**-0%**	**-27%**	**-20%**

Firstly, clan, collective titles with very high values of the positive deviation (equal or close to **+100%**) and very low values of the negative deviation (equal or close to **-0%**) can be distinguished: those include "lords of houses" and the "Northern"

[29] The whole deviation is produced by only one inscription (Na NAG 16) from the very end of the Ancient Period.

[30] The great value of the deviation is created by 1-2 inscriptions and consequently does not give grounds for any definite conclusions.

[31] As was indicated above, the positive deviation to the plural in this case can be explained by the "Northern" influence.

[32] See the previous two notes.

*qayl*s. *Secondly*, it is possible to isolate the group of the individual titles with very low values of the positive deviation (equal or close to **+0**) and sometimes noticeable values of the negative deviation: those include the Ancient clients, *qayl*s and bearers of a *nisbah*, as well as the Middle "Southern" *qayl*s and the Middle "Northern" *maqtawī*s (the same can be said about all the *maqtawī*s in general). *The third group* of titles occupies the intermediate position: in some cases those titles characterized the status of an individual person, in the other cases they would denote the collective status of whole clans. They include the Middle "Northern" clients and bearers of *nisbah*.

What immediately attracts one's attention is the fact that the phenomenon of the positive deviation is strictly confined to the Middle Period[33], and it is attested on a mass scale in "the North". For the Ancient Period it is not typical at all. What is also quite important is that there is an evident correlation between the mode of the use of the titles and the average numbers of the authors of the inscriptions installed by the bearers of these titles (see table 26):

[33] Some cases of the collective application of the qaylite title can be attested for the Late, Monotheistic Period (see for example Ry 520). It is also necessary to stress that the phenomenon of the positive deviation is not confined to the above-mentioned titles only. A very small number of cases of other collective clan titles can be found in the Middle Sabaic (and practically only in the Middle Sabaic) inscriptions: the positive deviation from the dual - *ʿqbt mlkn b-hgrn* ***X*** "governors of the king in the *hagar* **X**" (Ja 619,1-3); *ms³wdt mlkn*,"counsellors of the king" [Ja 2115 (CIAS II 39.11/o3 N1)]; the positive deviation from the singular - *'rs²w* ***X***, "priests of (the deity) **X**" (C 41, 1); *ḥwrw hgrn* ***X***, "citizens /?/ of the *hagar* **X**" (Lu 23 = Graf 2 = DJE 13,1-3) - Epigraphic South Arabian *ḥwrw hgrn* ***X*** seems to denote a certain stratum of the citizens of the South Arabian *hagar*s. Shifman compares the Sabaic *ḥwrw hgrn* with *ḥōrīm* of the Old Testament where it means "the free" and the "notables" (usually as a certain stratum within the "city" community - Shifman 1989, 81). This, of course, leads one to the supposition that *ḥwrw hgrn* ***X*** denotes competent (or even notable) members of a certain civil community. However, it must be taken into consideration that the Hebrew *ḥōrīm* might well be of the root **ḤRR** and thus irrelevant in this case. It is also more likely that the South Arabian denomination of the competent, notable citizens of *hagar*s would be *'bʿl hgrn* ***X*** (Loundine 1973 b; Lundin 1969 a; Beeston 1976 b, 4) rather than *ḥwrw hgrn* ***X***; whereas *ḥwrw* appear to have occupied a position below *'bʿl* (Gl 1573 a, 3-4). Even *'bʿl* would not always be the highest stratum of a civil community, as there could be at least one more stratum (*mr's*, "*city* leaders /?/") above them (Er 13 §8; in Sh 7 and 8 *mr's* [as well as *ms³wd* and *'qwl*] are more likely to be considered as a part of *'bʿl hgrn MR(Y)B*, "the competent citizens of the city Mārib". From my point of view it appears quite clear that *ḥwrw hgrn* ***X*** denotes a kind of formal membership in the civil community of the respective city. Hence, it does not seem strange at all that South Arabians could retain their citizenship with their original city community **X** even when residing in city **Y** (see e.g. Ja 2898 or *Shibʿanu* 1). In any case I would prefer to render *ḥwrw hgrn* ***X*** as "citizens (i.e. formal members) of (the civil community of) the *hagar* **X** (with acertain status within it)", rather than "settlers, immigrants, inhabitants *of town*" (Beeston *et al.* 1982, 73), or "settlers, inhabitants" (Biella 1982, 170); though its original meaning is indeed very likely to have been "settler, inhabitant".

Table 26. NUMBER OF AUTHORS OF THE INSCRIPTIONS INSTALLED BY THE BEARERS OF THE MAIN SABAIC TITLES (Summary)

ANCIENT PERIOD

	Clients		***Nisbah***		***Qayls***	
1 AUTHOR	26	**68%**	18	**82%**	5	**100%**
2 OR MORE	12	**32%**	4	**18%**	0	**0%**

MIDDLE PERIOD

	N	O	R	T	H	SOUTH
	Clients	***Nisbah***	***Qayls***	***'bˁl bytn* X**	***mqtwy***	***Qayls***
1 AUTHOR	34 **33%**	22 **38%**	17 **28%**	5 **31%**	45 **64%**	18 **72%**
2 OR MORE	68 **67%**	36 **62%**	43 **72%**	11 **69%**	25 **36%**	7 **28%**

The bearers of the individual titles act alone in the majority of cases, whereas the bearers of the collective, clan titles tend to avoid acting alone. In most cases they undertake socially important, epigraphically recorded actions, together with some of their clansmen. Consequently, for the titles which were used both in the Ancient and the Middle Periods the following regular pattern can be detected: the trend to the use of those titles as collective ones is accompanied by the trend towards the increase in the average number of the authors of the inscriptions installed by the bearers of those titles.

It is evident that the singular, dual and plural forms of the titles depend on the character of their use and the number of the authors of the respective inscriptions; as a result such a supposedly purely linguistic variable as the percentage of the singular, dual and plural forms of certain nouns in certain positions turns out to be a synthetic and sensitive indicator of the "individualization" and "collectivization" of the social relations behind respective titles. With regard to this synthetic variable the difference between the Ancient "individualized" relations and the "collectivized", "clan" ones of the Middle Period (with special position of *maqtawīs*) is most evident:

Table 27. FORMS OF THE MAIN SABAIC TITLES (Summary)

ANCIENT PERIOD

	Clients		*Nisbah*		*Qayls*	
Singular	35	**85%**	18	**82%**	4	**80%**
Dual	3	**7%**	3	**14%**	0	**0%**
Plural	3	**7%**	1	**5%**	1	**20%**

MIDDLE PERIOD

	N	O	R	T	H	SOUTH
	Clients	*Nisbah*	*Qayls*	*'b^{c}l bytn* **X**	*mqtwy*	*Qayls*
Sing.	19 **17%**	18 **30%**	2 **3%**	0 **0%**	47 **66%**	14 **54%**
Dl.	0 **0%**	2 **3%**	0 **0%**	0 **0%**	16 **23%**	3 **12%**
Pl.	90 **83%**	40 **67%**	62 **97%**	17 **100%**	8 **11%**	9 **35%**

All these transformations which took place in the North with the transition from the Ancient to the Middle Period were quite logically accompanied by the significant increase in the proportion of clans among the patrons of clients and the decrease in the proportion of individuals occupying this position (see table 19 above).

In general it seems possible to state the existence of the phenomenon of dissolution of the social status of an individual in the social status of his clan. This phenomenon was quite wide-spread in the "Middle North", whereas it was practically absent in the Ancient Period. To my mind this very phenomenon stands behind the "positive deviation". A person who describes himself as ***X** bn **Y** 'b^{c}l bytn **A** 'qwl s^{2c}bn **B** / 'fln / 'dm bn **Z**,* "**X** son of (the clan) **Y**, the lords of the house **A**, the *qayl*s of the tribe **B**, (or) the members of the tribe **F**, (or) the clients of (the clan) Banū **Z**" is a client, *qayl* &c not in his personal capacity, but as a member of a certain clan. It is his affiliation to this clan that imposes upon him the obligations and gives him the rights connected with the respective title.

This phenomenon seems to be quite typical for archaic societies. "*Je tiefer wir in der Geschichte zurückgehen, je mehr erscheint das Individuum, daher auch das producirende Individuum als unselbständig, einem grössern Ganzen angehörig: erst noch in ganz natürlicher Weise in der Familie und der zum Stamm erweiterten Familie; später in dem aus dem Gegensatz und Verschmelzung der Stämme hervorgehnden Gemeinwesen in seinen verschiedenen Formen*" (Marx 1976, 22). For example, Gurevich, while studying the "barbarian societies" of early Medieval Europe, maintained such characteristics of personality there as "its inseparability from the collectivity, and what is more its absorption by its clan, community, extended family; as a result an individual did not conceive of himself separately from his group, his personal status dissolved in the status of the group to which he was affiliated" (Gurevich 1968, 394).

As one can see, all that applies quite well to "Sabaean" society, but with one important reservation: the further back we go in Sabaean history, the more the individual appears to be **in**dependent.

The Middle "Sabaean" society seems to be more "archaic" in some respects than the Ancient one. That leads one to the supposition that a certain "archaization" of the Sabaean cultural-political area took place with the transition from the Ancient to Middle Period at the end of the 1st millennium BC. One of the main results of this process in the area might have been a considerable consolidation of clan organization, and the rise in its importance.

This supposition correlates quite well with the results of the analysis of the Sabaic onomastic formulae by Avanzini who comes to the following conclusions: in the Middle Period **Y** of the basic onomastic formula ***X** bn **Y*** was practically always a clan ("family") name (Avanzini 1991, 22). Yet "*la formule onomastique composée de deux membres avec nom de famille n'est pas toujours attestée dans la documentation sabéenne; il apparaît déjà clairment, après une première observation, que la documentation de la ville de Mārib et des régions voisines de la période des moukarribs de Saba, c'est-à-dire au début de la documentation, donne des indications différentes. Dans la formule onomastique: **X** bn **Y**, **Y** est généralement le nom du père et non de la famille*" (Avanzini 1991, 22). On the other hand, it is difficult not to agree with the following point Avanzini maintains with respect to the Sabaic onomastic formulae: "*Le nom individuel reste l'élément principal d'identification, mais* *l'individu est intégré à l'intérieur du groupe social soit en privilégiant le rapport avec son père soit en privilégiant le rapport avec sa lignée*" (Avanzini 1991, 23). So I would interpret the results of Avanzini's study of the Sabaic onomastic formulae as another important piece of evidence in support of the supposition that the Sabaean clan organization had become much stronger by the end of the Ancient Period than it was at its beginning.

In the following chapters I shall try to show that this supposition fits quite well into the general picture of ancient South Arabian history.

NOTES TO THE TABLES OF CHAPTER 1

Note to table 1: this table has been made on the basis of all the accessible inscriptions. Most of them come from the Sabaean cultural-political area of the Middle Period (= the Northern part of the area of the Middle Sabaic epigraphy). In this table (as well as in all the other tables) only titles explicitly mentioned by the authors in the initial formulae of their official self-identification have been taken into consideration.

1 AUTHOR - **Plural:** Er 22 §1; 40, 1; Ja 562, 1-2; 564, 1-2; 651, 1-4; 695, 1-3; 2867, 1-3.

2 AUTHORS - **Plural:** C 628 [= Fa 65 bis], 1-2; Gl 1320/I ≈ II, 1-3; Ja 670, 1-3.

3 OR MORE - **Plural:** C 172, 1 /?/; Ja 616, 1-3; 716, 1-3; 718, 1-4; 1819 [= VL 23 = Doe/W.Shirjān 19], 1-5; Na NAG 8, 1-5; Ry 538, 1-4.

Note to table 2: the table is made on the basis of all the accessible inscriptions. The overwhelming majority of them come from the Sabaean cultural-political area of the Middle Period (= the Northern part of the area of the Middle Sabaic epigraphy).

1 AUTHOR - **Singular:** C 140 (= Ga 31 [NES I/1] = DJE 24), 1-2; 226, 1-2; 289, 6; 352, 1-3; 405, 1-2; 407, 1-5; 447, 1-2; 528 [= Haram 30], 1-2; DJE 22; Er 13 §1; 15 §1; 20 §1; Gl 1540, 1-3; Gl A 788, 1; Ja 579, 1-4; 580, 1-3; 581, 1-3; 582, 1-5; 583 + 807, 1-4; 612, 1-5; 613, 1-5; 646, 1-4; 649, 1-5; 650, 1-3; 651, 1-7; 673, 1; 690, 1-3; 691 (= AM 851 = NAM 212 [CIAS II 39.11/ o7 N5]), 1-2; 708 (= NAM 1626 [CIAS II 39.11/ o2 N6]), 1-4; 710, 1; 739, 1-4; 749, 1-3; 757 bis (= NAM 1852 [CIAS II 39.11/ o9 N1]), 1-3; 758, 1-3; 2110 (= AM 848 = NAM 430 [CIAS II 39.11/ o2 N8]), 1-4; 2114 (= AM 856 = NAM 1410 [CIAS II 39.11/o5 N2]), 1-4; 2116 (= AM 858 = NAM 431 [CIAS II 39.11/ o4 N1]), 1-2; 2118 (= AM 862 = NAM 323 [CIAS II 39.11/o3/ N9]), 1-2; 2119 (= AM 864 = NAM 2372 [CIAS II 39.11/o7 N8]), 1-5; 2356 c [= VL 29c = Shirjān 9], 1-3; 2860 a; an; 2959 f; Na NAG 1, 1-3; Na NNSQ 14, 1-3; Pirenne/ sha'b Ma'alaja 1; R 3929, 1-4; 4107; 4420; 4577; Ry 513, 1-3; 514, 1-4; 592 A, 1-2; YM 394 [CIAS I 39.11/o6 N2], 1-2;

2 AUTHORS - **Dual:** C 314 + 954, 1-5; Er 26 §1; 27 §1; 69, 1-5; Fa 120, 1-3; Ja 572 (+ 573 + 593), 1-3; 578, 1-4; 614, 1-5; 632, 1-2; 652, 1-6; 700 (+ 814), 1-2; 713, 1-5; 2113 (= AM 855 = NAM 1448 [CIAS II 39.11/ o3 N5]), 1-3; Na NAG 11 [= Er 25], 1-8;

2 AUTHORS - **Plural:** Ry 515, 1-4;

3 AND MORE - **Singular:** Er 23 §1 /?/; Gl 1537, 1-2;

3 AND MORE - **Dual:** Er 21 §1; Kortler 2, 1-7;

3 AND MORE - **Plural:** C 287, 3-11, 12-15; Er 33 §1; Ja 615, 1-8; 616, 1-6; 661, 1-3; 2355 [= Shirjān 2], 1-9; Ry 538, 1-8; YM 438 [CIAS I 39.11/ o6 N 3], 3.

Note to table 6: the overwhelming majority of the Sabaic "qaylite" inscriptions (but not all of them) belongs to the Middle Period.

Description of cases:

1 AUTHOR - **Singular:** BF-BT 2, 1-2; BR/Yanbuq 38, 1-3; C 317, 1; 642, 1-2; 658, 1-2; Ja 489 A, 1; 2864, 1-2; 2867, 1; MAFRAY/ Sāri^{c} 6, 1-2; R 3958, 1-2; 4196, 1; 4231, 1-2; YMN 3, 1-2; 4, 1-2; 7, 1-2; 8, 1-2; 9, 1-2; 10, 1;

1 AUTHOR - **Dual:** MAFRAY/ d̠ī-Ḥadīd 1, 1-3; 2, 1-2 (each of MAFRAY/ d̠ī-Ḥadīd 1 and 2 has only 1 author; however, the title seems to belong individually to the author's "father" and "grandfather" in # 2, and it appears to belong to both the author and his "father" in # 1);

1 AUTHOR - **Plural:** C 41, 1; 282, 1-2; Er 1 §1; 5 §1; 13 §1; 22 §1; 28 §1; 40, 1-2 Ja 562, 1-3; 564, 1-2; 631, 1; 644, 1; 649, 1-4; 650, 1-2; 651, 1-4; 695, 1-3; 2862 [= MAFRAY/ al-Mi^csāl 7], 1-4; Na NAG 16, 1-2; R 3990, 1-3; 3993, 1-2; Ry 520, 1-3;

2 AUTHORS - **Singular:** C 314 + 954, 1-2;

2 AUTHORS - **Dual:** MAFRAY/ al-Maktūba 1, 1-2;

2 AUTHORS - **Plural:** C 40, 1-2; 187, 1-3; 315, 1-2; Er 18, 1-2; 19, 1-3; 26 §1; 37 §1; Gl 1320 I≈II, 1-4; Gr 23, 1-3; Ja 578, 1-2; 624 (+R 4194), 1; 629, 1-2; 658, 1-3; 670, 1-5; Na NAG 5, 1-3; 11 [= Er 25], 1-5; R 3968 + 3979 + Ga 21, 1 /?/; R 4187, 1-3; 4677, 1-2;

3 OR MORE - **Singular:** Av. Aqmar 1, 1;

3 OR MORE - **Plural:** ᶜAbadān, 1-2 /? - cp. Robin 1986, 192/; C 24, 1-4; 648, 1-3; Er 4 §1; 6 §1; 7 §1; 23 §1; Gl 1365, 1-3; Gr 22, 1-2 Ja 559, 1; 561, 1-2; 561 bis, 1-4; 615, 1-4; 616, 1-4; 626, 1-3; 666, 1-3; 716, 1-3; 1819 [= VL 23 = Doe/ W.Shirjān 19, 1-6; 2861 [= MAFRAY/ al-Miᶜsāl 9], 1-3; Kensdale 2 /?/; Na NAG 8, 1-6; R 4190, 1-4; 4712 [= Na NNSQ 69], 1-3; Robin-Bron/ Masǧad an-Nūr 1 [= BF-BT 6], 1-2; Ry 538, 1-5.

Note to table 7: 1 AUTHOR - **Singular:** Ja 489 A, 1;

1 AUTHOR - **Plural:** C 282, 1-2; Er 1 §1; 5 §1; 13 §1; 22 §1; 28 §1; Ja 562, 1-3; 564, 1-2; 631, 1; 644, 1; 649, 1-4; 650, 1-2; 651, 1-4; 695, 1-3; R 3990, 1-3; 3993, 1-2;

2 AUTHORS - **Singular:** C 314 + 954, 1-2;

2 AUTHORS - **Plural:** C 187, 1-3; 315, 1-2; Er 18, 1-2; 19, 1-3; 26 §1; 37 §1; Gl 1320 I≈II, 1-4; Gr 23, 1-3; Ja 578, 1-2; 624 (+ R 4194), 1; 629, 1-2; 658, 1-3; 670, 1-5; Na NAG 5, 1-3; 11 [= Er 25], 1-5; R 3968 + 3979 + Ga 21, 1 /?/; 4187, 1-3; 4677, 1-2;

3 OR MORE - **Plural:** C 24, 1-4; Er 4 §1; 6 §1; 7 §1; 23 §1; Gl 1365, 1-3; Gr 22, 1-2; Ja 559, 1; 561, 1-2; 561 bis, 1-4; 615, 1-4; 616, 1-4; 626, 1-3; 666, 1-3; 716, 1-3; Kensdale 2 /?/; Na NAG 8, 1-6; R 4190, 1-4; 4712 [= Na NNSQ 69], 1-3; Ry 538, 1-5.

Note to table 8: 1 AUTHOR - **Singular:** BF-BT 2, 1-2; C 658, 1-2; Ja 2864, 1-2; 2867, 1; MAFRAY-Sāriᶜ 6, 1-2; R 3958, 1-2; 4196, 1; YMN 3, 1-2; 4, 1-2; 7, 1-2; 8, 1-2; 9, 1-2; 10, 1;

1 AUTHOR - **Dual:** MAFRAY-d̲ī-Ḥadīd 1, 1-3; 2, 1-2;

1 AUTHOR - **Plural:** C 41, 1; Er 40, 1-2; Ja 2862 [= MAFRAY/ al-Miᶜsāl 7], 1-4;

2 AUTHORS - **Dual:** MAFRAY/ al-Maktūba 1, 1-2;

2 AUTHORS - **Plural:** C 40, 1-2;

3 OR MORE - **Singular:** Av. Aqmar 1, 1;

3 OR MORE - **Plural:** C 648, 1-3; Ja 1819 [= VL 23 = Doe/ W.Shirjān 19, 1-6]; 2861 [= MAFRAY/ al-Miᶜsāl 9], 1-3; Robin-Bron/ Masǧad an-Nūr 1 [= BF-BT 6], 1-2.

Note to table 10: *'bᶜl bytn* **X:** see table 1 + an inscription with unknown exact number of authors, but there is no doubt that their number was not less than 2 (Ja 671 + 788, 1-3).

"Northern" *qayl*s: 1 AUTHOR: see table 7;

2 OR MORE: see table 7 + 3 inscriptions with "2 or more" authors: C 181, 1-3; Fa 95 + 94, 1; Ja 671 + 788, 1-5. E.g. the beginning of C 181 looks as follows: ... *w]bn-hw* ... *bnw BTᶜ 'q[wl...*, "... and] his son (or sons) ... Banū BTᶜ, the *qayl*s..." (lines 1-2). There is no doubt here that the number of the authors was not less than 2. However, no further precision appears possible: *bn-hw* can mean both "his son" and "his sons" (see e.g. Bauer 1966, 58; Beeston *et al.* 1982, 29), whereas the plural form of *bnw* is not sufficient here to state that the number of authors was more than 2 (see below part **g.** of this Chapter).

*Maqtawī*s of the Middle Period: see note to table 25;

"Southern" *qayl*s: see table 8;

"Ancient" *qayl*s: C 317, 1; 642, 1-2; Na NAG 16, 1-2; R 4231, 1-2; 4638, 1.

Note to table 12: 1 AUTHOR - **Singular:** C 86, 1-2; 397, 1-3; 440, 1-2; 510 ≈ 511 [= Haram 16 ≈ 17], 1-4; 515 [= Haram 19], 1-3; 558, 1-3; 561, 1-3; 572, 1; 574, 1-2; 663, 1; 722, 1-2; Fa 88, 1; 119 (= YM 358 [CIAS I 39.11/ o3 N1]), 1-2; Gl 931; 1208, 1-2; 1636, 1-3; 1734 A; B; Ja 557; 570, 1; 683, 1; 694, 1-2; 711, 1-2; 723 (= NAM 2320 [CIAS II 39.11/ o4 N2]), 1-2; 741 ≈ 756, 1-3; 831, 1; 2870 [= R 4081 N 107 = Gl 1654], 1-2; 2927 b, 1-2; Na NNSQ 55; R 4062 N 186; 4079 N 79; 4147, 1; 4385 [= Bron 8], 1-2; 4405; 4411; 4438; 4444; 4656; 4674 [= Haram 37], 1-2 /?/; 4810; 5102 [= Ry 373], 1-3; Robin/ al-H̲azā'in 33; /Kāniṭ 25 /?/; Ry 394, 1-2; 501 [= Ja 2139], 1-2; 584, 1; 608; Schm/ Mārib 20, 1; 20, 2; 21, 1-2; /Samsara 9; YM 452 [CIAS I 39.11/ r9/ P12 N2], 1;

1 AUTHOR - **Plural:** C 397, 1-3; 410, 1-2; 531, 1; 534, 1-3; Fa 102 [= M.Bayḥān 9], 1; Ja 689, 1; 696 ≈ 697, 1-2; 725, 1; 726, 1-2; 2111 (= AM 849 = NAM 2357 [CIAS II 39.11/o7 N 2]), 1-2; 2112 (=

AM 854 = NAM 1619 [CIAS II 39.11/ o2 N 7]), 1-2; Na NAG 2, 1-3; 3, 1-2; R 4229, 1-2;

2 AUTHORS - **Singular:** C 376, 1-3; 496 [= MAFRAY/ Ḫirbat Saᶜūd 13], 1-3; Ga SF 1; R 4228, 1-5; 4387, 1; Schm/ Mārib 26;

2 AUTHORS - **Dual:** Fa 30, 2-3; Lu 1 [= Ja 410], 1;

2 AUTHORS - **Plural:** C 341, 1; 343, 1-2; 535, 1-3; 544, 1-2; Ja 704, 1-2; 725, 1; 730, 1-3; 2115 (= AM 857 = NAM 1627 [CIAS II 39.11/ o8 N 1], 1-3; Mü 1, 1; Ry 542 (= AM 844 = NAM 1631 [CIAS II 39.11/ o6 N7]), 1-3; YM 349 [CIAS I 39.11/o3 N4], 1-3; 350 [CIAS I 39.11/ o6 N 5], 1-3;

3 OR MORE - **Singular:** C 439, 1; R 5095, 2;

3 OR MORE - **Plural:** C 77, 1-3; 87, 1-3; 88, 1-3; 102, 1-5; 224, 1; 240, 1-4; 339, 1; 339 bis, 1-2; 340, 1-2; 357, 1-5; 416, 1-2; 449, 1-2; 536, 1-4; Er 16 [= M.Bayḥān 7], 1-2; Ga 9 [Ga AY II/6], 1; 14 [Ga AY II/10b], 1; Ga NES II/10c [C 214 + R 3998 + C 199 + R 4001]; Gl 1438, 1-3; 1725, 1-2; A 783, 1-2; Ja 707 (= AM 852 = NAM 2358 [CIAS II 39.11/ o6 N8]), 1-4; 712, 1-4; 2223, 1-3; 2871, 1-2; Na NNSQ 67 [= Gl 1431], 1-2; NAM 281 [CIAS II 95.11/o3 N 2], 1-3; R 3974, 1; 3976, 1-2; 3977, 1-3; 3991, 1-3; 4033, 1-1a; 4063 [= Ja 519], 1-2; 4151, 1-2; 4188, 1-3; 4636, 1-4; 5095, 1; Robin/ Rayda 1, 1-2; Ry 505 [= Ja 2140], 1; YM 396 [CIAS I 95.11/ o3], 1-2 /?/.

Note to table 13: 1 AUTHOR - **Singular:** C 440, 1-2 /?/; 510 ≈ 511 [= Haram 16 ≈ 17], 1-4; 515 [= Haram 19], 1-3; 561, 1-3; 722, 1-2; Fa 88, 1; Gl 931; 1636, 1-3; Ja 557; 831, 1; 2870 [= R 4081 N 107 = Gl 1654], 1-2; 2927 b, 1-2; R 4385 [= Bron 8], 1-2; 4405; 4411; 4438; 4810; 5102 [= Ry 373], 1-3 /?/; Ry 584, 1; 608; Schm/ Mārib 20, 1; 20, 2; 21, 1-2; /Samsara 9; YM 452 [CIAS I 39.11/ r9/ R 12 N 2], 1;

2 AUTHORS - **Singular:** C 376, 1-3; 496, 1-3; Ga SF 1; R 4228, 1-5; Schm/ Mārib 26;

2 AUTHORS - **Dual:** Lu 1 [= Ja 410], 1-2; Fa 30, 2-3;

3 OR MORE - **Singular:** C 439, 1; R 5095, 2;

3 OR MORE - **Plural:** R 5095, 1.

Note to table 14: 1 AUTHOR - **Singular:** C 86, 1-2; 397, 1-3; 572, 1; 663, 1; Fa 119 (= YM 358 [CIAS I 39.11/ o3 N1]), 1-2; Gl 1208, 1-2; Ja 570, 1; 683, 1; 694, 1-2; 711, 1-2; 723 (= NAM 2320 [CIAS II 39.11/ o4 N2]), 1-2; 741 ≈ 756, 1-3; Na NNSQ 55 /?/; R 4147, 1; 4656 /?/; 4674 [= Haram 37], 1-2 /?/; Robin/ Kāniṭ 25 /?/; Ry 394, 1-2 /?/;

1 AUTHOR - **Plural:** C 397, 1-3; 410, 1-2; 531, 1; 534, 1-3; Fa 102 [= M.Bayḥān 9], 1; Ja 689, 1; 696 ≈ 697, 1-2; 725, 1; 726, 1-2; 2111 (= AM 849 = NAM 2357 [CIAS II 39.11/o7 N 2]), 1-2; 2112 (= AM 854 = NAM 1619 [CIAS II 39.11/o2 N 7]), 1-2; Na NAG 2, 1-3; 3, 1-2; R 4229, 1-2;

2 AUTHORS - **Plural:** C 341, 1; 343, 1-2; 535, 1-3; 544, 1-2; Ja 704, 1-2; 725, 1; 730, 1-3; 2115 (= AM 857 = NAM 1627 [CIAS II 39.11/o8 N 1]), 1-3; Mü 1, 1; Ry 542 (= AM 844 = NAM 1631 [CIAS II 39.11/ o6 N7]), 1-3; YM 349 [CIAS I 39.11/ o3 N4], 1-3; 350 [CIAS I 39.11/ o6 N 5], 1-3;

3 OR MORE - **Plural:** C 77, 1-3; 87, 1-3; 88, 1-3; 102, 1-5; 224, 1; 240, 1-4; 339, 1; 339 bis, 1-2; 340, 1-2; 357, 1-5; 416, 1-2; 449, 1-2; 536, 1-4; Er 16 (= M.Bayḥān 7), 1-2; Ga 9 [Ga AY II/6], 1; 14 [Ga AY II/10b], 1; Ga NES II/10c [C 214 + R 3998 + C 199 + R 4001]; Gl 1438, 1-3; 1725, 1-2; A 783, 1-2; Ja 707 (= AM 852 = NAM 2358 [CIAS II 39.11/ o6 N8]), 1-4; 712, 1-4; 2223, 1-3; 2871, 1-2; Na NNSQ 67 [= Gl 1431], 1-2; NAM 281 [CIAS II 95.11/ o3 N 2], 1-3; R 3974, 1; 3976, 1-2; 3977, 1-3; 3991, 1-3; 4033, 1-1a; 4063 [= Ja 519], 1-2; 4151, 1-2; 4188, 1-3; 4636, 1-4; Robin/ Rayda 1, 1-2; YM 396 [CIAS I 95.41/ o3], 1-2 /?/.

Note to table 18: this table (as well as the analogous ones) has been made taking into consideration the inscriptions which are known to belong to two or more authors, i.e. due to lacunae &c at the beginning of such inscriptions the exact number of authors cannot be established. E.g. the beginning of R 4725 (+ 3972) looks as follows: [lacuna...]*MN bnw SLMN 'dm bny WRKN*, "...MN, the sons (of the clan) SLMN, the clients of Banū WRKN". Such an inscription might have three or more authors; but it could have two authors as well. The plural form *bnw*, "sons (of)", excludes the possibility of one author, but it does not exclude the possibility of two. Indeed, as has been mentioned above (see part **g.** of this chapter), in the Middle Sabaic inscriptions the plural sometimes is used instead of the dual, as a result of a linguistic trend towards the supplanting of the dual by the plural. For example, the authors of C 343 identify themselves as *H]ᶜN Y'ZM w-bny-hw YḤMD YĠBR bnw SMYᶜM 'dm bn BTᶜ* (lines 1-2), "H]ᶜN Y'ZM and his son YḤMD YĠBR, the sons of (the clan) SMYᶜM, the clients of Banū BTᶜ", employing the plural form *bnw*, though their number is only two. Hence, the only thing which we can say about the inscriptions of the "R 4725 type" is that they had "2 or more" authors. It was impossible to take such inscriptions into consideration in the previous tables of "three-in-three" type. However, it is completely possible to take them into account in the tables of the present type. That is why there is sometimes a certain difference in the summary figures presented by the tables of those two types - the present table takes into account some inscriptions which could not be

considered in the previous tables. E.g. the number of the Middle "Sabaean" client inscriptions with "2 or more" authors is arrived at by the summing up of the number of inscriptions with two authors (from table 14) + the number of inscriptions with "3 or more" authors (from table 14) + the number of all the relevant inscriptions of the "R 4725 type".
Description of cases:
ANCIENT PERIOD - 1 AUTHOR: see table 13;
2 OR MORE: see table 13 + R 3911, 1; 4349, 1-2;
"MIDDLE NORTH" - 1 AUTHOR: see table 14;
2 OR MORE: see table 14 + C 30, 1-2; 107, 1; 211/ I [= DJE 5/ I], 1-2; 331, 1; 345, 1; 398, 1-3; 432, 1; ᶜInān 29; Ja 812; R 3971, 1; 4030, 1-2; 4142, 1-3; 4648, 1-2; 4651, 1-2; 4659, 1-3; 4706, 1; 4725 + 3972, 1; 4990, 1-2; Robin/ Rayda 4, 1-3.

Note to table 19: The table takes into consideration all the bearers of the cliental status, both men (**'dm**) and women (**'mh**). Only patrons mentioned by clients in the initial formulae of the official self-identification are taken into consideration.
ANCIENT PERIOD - **Clans**: C 440, 1-2; 722, 1-2; Fa 30, 2-3; 88, 1; Gl 1636, 1-3; Lu 8, 1; R 3911, 1; 4189, 1-2; 4349, 1-2; 4385 [= Bron 8], 1-2; 5095, 2; Ry 608 /?/;
Individual monarchs: C 439, 1; 496, 1-3; 510 ≈ 511 [= Haram 16 ≈ 17], 1-4; 515 [= Haram 19], 1-3; Ga SF 1; Gl 931; Ja 557; 2927 b, 1-2; R 4228, 1-5; 4405; 4438; 4810; Ry 584, 1; Schm/ Mārib 20, 1; 20, 2; 21, 1-2; 26; /Samsara 9; Y.85.AQ/17 = Er 43 [/?/ - cf. Beeston 1991 b, 56-57];
Individual persons: C 376, 1-3; Ja 831, 1; R 4081 N 107 [= Gl 1654 = Ja 2870], 1-2; 5095, 1; 5102 [= Ry 373], 1-3;
MIDDLE PERIOD, the North - **Clans**: C 30, 1-2; 77, 1-3; 86, 1-2; 87, 1-3; 88, 1-3; 102, 1-5; 107, 1; 211/I [= DJE 5 I], 1-2; 240, 1-4; 303, 1-2; 331, 1; 339, 1; 339 bis, 1-2; 340, 1-2; 341, 1; 343, 1-2; 357, 1-5; 397, 1-3; 410, 1-2; 416, 1-2; 432, 1; 449, 1-2; 504, 1-2; 536, 1-4; 560, 1-3; 572, 1; 663, 1; Er 34; Fa 119 (= YM 358 [CIAS I 39.11/o3 N1]), 1-2; Ga 14 [AY II/10b], 1; NES II/10c [C 214 + R 3998 + C 199 + R 4001]; Gl 1208, 1-2; 1438, 1-3; 1725, 1-2; Gl A 783, 1-2; ᶜInān 29; Ja 683, 1; 689, 1; 696 ≈ 697, 1-2; 704, 1-2; 707 (= AM 852 = NAM 2358 [CIAS II 39.11/o6 N8]), 1-4; 711, 1-2; 712, 1-4; 721, 1-2; 722, 1-3; 726, 1-2; 730, 1-3; 731 (= AM 853 = NAM 2375 [CIAS II 39.11/ o3 N10]), 1-2; 741 ≈ 756, 1-3; 2111 (= AM 849 = NAM 2357 [CIAS II 39.11/ o7 N2]), 1-2; 2871, 1-2; Mü 1, 1; Na NAG 2, 1-3; 3, 1-2; Na NNSQ 55; 67 [= Gl 1431], 1-2; NAM 281 [CIAS II 95.11/o3 N2], 1-3; 2494 [CIAS II 39.11/ o3 N6], 1-2; R 3956 [= Haram 35], 1; 3970, 1; 3971, 1; 3973, 1; 3974, 1; 3976, 1-2; 3977, 1-3; 3991, 1-3; 4030, 1-2; 4033, 1-1a; 4052, 1; 4063 [= Ja 519], 1-2; 4147, 1; 4151, 1-2; 4229, 1-2; 4648, 1-2; 4651, 1-2; 4656; 4659, 1-3; 4674 [= Haram 37], 1-2; 4706, 1; 4725 + 3972, 1; 4770, 1; 4990, 1-2; Robin/ Rayda 1, 1-2; 4, 1-3; Ry 394, 1-2; YM 396 [CIAS I 95.41/ o3], 1-2;
Royal power: C 397, 1-3; 398, 1-3; 531, 1; 534, 1-3; 535, 1-3; 544, 1-2; Fa 102 [= M.Bayḥān 9], 1; Ga 9 [Ga AY II/6], 1 /?/; Ja 570, 1; 694, 1-2; 723 (= NAM 2320 [CIAS II 39.11/ o4 N2]), 1-2; 784; 812; 2112 (= AM 854 = NAM 1619 [CIAS II 39.11/ o2 N7]), 1-2; 2115 (= AM 857 = NAM 1627 [CIAS II 39.11/ o8 N1]), 1-3; 2223, 1-3; R 4142, 1-3; 4188, 1-3; 4636, 1-4; Ry 542 (= AM 844 = NAM 1631 [CIAS II 39.11/ o6 N7]), 1-3; YM 349 [CIAS I 39.11/ o3 N4]), 1-3; 350 [CIAS I 39.11/o6 N5], 1-3; these are the inscriptions whose authors identify themselves as *'dm mlkn* (with variants);
Individual monarchs: Er 16 [= M.Bayḥān 7], 1-2;
Individual persons: C 581, 1-3.

Note to table 20: *MAQTAWĪS* - **Clans**: C 447, 1-2; DJE 22; Gl A 788, 1; Ja 757 bis (= NAM 1852 [CIAS II 39.11/ o9 N1]), 1-3; R 4577, 1-2;
MAQTAWĪS - **Royal power**: C 405, 1-2; Ja 749, 1-3; 2118 (= AM 862 = NAM 323 [CIAS II 39.11/ o3 N9]), 1-2;
MAQTAWĪS - **Individual monarchs**: C 314 + 954, 1-5; 407, 1-5; Er 13 §1; 15 §1; 20 §1; 21 §1; 23 §1; 26 §1; 69, 1-5; Ja 572, 1-3; 578, 1-4; 579, 1-4; 580, 1-3; 581, 1-3; 582, 1-5; 583 [+ 807], 1-4; 612, 1-5; 613, 1-5; 614, 1-5; 615, 1-8; 616, 1-6; 646, 1-4; 649, 1-5; 650, 1-3; 651, 1-7; 652, 1-6; 660, 1-5; 661, 1-3; 2110 (= AM 848 = NAM 430 [CIAS II 39.11/ o2 N8]), 1-4; 2114 (= AM 856 = NAM 1410 [CIAS II 39.11/ o5 N2]), 1-4; 2119 (= AM 864 = NAM 2372 [CIAS II 39.11/ o7 N3]), 1-5; Kortler 2, 1-7; Na NAG 11 [= Er 25], 1-8; R 3929, 1-4; Ry 538, 1-8;
MAQTAWĪS - **Individual persons**: C 140 (= Ga 31 [NES I/1] = DJE 24), 1-2; 226, 1-2; 287, 3-11, 12-15; 352, 1-3; 528 [= Haram 30], 1-2; Er 27 §1; 33 §1; Fa 120, 1-3; Ja 632, 1-2; 690, 1-3; 691 (= AM 851 = NAM 212 [CIAS II 39.11/ o7 N5]), 1-2; 700 [+ 814], 1-2; 708 (= NAM 1626 [CIAS II 39.11/ o2 N6]), 1-4; 713, 1-5; 739, 1-4; 758, 1-3; 2113 (= AM 855 = NAM 1448 [CIAS II 39.11/ o3 N5]), 1-3; 2116 (= AM

858 = NAM 431 [CIAS II 39.11/ o4 N1]), 1-2; 2860a; Na NAG 1, 1-3; Na NNSQ 14, 1-3; R 4420; Ry 592 A, 1-2; YM 438 [CIAS I 39.11/ o6 N3], 1-3.

Note to table 21: 1 AUTHOR - **Singular:** C 84, 1; 311; 359, 3-4; 440, 1-2; 466, 4-5; 485 [= Bron 3]; 518 [= Haram 49], 1; 532 [= Haram 33], 1-2; 570; 721; 829 [= Gl A 784]; 969, 1; 970, 3-5; Gl 932; 1536; 1538; 1542; 1543; 1636, 1-4; 1637, 1-3; Ja 698, 1-2; 706, 1; 717, 1; 741 ≈ 756, 1-2; 2918 e, 1; f, 1; 2927 b, 1; 2928 a, 1; 2942 a; al-Kāfir 10; Kortler 4, 1-3; NAM 230 (= AM 222 [CIAS II 95.11/ o8 N1]), 1; R 3957 [= Haram 36], 1-2; 4153, 1-2; 4205, 1-2; 4525, 1-2; Robin/ al-Ḫazā'in 19; 20; Ry 605, 1-3; Sh II-93; YM 375 [CIAS I 95.41/ r4], 1-2; 386 [CIAS I 35.91/ o6/ P53], 1; 394 [CIAS I 39.11/ o6 N2], 1; 1064, 1-2;

1 AUTHOR - **Plural:** C 397, 1-3; 534, 1-2; Er 36 §1; Ja 2112 (= AM 854 = NAM 1619 [CIAS II 39.11/ o2 N7]), 1; 2355 [= Doe/ W.Shirjān 2], 3, 4; Lu 23 [= DJE 13], 1-2; Ry 591, 2-3; YM 392 [CIAS I 39.11/ o6 N1], 1;

2 AUTHORS - **Singular:** C 716 [= Kamna 11], 1-3;

2 AUTHORS - **Dual:** C 715 [= Haram 26], 1-3; Ja 401 [= YM 263], 1; R 4663, 1-2;

2 AUTHORS - **Plural:** C 534; 535; Er 27 §1; 37 §1; Ja 693, 1-2; 704, 1-2; 727, 1-3; 2115 (= AM 847 = NAM 1627 [CIAS II 39.11/ o8 N1]), 1-3; NAM 2494 [CIAS II 39.11/ o3 N6], 1-2; R 4663, 1-2; Ry 375 (= AM 104 = NAM 1583 [CIAS II 39.11/ o5 N3]), 1-2; 542 (= AM 844 = NAM 1631 [CIAS II 39.11/ o6 N7]), 1-3; YM 350 [CIAS I 39.11/ o6 N5], 1-2;

3 OR MORE - **Singular:** C 287, 1-8; 349; R 4109, 1-5;

3 OR MORE - **Dual:** R 5095,1; 5095, 1-2;

3 OR MORE - **Plural:** C 102, 1-4; 180, 1-2; 224, 1; 536; Fa 127 [= Haram 53], 1; Ja 621, 1-3; 707 (= AM 852 = NAM 2358 [CIAS II 39.11/ o6 N8]), 1-4; 712, 1-3; 738, 1-3; 740, 1-3; 767, 1-4; R 4188, 1-3; 4636, 1-4; Ry 455; *Shibᶜanu* 1, 1-3.

With respect to the inscriptions C 485 [= Bron 3]; Gl 932; 1536; 1538; 1542; 1543; 1636; Ja 2927 b; 2928 a and 2942 a it must be noted that their authors mention *GRBYN* as their "title". *GRBYN* has the form of *nisbah*; however, it seems to mean something like "stonemason" rather than the affiliation to a hypothetical tribe *Garbān (Beeston 1976 a, 412-413; Beeston *et al.* 1982, 50). Beeston rightly remarks that "here we have no direct evidence that such craftsmen were regarded as a "tribe", but a certain significance attaches to the fact that it is a *nisba* form, and these forms are normally used in Sabaic to denote membership of groups for which we have certain evidence of their being tribal names" (Beeston 1979 a, 117); these considerations appear especially reasonable if we take into account a clear case of a professional group being designated as *shaᶜb*, "tribe", in ᶜInān 22 (see also Beeston 1979 a, 117-118). In any case it must be stressed that *grbyn* forms a small minority of all the cases; and its deletion from the sample would not affect the general picture significantly.

Note to table 22: 1 AUTHOR - **Singular:** C 311; 440, 1-2; 466, 4-5; 518 [= Haram 49], 1; 570; 970, 3-5; Gl 932; 1636, 1-4; 1637, 1-3; Ja 2918 e, 1; f, 1; 2927 b, 1; 2928 a, 1; 2942 a; R 4525; Ry 605, 1-3; YM 375 [CIAS I 95.41/ r4], 1-2; 1064, 1-2;

2 AUTHORS - **Dual:** Ja 401 [= YM 263], 1;

3 OR MORE - **Dual:** R 5095, 1; 5095, 1-2.

Note to table 23: 1 AUTHOR - **Singular:** C 84, 1; 359, 3-4; 532 [= Haram 33], 1-2; Ja 698, 1-2; 706, 1; 717, 1; 741≈756, 1-2; al-Kāfir 10; Kortler 4, 1-3; NAM 230 (= AM 222 [CIAS II 95.11/ o8 N1]), 1; R 3957 [= Haram 36], 1-2; Sh II-93; YM 386 [CIAS I 35.91/o6/ P53], 1 /?/; 394 [CIAS I 39.11/ o6 N2], 1;

1 AUTHOR - **Plural:** C 397, 1-3; 534, 1-2; Er 36 §1; Ja 2112 (= AM 854 = NAM 1619 [CIAS II 39.11/ o2 N7]), 1; Lu 23 (=DJE 13); Ry 591, 2-3; YM 392 [CIAS I 39.11/ o6 N1], 1;

2 AUTHORS - **Singular:** C 716 [= Kamna 11], 1-3;

2 AUTHORS - **Dual:** C 715 [= Haram 26], 1-3; R 4663, 1-2;

2 AUTHORS - **Plural:** Er 27 §1; 37 §1; C 534, 1-2; 535, 1-2; Ja 693, 1-2; 704, 1-2; 727, 1-3; 2115 (= AM 857 = NAM 1627 [CIAS II 39.11/ o8 N1]), 1-3; NAM 2494 [CIAS 39.11/ o3 N6], 1-2; R 4663, 1-2; Ry 375 (= AM 104 = NAM 1583 [CIAS II 39.11/ o5 N3]), 1-2; 542 (= AM 844 = NAM 1631 [CIAS II 39.11/o6 N7]), 1-3; YM 350 [CIAS I 39.11/ o6 N5], 1-2;

3 OR MORE - **Singular:** C 287, 1-8; 349;

3 OR MORE - **Plural:** C 102, 1-4; 180, 1-2; 224, 1; 536; Fa 127 [= Haram 53], 1; Ja 621, 1-3; 707 (= AM 852 = NAM 2358 [CIAS II 39.11/ o6 N8]), 1-4; 712, 1-3; 738, 1-3; 740, 1-3; 767, 1-4; R 4188, 1-3; 4636, 1-4; *Shibᶜanu* 1, 1-3.

Note to table 25: these data have been arrived at on the basis of tables 1, 7, 8, 13, 14, 22 and 23. The notes to these tables contain detailed description of the cases of the use of the majority of these titles. I have

not adduced yet such descriptions for the Ancient *qayl*s and the "Middle Northern" *maqtawīs*, and I make it below:
The Ancient *qayls*: 1 AUTHOR - **Singular:** C 317, 1; 642, 1-2; R 4231, 1-2; 4638, 1 /?/;
1 AUTHOR - **Plural:** Na NAG 16, 1-2.
The "Middle Northern" *maqtawīs*: 1 AUTHOR - **Singular:** C 140 (= Ga 31 [NES I/1] = DJE 24), 1-2; 226, 1-2; 289, 6; 352, 1-3; 405, 1-2; 407, 1-5; 528 [= Haram 30], 1-2; DJE 22; Er 13 §1; 15 §1; 20 §1; Gl A 788, 1; Ja 579, 1-4; 580, 1-3; 581, 1-3; 582, 1-5; 583 + 807, 1-4; 612, 1-5; 613, 1-5; 646, 1-4; 649, 1-5; 650, 1-3; 651, 1-7; 690, 1-3; 691 (= AM 851 = NAM 212 [CIAS II 39.11/ o7 N5]), 1-3; 708 [= NAM 1626 [CIAS II 39.11/ o2 N6]), 1-4; 710, 1; 739, 1-4; 749, 1-3; 757 bis (= NAM 1852 [CIAS II 39.11/ o9 N1]), 1-3; 758, 1-3; 2110 (= AM 848 = NAM 430 [CIAS II 39.11/ o2 N8]), 1-4; 2114 (= AM 856 = NAM 1410 [CIAS II 39.11/ o5 N2]), 1-4; 2116 (= AM 858 = NAM 431 [CIAS II 39.11/ o4 N1]), 1-2; 2118 (= AM 862 = NAM 323 [CIAS II 39.11/ o3 N9]), 1-2; 2119 (= AM 864 = NAM 2372 [CIAS II 39.11/ o7 N8]), 1-5; 2860 a; 2959 f; Na NAG 1, 1-3; Na NNSQ 14, 1-3; R 3929, 1-4; 4420; 4577, 1-2; Ry 592 A, 1-2; YM 394 [CIAS I 39.11/o6 N2], 1-2;

2 AUTHORS - **Dual:** C 314 + 954, 1-5; Er 26 §1; 27 §1; 69, 1-5; Fa 120, 1-3; Ja 572, 1-3; 578, 1-4; 614, 1-5; 632, 1-2; 652, 1-6; 700 + 814, 1-2; 713, 1-5; 2113 (= AM 855 = NAM 1448 [CIAS II 39.11/ o3 N5]), 1-3; Na NAG 11 [= Er 25], 1-8;

3 OR MORE - **Singular:** Er 23 §1 /?/;

3 OR MORE - **Dual:** Er 21 §1; Kortler 2, 1-7;

3 OR MORE - **Plural:** C 287, 3-11, 12-15; Er 33 §1; Ja 615, 1-8; 616, 1-6; 661, 1-3; Ry 538, 1-8; YM 438 [CIAS I 39.11/ o6 N 3], 3.

Note to table 26: *qayl*s: see table 10 (with notes).
'b^cl bytn: see tables 1 and 10 (with notes) minus 3 "Southern" insscriptions (Er 40; Ja 1819 [= VL 23 = Shirjān 19]; 2867).
maqtawīs: see note to table 25.
Clients - see table 18.
Bearers of *"nisbah"*: the Ancient Period: see table 22 + for **2** OR MORE: Gl 1572, 1-2.
The Middle Period: see table 23 + for **2** OR MORE: C 29, 1; ^cInān 29; Ja 747, 1-2; R 4142, 1-2.

Note to table 27: in addition to the previously used inscriptions this table takes into consideration the inscriptions with an unknown number of authors but with remaining title of the authors. It was impossible to consider these inscriptions in the previous tables.

***The Ancient Period*:**

QAYLS: see table 10;
CLIENTS (*^cbd/ 'dm*): **the singular**: see table 13 + R 4189, 1-2; 4360;
the dual: see table 13 + Lu 8, 1;
the plural: see table 13 + R 3911, 1; 4349, 1-2;
NISBAH: **the singular** and **the dual**: see table 22;
the plural: see table 22 + Gl 1572, 1-2.

***The Middle Period, the "North"*:**

QAYLS: **the singular**: see table 7;
the plural: see table 7 + C 181, 1-3; Fa 95 + 94, 1; Gl 1180, 1-3; Ja 671 + 788, 1-5; R 4191, 1; 4658, 1; 4676, 1-3.
CLIENTS: **the singular**: see table 14;
the plural: see table 14 + C 30, 1-2; 107, 1; 211/I [= DJE 5 I], 1-2; 211/II [= DJE 5 II], 1; 281, 1; 303, 1-2; 331, 1; 345, 1; 398, 1-3; 432, 1 /?/; ^cInān 29; Ja 784; 812; R 3970, 1; 3971, 1; 3973, 1; 4030, 1-2; 4142, 1-3; 4648, 1-2; 4651, 1-2; 4659, 1-3; 4706, 1; 4725 [+ 3972], 1; 4770, 1; 4990, 1-2; Robin/ Rayda 4, 1-3;
"LORDS OF HOUSES": see tables 1 and 26 + C 202 [= DJE 4], 1;
NISBAH: **the singular** and **the dual**: see table 23;
the plural: see table 23 + C 29, 1; ^cInān 29; Ja 747, 1-2; 2107 (= AM 841 = NAM 429 [CIAS II 39.11/ o2 N2]), 1-3; R 4142, 1-2; 4149, 1;
MAQTAWĪS: **the singular**: see note to table 25 + Ja 660, 1-5;
the dual and **the plural**: see table 25.

***The "South"*:**

QAYLS: **the singular** and **the dual**: see table 8;
the plural: see table 8 + Moretti 1, 1.

CHAPTER II
FROM CLAN TITLES TO CLAN NAMES?

The process of "archaization" of the Sabaean cultural-political area seems to have brought as one of its results such a peculiar phenomenon as the probable transformation of the names of certain Ancient administrative posts into the names of some Middle "Sabaean" clan groups. It can be maintained with confidence with respect to the Middle "Sabaean" clan *bnw ḏ-KBR-'QYNM* and with less confidence to such clan names as *KBR-ḪLL*, *KBR-'ḤS^{3}RN*, *ḏ-ĠYMN*, *ḏ-M'ḎNM*, *RS^{2}WN* and some others.

Kbr-'QYNM can be translated as "the *kabīr*, the elder of 'QYNM". On the other hand, *'qynm* is not necessarily a proper name. It can also be considered as the absolute plural form for *qyn*, *"qayn"*. But *qayn* is quite a well-known administrative post of the Ancient Period. "The term *qyn* (pl.*'qyn*) frequently occurs in the Sabaean inscriptions (Gl 1719 + 1717 + 1718, 2; Ja 550, 1; 552, 1; 554; 555, 1, 3; 556 &c), always as an author's title. This title can relate an author to a deity (Ja 556: *qyny/hwbs/w'lmqh*; Ja 554: *qyn/'lmqh*), mukarrib (Gl 1719 + 1717 + 1718, 2-3: *qyn/ydʿ'l*), city (Ja 555, 3: *qyn/mryb*) or clan (Ja 550, 1: *qyn/sḥr*[1]). The real meaning of the title is still not completely clear, but it can be said with confidence that it denoted a certain official of the state apparatus or even some clan-tribal magistracy" (Lundin 1971, 229; see also: Rhodokanakis 1927, 131-132; J.Ryckmans 1951, 25, 33-34, 146-147; Grohmann 1963, 130; Robin 1981 c, 266; Robin, Ryckmans 1982 a, 109-110 &c). In the light of all that Lundin considers *kbr-'qynm* as "a board of qayns, officials with certain functions" (Lundin 1971, 229).[2]

Lundin, basing himself on Beeston (1937, 71, 73),[3] tends to consider *kbr*

---

1 In my view SḤR is more likely to denote in this inscription the well-known Sabaean deity (see for example Höfner 1970, 253, 271-272) and not the clan *ḏ-SḤR* in some way related to this deity.

2 Though to my mind it would be more logical to consider *kbr 'qynm* rather as a "chairman" of this board.

3 In his turn Beeston based himself in this point on Rhodokanakis (see Beeston 1975 c, 192).

'ḥs³rn as "a board of tax-collectors" (Lundin 1971, 229).[4] Incidentally, in his recently published autobiography, Beeston maintains with respect to Beeston 1937 that "there is not much in it with which I would now agree" (Beeston 1987 a, XVI). So he has reconsidered the above-mentioned interpretation of *'ḥs³rn* as "tax-collectors" and now he tends to understand it as something like a lower stratum of population comparable with the Hadrami *ḍuᶜafā'* (Beeston 1975 c, 192).[5] Yet it does not change the essence of the matter, as such an interpretation also permits the consideration of *kbr 'ḥs³rn* as an administrative post, an official in charge of that category of the population. Lundin even supposes, basing himself again on Beeston 1937 (p.73), that *kbr ḫll* could mean something like "kabirs of the legislators /?/" (Lundin 1971, 230).

The most important fact is that, if the statements that the three above-mentioned combinations could denote certain administrative positions are true (and that seems to be really plausible with respect to *kbr 'qynm* only), it will be valid exclusively for the Ancient Period, because in the Middle Sabaic inscriptions all the three combinations were certainly used only as clan names (C 80, 13; 618; Fa 121; Er 6 §1; 13 §1; Ja 615; 684, 2-4, 13-14; 696 ≈ 697; 711, 8-10; 739, 2-4, 13-14; 758, 1-3, 16-18; 816; Na NAG 19 [= Lu 17 = YM 363 = CIAS I 95.41/ p6] R 4130, 2 &c).

In the Middle Sabaean cultural-political area the very post of *qayn* seems to be completely extinct. All the cases when this office is mentioned occur in the inscriptions of the Ancient Period. Yet what remained in the area was a clan (occupying quite a prominent position) with a name whose literal translation would be "the senior *qayn*". The name of this administrative post has completely lost its substance, its previous social meaning; in the Middle Period it is neither an office, nor a title, it has become just a name of one of the "Sabaean" clans.[6]

Thus, the names of the administrative posts of the Ancient Period, which

---

4 Here again it would seem to me more logical to consider *kbr 'ḥs³rn* rather as a "chairman" of that board.

5 To my mind the fact that in C 601, 4 'ḤS³RN is listed among the most noble Sabaean clans makes this hypothesis look implausible.

6 This phenomenon has already been noticed by Robin who maintains the following: "A l'origine le terme *kbr-'qynᵐ* désigne manifestement une fonction: "chef d'administrateurs" ou mieux "administrateur en chef"... Nous serions enclin à supposer qu'à Sibām le *kbr-'qynᵐ*, l'administrateur en chef, était au service de la divinité fédérale, *'lmqh*, et qu'il se trouvait là en raison de la présence du sanctuaire fédéral. Cette fonction dut être exercée héréditairement: en effet, au bout d'un certain temps, tous les descendents des premiers *kbr-'qynᵐ* revendiquent ce titre qui deviendra finalement un véritable nom de lignage" (Robin 1981 c, 266; see also Beeston 1979 a, 117).

ceased to be either posts or titles in the Middle Period, can change into the clan names.[7]

With respect to *kbr-ẖll*, from my point of view the most probable version of the evolution would be that from *kbr H̱LL* as an elder of the clan H̱LL in the most ancient period[8], to *ḏ-KBR-H̱LL* as the senior (socially and "genealogically"?) subclan within this clan in the Middle Period. In the first stage of this process the position of the elder of the clan seems to have been occupied by the "first-born"[9] who might have been a member of any lineage of the clan. Then this position seems to have been monopolized by a certain subclan (namely Banū ḤZFRM[10] ?), and finally, by the Middle Period, when no real *kabīr*s of H̱LL are mentioned, *ḏ-KBR-H̱LL* is used as a name of this subclan of H̱LL. *KBR-H̱LL*, literally "the elder of (the clan) H̱LL" in this period seems to denote any member of this subclan (C 80, 13; 618, 1; Ja 711, 9; Na NAG 19 = Lu 17, 1 &c).[11]

One of the Middle Sabaean clans had the name *RS^{2}W(Y)N* (R 4815[12]; Er 27; 34; &c). The literal meaning of *rs^{2}w* is "priest", and J.Ryckmans has shown that such a meaning appears not to be completely fortuitous in this case, as some of the members of this clan seem to have been performing priestly functions (Ryckmans 1974 b, 493).[13] It is possible to ask if this is not another example of the

---

[7] I would mention that the most ancient case of what seems to be a name of the administrative post transformed into a clan name (*MRFDM bn ᶜMSMᶜ bn 'QYN MRYB*) comes from one of the most ancient Sabaic inscriptions (MAFRAY-al-Balaq al-Ğanūbī 1 ≈ Gl 1719+1717+1718, 1-2). Yet at that time this transformation does not appear to have been durable and definitive, as later in the Ancient Period we find *qyn MRYB* as a doubtless administrative post and certainly not a clan name (Ja 555,3: *w-ywm t'bh-hw qyn MRYB*, "and when he was appointed as a *qayn* of Mārib").

[8] See Gl 1679, 1, 2, 3; 1687, 1, 2; 1773 a, 1; b, 1 = Ja 2848 y, 1, 2, 3, 4, 11, 12, whose authors denote themselves as *bkr H̱LL w-kbr-hmw* "the first-born of H̱LL and the *kabīr* of them (i.e. the clan H̱LL)".

[9] Determined for example through the procedure described by Strabo (XVI.4.3).

[10] For example in the Middle Sabaean eponym datings *bn ḏ-KBR-H̱LL* and *bn ḤZFRM* seem to be interchangeable (see for example Lundin 1971, 40, 180); on the other hand, Banū ḤZFRM appears to be just a subclan of the clan H̱LL (see for example Gl 1690, 1, 2; 1752, 1; 1757 b; 1775, 1, 2 &c; Beeston 1956, 30; Lundin 1971, 54-55 &c). It must be maintained, however, that the identification of Banū ḏ-KBR-H̱LL and Banū ḤZFRM has been recently challenged by Robin (1993).

[11] I would suppose the same scheme of evolution with respect to *KBR 'ḤS^{3}RN*, though the history of this subclan is too poorly documented to provide any real substantiation for this hypothesis.

[12] The end of the Ancient Period.

[13] Though Jamme is quite right when he maintains that it is not valid for some other members of this clan (Jamme 1976, 175).

transformation of the name of a (priestly) post into the name of the clan, occurring as a result of monopolization of the priestly functions of a certain deity by a certain clan.[14] If so, this transformation must have occurred in the Ancient Period, as the clan RS²WN is already attested to in this epoch (C 399, 2; Ja 2927 m; 2929; R 4766, 2 &c).[15]

The general scheme of the evolution may be reconstructed as follows:

an individual title - name of a certain administrative post

↓

(monopolization of the title by a certain clan)

↓

a collective clan title

↓

(supplanting of the clan name by the name of the title)

↓

a clan name

One of the intermediate stages of this process may be reflected in Gl 1533 = Ja 2855. This inscription was installed in Ṣirwāḥ in the fourth century BC approximately (according to palaeographic evidence). The text seems to represent a record of the discharge of a debt by a certain Abkarib from the clan ᶜInān (*'BKRB bn ᶜNNN*). Abkarib inherited this debt from one of his ancestors (*'bh-hw* - line 5) for whom in his time 400 *blṭ* coins were paid by a certain Nasha'karib from the clan Habāb (*NS²'KRB d̲-ḤBB*) in response to some financial demand (*s'l* - line 5).[16] By the moment when the document was being drawn up, neither Nasha'karib Dhū-Ḥabāb, nor the above-mentioned Abkarib's ancestor (who ran into debt) seems to have been

---

[14] The same supposition could be made with respect to the Sabaean clan d̲-SḤR, that seems to have been in a special relation with the deity SḤR (C 391; Ja 567; R 4146; &c). It might have been the clan which monopolized the post of the *qayn* of SHR (mentioned in C 375=Ja 550,1).

[15] For some other probable cases of the transformation of the clan titles into the clan names see Korotayev 1994 d.

[16] I.e. a certain ancestor of Abkarib b. ᶜInān had to pay this really considerable sum in response to some financial demand, but this ancestor does not seem to have had this money, and it was paid by Nasha'karib Dhū-Ḥabāb. Thus the ancestor became a debtor of the clan Ḥabāb, and finally the debt was discharged by one of his descendants, Abkarib.

alive. As a result the debt of the ancestors is discharged by one of their descendants, whereas the descendants of the creditor act as the recipients of the payment.

The full official identification of the "creditor" looks as follows: *NS²'KRB ḏ-ḤBB 'qyn ṢRWḤ*, "Nasha'karib of (the clan) Ḥabāb, the *qayn*s of Ṣirwāḥ", where the title *qayn* is used explicitly in the plural (*'qyn*), and consequently it relates to the clan Ḥabāb and not to Nasha'karib; in this inscription we deal with an extremely rare case of a collective clan title used in an Ancient (not a Middle) text.

Abkarib b. ᶜInān pays "the debt of his ancestors" to a group described as *'ly st 'qyn ṢRWḤ* (line 2), something like "those of the six *qayn*s of Ṣirwāḥ",[17] or "those of the authority of the *qayn*s of Ṣirwāḥ".[18] But as we could see "*qayn*s of Ṣirwāḥ" are identical with Dhū-Ḥabāb clan. The recipient of Abkarib's (and consequently the Inanids') payment is certainly the clan Ḥabāb (lines 11 and 15), hence the combination *'ly st 'qyn ṢRWḤ* is identical with *ḏ-ḤBB*, "(the clan) Dhū-Ḥabāb" (line 15). The fact that "six *qayn*s of Ṣirwāḥ" denote a clan and not a collegium of the officials seems to be underlined by the use of the relative pronoun *'ly* (the accusative plural for *ḏ-*: see for example Beeston *et al.* 1982, 37). It would not be appropriate at all in the case of a "collegium of the officials" (Beeston 1984 b, 34), but it was extensively used (parallel with the noun *bn/bny/bnw* "son/sons") for the designation of the clan affiliation (Beeston 1978 a, 15-16).

On line 11 the same clan is denoted as *bn byt ḏ-ḤBB w-'qyn ṢRWḤ*, "the sons[19] of the house Dhū-Ḥabāb and (of) the *qayn*s of Ṣirwāḥ", and on line 15 it is designated simply as *ḏ-ḤBB*.

Thus in the inscription under consideration "those of the six *qayn*s of Ṣirwāḥ", "Ḥabāb, the *qayn*s of Ṣirwāḥ", "Ḥabāb and *qayn*s of Ṣirwāḥ" and simply "Dhū-Ḥabāb" denote the same clan group. The monopolization by the clan Dhū-Ḥabāb of the posts of the *qayn*s in Ṣirwāḥ might have led to the situation when the designation "the *qayn*s of Ṣirwāḥ" became identical with the notion "(the clan) Dhū-Ḥabāb". As a result a

---

17 Similar translations were proposed by Höfner (1973, 30) and Jamme (1976, 88).

18 According to Beeston's proposal (Beeston 1976 a, 409-410; Beeston 1984 b, 34). Beeston's argumentation appears not entirely convincing to me, but I shall not analyze it in detail here (for full analysis see Korotayev 1990 a, Appendix 4, 80-83), because this proposal does not change the general sense of the inscription. In any case the probable difference is completely irrelevant for the subject of this chapter: both "those of the six *qayn*s of Ṣirwāḥ" and "those of the authority of the *qayn*s of Ṣirwaḥ" could be interpreted as a clan title developed into a clan name.

19 For the use of *bn Z* for the designation of whole clans, see Korotayev 1994.

new expression of the affiliation to this clan appeared, yet the old one did not disappear, and for some time both of the designations were used simultaneously. This situation is reflected in the inscription under consideration: in one case the new name is used, in another place the old one is employed, in the two other cases both of the designations are used together. Incidentally, two different modes are employed. Finally, one has an impression that the compiler of the document has used all the possible variants of the designation of one clan group - perhaps for "stylistic" purposes. It is evident that just a step remains from such a situation to the final transformation of the name of the administrative post into the clan name.

This step seems to have been made in Bakilite Shibām where the name of the administrative post "the senior *qayn*" monopolized by a certain clan appears to have finally and irrevocably supplanted the old name of the clan dominating in the Shibamite tribe.[20]

Due to unknown causes, this step was not made in Ṣirwāḥ. The clan Dhū-Ḥabāb continued dominating in this tribe at least till the end of the Middle Period. In this period this clan acquired the qaylite title (Er 23; 28; Ja 649 &c), but all this time it kept its old name, Dhū-Ḥabāb.[21] The trend towards the supplanting of the old clan name by the name of the administrative post monopolized by the clan was not completed. The old name survived and the new name of the clan dominating in Ṣirwāḥ disappeared.[22]

---

[20] The intermediate situation in this case might be reflected in C 132, but this text is too fragmentary to make any far-reaching conclusions on its basis.

[21] Though adding sometimes to it the names of other clans, with which it formed clan alliances - a usual practice in the Middle Sabaean cultural-political area (see e.g. Korotayev 1995 a, Chapter VI).

[22] Incidentally, when reading the text of Gl 1533 = Ja 2855 it is difficult to avoid the supposition that the *'qyn ṢRWḤ* element of the combination *ḏ-ḤBB 'qyn ṢRWḤ* might have been used to distinguish the senior lineage of the Dhū-Ḥabāb clan. For some other probable instances of such transformations see Korotayev 1994 d.

CHAPTER III
QUANTITATIVE ANALYSIS
OF SABAIC POSSESSIVE PRONOMINAL SUFFIXES

a. Introduction

The phenomenon of "positive deviation" analyzed in Chapter 1 is not only confined to the use of some Middle Sabaic titles. The use of the plural where the singular or the dual are expected can be observed as well in some other fields.

One of the most evident fields in which this phenomenon is prevalent is the use of the possessive pronominal suffixes with the word *'rḍ/t*, "land/s". Indeed, a single author of a Middle "Sabaean" ("Northern") dedicatory inscription seeking good crops from a deity would never mention *'rḍ-hw*, "**his** land", but would always use the combination *'rḍ-hmw*, "**their** land", where "their", as will be shown below, almost always means "belonging to his clan" (see for example C 282, 13; Er 5 §6; 22 §1, 2; 24 §2; 28 §2; 29 §2; 36, 6, 12; Ja 601, 17; 602 [= Na NAG 7], 17; 628, 23; Na NAG 2, 8; Ry 394, 6-7 &c).

In all the Ancient Sabaic texts we have only five cases of the use of the combination under consideration. But in **all** of these cases the **singular** form of the pronominal suffix is used: an Ancient author would always speak about "**his** (and not **their**) land/s" (*'rḍ/t-hw*: C 37, 2; 356, upper edge; 576 /?/; Ja 555, 3; YM 453 [CIAS I 39.11/r9/P12 N4], 2-3).[1] Quite surprisingly, notwithstanding the very small number of cases, the "Middle South" shows again an intermediate picture (the singular with one author in C 658, 3 and the plural with two authors in R 4194, 3).

b. "Land property words"

The possessive pronominal suffixes were also used with other words denoting different kinds of land property such as *ᶜbr(t)*, "terraced fields", *'nẖl*, "palm groves",

[1] It appears also quite easy to find a similar combination, *'rḍ-s*, "his land", in Qatabanic inscriptions (the Ancient and Early Middle Period: Ja 2360 [= Q 700], 3; R 3858 [= Q 74], 14 [a "Sabaeism", *'rḍ-hw*]; 4330 [= Ry 388 = Q 178], 2. It does not appear fortuitous as we shall see below.

ms²ymt, "fields", *'srr*, "cultivated lands beside flood-bed", *'ᶜnb, 'wyn*, "vineyards", *mfnt*, "irrigated lands", *'mṭr*,"rain-watered fields", *tbqlt*, "plantations" &c. However, the number of cases when each of those words is used with the pronominal suffixes is usually too small for the application of any quantitative methods, but we shall obtain quite a representative sample if we consider all the words denoting various kinds of land possessions (including *'rḍ/t*) together. The general picture of the use of the possessive pronominal suffixes with this kind of words looks as follows:

Table 28. USE OF THE POSSESSIVE PRONOMINAL SUFFIXES WITH THE WORDS DESIGNATING ALL THE TYPES OF LAND PROPERTY (on the basis of all the accessible Sabaic inscriptions)

	1 AUTHOR	2 AUTHORS	3 OR MORE
Singular	47 **36%**	0	0
Dual	0	10 **16%**	0
Plural	84 **64%**	52 **84%**	100 **100%**
TOTAL	131 **100%**	62 **100%**	100 **100%**

As usual, a mixed picture of the use of the pronominal suffixes can be explained through the difference in their application in the Ancient and the Middle Period, as well as in the "North" and "South".

For the "Middle North" we have the following picture (see table 29):

Table 29. USE OF THE POSSESSIVE PRONOMINAL SUFFIXES WITH THE WORDS DESIGNATING ALL THE TYPES OF LAND PROPERTY (the Sabaean cultural-political area ["North"] in the Middle Period)

	1 AUTHOR	2 AUTHORS	3 OR MORE
Singular	2 **3%**	0	0
Dual	0	0	0
Plural	77 **97%**	49 **100%**	64 **100%**
TOTAL	79 **100%**	49 **100%**	64 **100%**

As we can see, the positive deviation here is very high (**+97%** from the singular and **+100%** from the dual). I would stress that both "Middle Northern" cases of the use of the *-hw*, "his", suffix with the words denoting land property seem to come from the inscriptions from the Sabaean Lowlands (the area of Mārib) - C 584, 2-3 and Fa 61, 3; for the "Middle Highlands" the value of the positive deviation appears maximum both for the dual and the singular. That seems to be an indicator (though a relatively weak one) of the probable fact that in the "Middle Northern" Lowlands the land property relations were less collectivized than in the Highlands, and the Ancient "individualistic" tradition was not so completely extinct in the Middle Period here as it seems to have been in the "Sabaean" Highlands.

The picture for the Ancient Period looks as follows:

Table 30. USE OF THE POSSESSIVE PRONOMINAL SUFFIXES WITH THE WORDS DESIGNATING ALL THE TYPES OF LAND PROPERTY (the Ancient Period)

	1 AUTHOR	2 AUTHORS	3 OR MORE
Singular	33 **100%**	0	0
Dual	0	10 **91%**	0
Plural	0	1 **9%**	4 **100%**
TOTAL	33 **100%**	11 **100%**	4 **100%**

It is not difficult to see that the Ancient picture differs dramatically from the "Middle Northern" one. Indeed, the positive deviation from the singular is simply absent (**+0%**). An Ancient single author (in a complete contrast to a "Middle Northern" one) always mentions "**his**" land possessions. The positive deviation from the dual is minimum (**+9%**). All the positive deviation in this case is created by only one inscription (Gl 1352 + 1354 = R 4626, 1) coming from the end of the Ancient Period. It is not surprising at all, as one would expect that the above-mentioned transformation from the "individualistic" Ancient Period to the "collectivistic" Middle one must have begun at least at the end of the Ancient Period.[2] As a result the social relations of the end of the Ancient Period turn out to have some characteristics of both

[2] Some evidence for that has already been presented above in Chapter 2.

of the Periods, occupying more or less intermediate position between them.[3]

The intermediate position of the "Middle South" is even more evident:

Table 31. USE OF THE POSSESSIVE PRONOMINAL SUFFIXES WITH THE WORDS DESIGNATING ALL THE TYPES OF LAND PROPERTY (Himyarite-Radmanite cultural-political area ["South"] in the Middle Period)

	1 AUTHOR	2 AUTHORS	3 OR MORE
Singular	12 **67%**	0	0
Dual	0	2 **33%**	0
Plural	6 **33%**	4 **67%**	13 **100%**
TOTAL	18 **100%**	6 **100%**	13 **100%**

To facilitate the comparison tables 29-31 are presented below in the following form.

Table 32. USE OF THE POSSESSIVE PRONOMINAL SUFFIXES WITH THE WORDS DESIGNATING ALL THE TYPES OF LAND PROPERTY **BY SINGLE AUTHORS** (Comparative table)

	ANCIENT PERIOD	MIDDLE PERIOD "NORTH"	MIDDLE PERIOD "SOUTH"
Singular	33 **100%**	2 **3%**	12 **67%**
Plural	0 **0%**	77 **97%**	6 **33%**
TOTAL	33 **100%**	79 **100%**	18 **100%**

It is also reasonable to compare the "Ancient Period" and the "Northern" and "Southern" areas of the Middle Period with respect to the number of the authors of the corresponding inscriptions, i.e. according to the variable which can reflect as well

[3] C 611 and R 4815, which can be dated to the very end of the Ancient Period (Nebes 1987, 83) seem to provide more proof in support of this statement, because, though no positive deviation can be observed in these two texts, they display a picture of evident collective clan ownership, i.e. a "Middle Sabaean" type of relations.

the level of "individualization and collectivization" of the social relations of a certain type.

Table 33. NUMBER OF AUTHORS OF THE INSCRIPTIONS MENTIONING LAND POSSESSIONS (Comparative table).

	ANCIENT PERIOD	MIDDLE PERIOD "NORTH"	MIDDLE PERIOD "SOUTH"
1 author	33 **66%**	79 **38%**	18 **44%**
2 or more	17 **34%**	128 **62%**	23 **56%**
TOTAL	50 **100%**	207 **100%**	41 **100%**

In general this table seems to confirm the preliminary results we have at the moment: the "Ancient" social relations appear to be more "individualistic" than those of the "Middle North". The "South", as usual, occupies an intermediate position.

Finally, let us consider the inscriptions according to one more variable. As has been shown in Chapter 1, there is an indicator which appears to be most synthetic and sensitive. This is the relative proportion of the singular, dual and plural forms[4] (see table 34):

Table 34. FORMS OF POSSESSIVE PRONOMINAL SUFFIXES USED WITH THE WORDS DESIGNATING AUTHORS' LAND PROPERTY OF VARIOUS KINDS (Version 1)

	ANCIENT PERIOD	MIDDLE PERIOD "NORTH"	MIDDLE PERIOD "SOUTH"
Singular	36 **63%**	2 **0.7%**	12 **29%**
Dual	12 **21%**	0 **0%**	2 **5%**
Plural	9 **16%**	275 **99.3%**	27 **66%**
TOTAL	57 **100%**	277 **100%**	41 **100%**

[4] It is also quite important that the study of this variable allows one to use the inscriptions with a unknown number of authors. It is impossible to use them while dealing with the other variables.

The singular and dual forms reflect the cases of the possession of land by certain individuals. *'rḍ-hmy,* "the land of them both", is the land of two concrete individuals. Hence it is quite close to *'rḍ-hw,*"his land", and it is really distant from the Middle "Sabaean" *'rḍ-hmw,* "their land", which does not seem to designate the land possessions of concrete authors of certain inscriptions (even when such inscriptions have three or more authors). The best indicator to that is the fact that a single author of a Middle "Sabaean" inscription would usually mention **"their"** (-*hmw*) land possessions and practically never **"his"** (-*hw*) - see above. Hence it is reasonable to treat the singular and dual forms reflecting the individual possessions together, contrasting them with the plural form of the pronominal suffix which seems to reflect as a rule[5] the collective land possessions:

Table 35. FORMS OF POSSESSIVE PRONOMINAL SUFFIXES USED WITH THE WORDS DESIGNATING AUTHORS' LAND PROPERTY OF VARIOUS KINDS (Version 2)

	ANCIENT PERIOD	MIDDLE PERIOD "NORTH"	MIDDLE PERIOD "SOUTH"
Sg.+Dl.	48 **84%**	2 **0.7%**	14 **34%**
Plural	9 **16%**	275 **99.3%**	27 **66%**
TOTAL	57 **100%**	277 **100%**	41 **100%**

Thus, the variable gives us the same picture that was arrived at according to almost all the other indicators: the "individualistic" Ancient Period[6] distinctly contrasts with the "collectivistic" Middle North; the "Middle South" occupies again an intermediate position.

[5] At least in the Middle Sabaean inscriptions.

[6] The singular and dual forms of the possessive pronominal suffixes used with the words designating various kinds of land possessions are perfectly normal not only in the Ancient Sabaic inscriptions, but in the Ancient Minaic (Madhabian - e.g. Haram 2, 15; Kamna 5, 4; R 2754 [= M 16 = Haram 27], 2; 2791 [= M 45], 3 /?/; 3310 B [= M 297 B = Haram 42 B], 4 /?/) and Ancient and Early Middle Qatabanic texts (e.g. Ja 2360 [= Q 700], 3; 2366 [= Q 700], 3; 3537 [= Q 34], B; R 3854 [= Q 72], 3, 4, 5, 7; 3856 [= Q 73], 1, 3; 3858 [= Q 74], 14; 4330 [= Ry 388 = Q 178], 2; 4335 [= Q 182], 2) as well, which leads one to the supposition that the land property relations where as "individualized" in the Ancient Madhabian and Ancient and Early Middle "Qatabanian" communities as they were in the Ancient Sabaean cultural-political area. Hence, there are some grounds to speak about a general "Ancient Sayhadic" pattern of individualized land-property relations.

It is very remarkable that almost all the cases of the use of the land property words with the plural pronominal suffixes in the Ancient Sabaic inscriptions come from the end of this Period (Fa 124, 7; Ja 2834, 3;[7] Gl 1694, 1; R 3911, 3, 4; 3915, 2; 4626 [= Gl 1352 + 1354], 1; 4627, 3). It may be considered as another piece of evidence in support of the supposition that the "archaization" of the Sabaean cultural-political area began at the end of the Ancient Period; the processes, which resulted in the Middle Sabaean model of social relations, developed at the end of the 1st millenium BC.

Hence, the study of the use of the possessive pronominal suffixes with "land property words" leads one to the following preliminary suppositions with respect to the land property relations:

1) In the Middle Period in the Sabaean cultural-political area (= the Northern part of the area of the Middle Sabaic epigraphy = the "Middle North"), the land property relations were very weakly "individualized". Land possessions of any kind were usually considered here as a property of certain groups and not of individual persons.

2) In a sharp contrast with it, the analogous complex of relations in the Ancient Period was much more individualized. The land possessions mentioned in the inscriptions were usually considered to belong to individual persons and not to groups.

3) The level of the "individualization" of this complex of relations seems to have decreased at the end of the Ancient Period. It leads one to the supposition that the processes of "archaization" might have begun at that time.

4) In the Himyarite-Radmanite cultural-political area (= the Southern part of the area of the Middle Sabaic epigraphy = the "Middle South") in the Middle Period these relations seem to have been significantly more individualized than in the "North" (but considerably less individualized than the "Ancient" relations). The Ancient "individualistic" tradition seems to have been preserved in the South[8] much better than in the North.

---

[7] In this case a clan name is used. As stated above, it can be considered as an equivalent of the plural possessive pronominal suffix. I can add eight more similar cases occuring in the Sabaic inscriptions of the end of this Period (see e.g. Nebes 1988, 74): C 611, 2, 4, 6, 8; R 4815, 2, 3, 6, 7.

[8] Most of its territory was a part of the Qatabanian cultural-political area in the Ancient Period, yet Ancient Qatabanian society seems not to have differed significantly from the Ancient Sabaean one with respect to land property relations (in addition to what has been referred to above see also e.g. Bauer 1965 b; Lundin 1971, 233-245; 1987 a).

5) There are some grounds to suppose that the "archaization" of land property relations in the Sabaean Lowlands was not so complete as it was in the "Sabaean" Highlands.[9]

One may notice that not all of the above-stated conclusions are new in the area of Epigraphic South Arabian studies. For example, the study of the land property relations in the Ancient Sabaean cultural-political area has shown that in the Ancient Period evident processes in formation of individual private land ownership took place (Bauer 1964, 19-20; 1965 b, 209-217; Lundin 1965 b; 1971, 233-245).[10] However, the "archaization" of land property relations has not been noticed yet, hence the above-stated suppositions might be of some interest.

c. "Words designating buildings"

It might be useful to consider the use of the possessive pronominal suffixes with the other words designating immovable property, i.e. words denoting constructions of various types like "house" (*byt*)[11], "well" (*b'r*), "irrigation dike"

---

9 In addition to what has been referred to above, I would also mention that we have considerable evidence of the sale and purchasing of immovable property in the Middle Sabaean Lowlands (e.g. Alfiery 1 [CIAS I 28.11/p7]; C 435; 609; Fa 112-115; R 3959; the area of some of these transactions includes in addition to the Lowlands the special "royal district" in the Highlands, the area of Ṣanᶜā' - Shaᶜūb]), whereas almost no transactions of this kind are attested in the tribal "Sabaean" Highlands. However, even in the Lowlands in the Middle Period such transactions envolved whole clans rather than individuals only.

10 Incidentally such inscriptions as C 37 or a recently published "land decree" from Ḥadaqān (Lundin 1987 b) show that these processes developed not only in the Lowlands, but also in some areas of the Highlands. So Lundin's supposition that in the 4th-3rd centuries BC individual private land property forms close to the classical Greek ones existed in the area of Ḥadaqān seems to be plausible (Lundin 1987 b, 97). Yet his statement that this type of land property relations "is possible to consider as typical for all of South Arabia in the 4th-1st centuries BC"(*Ibidem*) does not appear to be really well corroborated. Indeed, Lundin has only provided more or less convincing evidence with respect to one of the Highland communities of the 4th-3rd centuries BC and for the Qatabanian civil community of the 2nd-1st centuries BC (Lundin 1987 a and b). Lundin's statement does not seem to be really convincing, because it does not take into consideration the existence in Ancient South Arabia of the vast "barbarian", "tribal" periphery in addition to the centres of civilization which in the Ancient Period appear to have been numerous in the internal Lowlands but scanty in the Highlands. The evident diversity of ancient Yemeni communities does not permit us to project the conclusions arrived at for two communities on to the whole of ancient South Arabia.

11 *byt*, "house", does not always mean simply a certain structure, dwelling. Quite often it denotes a certain "house community". For example this meaning is most probable when the authors ask a deity for the well-being and the prosperity (*wfy, l-d̲t nᶜmt w-tnᶜmn*) of them and "their house" (*byt-hmw*: C 530, 7; Ja 630, 16; Gl 1537, 5 &c). Incidentally "house" has similar meanings in practically all modern languages. Something more than just a dwelling is also denoted by *byt* in Ja 615, 20-21 (*'rḍ w-'srr w-mfnt w-ms²ymt byt-hmw*, "the land, wadi-side cultivation, irrigated plots and fields of their house"), Ja 730, 8-9 (*'fql yfqlnn ᶜdy byt-hmw*, "the crops they gather in their house") &c. However, very often *byt* denotes just a certain structure (C 4, 2; 6, 3; 17, 4; Lu 21 = DJE 12, 2; Ga 2, 1; 3, 2; 6, 1 &c). I believe that *byt* as a "house community" also included "house-dwelling" in its semantic field: when authors seek the well-being of their house the well-being of their dwelling was also implied, the well-being of the house community was impossible without the well-being of their dwelling. It is quite evident that a certain structure existed behind

(*m'hd*), "irrigation canal or bund" (*ḥrt*), "secondary canal" (*fnwt*), "tank, cistern, basin" (*m'gl, krf*), different substructures of house complexes (*ms³wd, ṣrḥt, mwrt* &c) &c.[12] The general picture of the use of the suffixes with this class of words looks as follows:

Table 36. USE OF THE POSSESSIVE PRONOMINAL SUFFIXES WITH THE WORDS DESIGNATING THE MAIN TYPES OF BUILDINGS (on the basis of all the accessible Sabaic inscriptions)

	1 AUTHOR	2 AUTHORS	3 OR MORE
Singular	48 **53%**	1 **3%**	0
Dual	0	8 **21%**	0
Plural	43 **47%**	30 **76%**	107 **100%**
TOTAL	91 **100%**	39 **100%**	107 **100%**

Table 37. USE OF THE POSSESSIVE PRONOMINAL SUFFIXES WITH THE WORDS DESIGNATING THE MAIN TYPES OF BUILDINGS (the Ancient Period)

	1 AUTHOR	2 AUTHORS	3 OR MORE
Singular	23 **96%**	0	0
Dual	0	5 **62.5%**	0
Plural	1 **4%**	3 **37.5%**	2 **100%**
TOTAL	24 **100%**	8 **100%**	2 **100%**

Table 38. USE OF THE POSSESSIVE PRONOMINAL SUFFIXES WITH THE WORDS FOR

any *byt* mentioned in the inscriptions, and that has led me to consider *byt* as one of the "words denoting buildings".

[12] Only funerary and public structures have not been taken into consideration.

BUILDINGS (the Sabaean cultural-political area ["North"] in the Middle Period)

	1 AUTHOR	2 AUTHORS	3 OR MORE
Singular	4 **13%**	1 **5%**	0
Dual	0	0	0
Plural	27 **87%**	20 **95%**	73 **100%**
TOTAL	31 **100%**	21 **100%**	73 **100%**

Table 39. USE OF THE POSSESSIVE PRONOMINAL SUFFIXES WITH THE WORDS DESIGNATING ALL THE MAIN TYPES OF BUILDINGS (the Himyarite-Radmanite cultural-political area ["South"] in the Middle Period)

	1 AUTHOR	2 AUTHORS	3 OR MORE
Singular	17 **63%**	0	0
Dual	0	4 **33%**	0
Plural	10 **37%**	8 **67%**	17 **100%**
TOTAL	27 **100%**	12 **100%**	17 **100%**

The data of tables 37-39 could be also presented in the following form:

Table 40. USE OF THE POSSESSIVE PRONOMINAL SUFFIXES WITH THE WORDS DESIGNATING ALL THE MAIN TYPES OF BUILDINGS **BY SINGLE AUTHORS** (Comparative table)

	ANCIENT PERIOD	MIDDLE PERIOD	
		"NORTH"	**"SOUTH"**
Singular	23 **96%**	4 **13%**	17 **63%**
Plural	1 **4%**	27 **87%**	10 **37%**
TOTAL	24 **100%**	31 **100%**	27 **100%**

The "synthetic" variables are presented in tables 41-43:

Table 41. NUMBER OF AUTHORS OF THE INSCRIPTIONS MENTIONING THEIR BUILDINGS (Comparative table)

	ANCIENT PERIOD	MIDDLE PERIOD "NORTH"	MIDDLE PERIOD "SOUTH"
1 author	24 **65%**	31 **20%**	27 **47%**
2 or more	13 **35%**	124 **80%**	30 **53%**
TOTAL	37 **100%**	155 **100%**	57 **100%**

Table 42. FORMS OF THE POSSESSIVE PRONOMINAL SUFFIXES USED WITH THE WORDS DESIGNATING AUTHORS' BUILDINGS OF VARIOUS KINDS (Version 1)

	ANCIENT PERIOD	MIDDLE PERIOD "NORTH"	MIDDLE PERIOD "SOUTH"
Singular	28 **58%**	5 **2%**	19 **28%**
Dual	8 **17%**	0 **0%**	5 **7%**
Plural	12 **25%**	196 **98%**	45 **65%**
TOTAL	48 **100%**	201 **100%**	69 **100%**

Table 43. FORMS OF THE POSSESSIVE PRONOMINAL SUFFIXES USED WITH THE WORDS DESIGNATING AUTHORS' BUILDINGS OF VARIOUS KINDS (Version 2)

	ANCIENT PERIOD	MIDDLE PERIOD "NORTH"	MIDDLE PERIOD "SOUTH"
Sg.+Dl.	36 **75%**	5 **2%**	24 **35%**
Pl.	12 **25%**	196 **98%**	45 **65%**
TOTAL	48 **100%**	201 **100%**	69 **100%**

As we can see, the complex of property relations in structures did not differ considerably from that in land. Here again the "collectivistic North" contrasts with the "individualistic Antiquity";[13] the "South" is again somewhere in the middle.

It is quite remarkable that all the cases of the use of the singular form in the Middle North occur in the inscriptions from the Sabaean Lowlands (the areas of Mārib and Nashq - Nashān in al-Jawf: C 584, 2; 939, 3-4; 982, 1-2; Ja 619, 12; R 4730).[14] Most cases of the use of the plural forms in the Ancient inscriptions come from the end of this Period (C 378, 4-5; Fa 124, 6; Gl 1592, 3; R 3911, 2, 3; 4198, 1-2, 2; Robin/ Ṣirwāḥ 7, 6; Y.81.C.0/ 1, 3).

d."Immovable property words" in general

Both classes of words designating the two main kinds of immovable property show more or less identical pictures of their usage of the possessive pronominal suffixes. Hence, the picture of the use of the suffixes with "immovable property words" in general turns out to be identical with that which was observed with respect to both of the above-mentioned types.

---

[13] One may also notice, that in the Ancient Sabaean inscriptions in expressions of the formula ***X* *d̲t byt* *Y***, "X of the house of Y", one finds a name of an individual (and not clan) in Y position (C 551; I 3; Na NNSQ 27; AQ/17 = Er 43; see also Lundin 1974 a). The singular and dual forms of the possessive pronominal suffixes used with the words designating various kinds of buildings are perfectly normal not only in the Ancient Sabaic inscriptions, but in the Ancient Minaic (Madhabian) and Ancient and Early Middle Qatabanic texts as well (Madhabian inscriptions - e.g. Haram 2, 11; R 2789 [= M 43], 2; 2791 [= M 45], 3-4, 4; 2843 [= M 95 = Kamna 12], 4; 2949 [= Ta 148 = M 168], 3; 2953 [= Ta 153 = M 173], 2; 4728 [= Ja 422 = M 381], 2; 4731 [= Ja 412 = M 382], 2; 4834 [= M 383], 1; Qatabanic texts - e.g. Be 9 [= Q 240], 5; Doe 5, 2; HI 61 [= Q 264], 3; Ja 118 [= Q 265], 2; 119 [= Q 266], 2; 2357 [= Q 691], 1; 2360 [= VL 6 = Q 694], 9; 2366 [= Q 700], 5; 2457 [= Q 790], 2; NAM 1646 [CIAS II 49.81/ r9/ N1 = Q 909], 1; R 3882 [= Q 82], 2-3; 3962 [= Q 99], 3; 3964 [= VL 12 = Ry 495 = Q 101], 1-2; 4273 [= Q 167], 3; 4332 [= Doe /Am ᶜAdīya 1 = Ja 1096 = Q 179], 1; 4337 B [= Q 186 B], 12; Ry 463 [= Q 860], 2; YMN 2, 5-6). As one can see, the immovable property relations in all the main centres of the Ancient South Arabian civilization (for which we have relevant data) appear essentially similar. Not only in the Ancient Sabaean cultural area but also in the Ancient Madhabian and Qatabanian ones were they rather "individualistic". Incidentally, inscriptions YMN 1 and 2 demonstrate quite impressively the evident link between the "individualistic" Ancient Qatabanian tradition and the one of the relatively "individualistic" Himyarite-Radmanite Area of the Middle Period (= the Southern half of the area of the Middle Sabaic epigraphy). These two inscriptions of the 1st century AD represent practically the same text reproduced both in Qatabanic (YMN 1) and Sabaic (YMN 2); and its author mention "his *bayt*" both in Qatabanic (YMN 1, 5-6: *by[t]-s*) and Sabaic (YMN 2, 6-7: *byt-hw*).

[14] The provenance of YM 544 [CIAS I 95.41/ b4] is unknown.

Table 44. USE OF THE POSSESSIVE PRONOMINAL SUFFIXES WITH THE WORDS DESIGNATING ALL THE MAIN TYPES OF IMMOVABLE PROPERTY (on the basis of all the accessible Sabaic inscriptions)

	1 AUTHOR	2 AUTHORS	3 OR MORE
Singular	95 **43%**	1 **1%**	0
Dual	0	18 **18%**	0
Plural	127 **57%**	82 **81%**	207 **100%**
TOTAL	222 **100%**	101 **100%**	207 **100%**

Table 45. USE OF THE POSSESSIVE PRONOMINAL SUFFIXES WITH THE WORDS DESIGNATING ALL THE MAIN TYPES OF IMMOVABLE PROPERTY (the Ancient Period)

	1 AUTHOR	2 AUTHORS	3 OR MORE
Singular	56 **98%**	0	0
Dual	0	15 **79%**	0
Plural	1 **2%**	4 **21%**	6 **100%**
TOTAL	57 **100%**	19 **100%**	6 **100%**

Table 46. USE OF THE POSSESSIVE PRONOMINAL SUFFIXES WITH THE WORDS DESIGNATING ALL THE MAIN TYPES OF IMMOVABLE PROPERTY (the Sabaean cultural-political area ["North"] in the Middle Period)

	1 AUTHOR	2 AUTHORS	3 OR MORE
Singular	6 **5%**	1 **1%**	0
Dual	0	0	0
Plural	104 **95%**	69 **99%**	137 **100%**
TOTAL	110 **100%**	70 **100%**	137 **100%**

Table 47. USE OF THE POSSESSIVE PRONOMINAL SUFFIXES WITH THE WORDS FOR ALL THE MAIN TYPES OF IMMOVABLE PROPERTY ("South" in the Middle Period)

	1 AUTHOR	2 AUTHORS	3 OR MORE
Singular	29 **64%**	0	0
Dual	0	6 **33%**	0
Plural	16 **36%**	12 **67%**	30 **100%**
TOTAL	45 **100%**	18 **100%**	30 **100%**

To facilitate the comparison tables 45-47 are presented below in the following form:

Table 48. USE OF THE POSSESSIVE PRONOMINAL SUFFIXES WITH THE WORDS FOR ALL THE MAIN TYPES OF IMMOVABLE PROPERTY **BY SINGLE AUTHORS** (Comparative table)

	ANCIENT PERIOD	MIDDLE PERIOD	
		"NORTH"	**"SOUTH"**
Singular	56 **98%**	6 **5%**	29 **64%**
Plural	1 **2%**	104 **95%**	16 **36%**

The general "synthetic" variables are presented in tables 49-51:

Table 49. NUMBER OF AUTHORS OF THE INSCRIPTIONS MENTIONING IMMOVABLE PROPERTY (Comparative table)

	ANCIENT PERIOD	MIDDLE PERIOD	
		"NORTH"	**"SOUTH"**
1 author	57 **66%**	110 **30%**	45 **46%**
2 or more	30 **34%**	252 **70%**	53 **54%**

Table 50. FORMS OF POSSESSIVE PRONOMINAL SUFFIXES USED WITH THE WORDS DESIGNATING AUTHORS' IMMOVABLE PROPERTY OF VARIOUS KINDS (Version 1)

	ANCIENT PERIOD	MIDDLE PERIOD	
		"NORTH"	"SOUTH"
Singular	64 **61%**	7 **1%**	31 **28%**
Dual	20 **19%**	0 **0%**	7 **6%**
Plural	21 **20%**	471 **99%**	72 **65%**

Table 51. FORMS OF POSSESSIVE PRONOMINAL SUFFIXES USED WITH THE WORDS DESIGNATING AUTHORS' IMMOVABLE PROPERTY OF VARIOUS KINDS (Version 2)

	ANCIENT PERIOD	MIDDLE PERIOD	
		"NORTH"	"SOUTH"
Sg.+Dl.	84 **80%**	7 **1%**	38 **35%**
Plural	21 **20%**	471 **99%**	72 **65%**

Finally, the summary comparative tables for the main variables:

Table 52. USE OF THE POSSESSIVE SUFFIXES IN SINGLE-AUTHOR INSCRIPTIONS

	ANCIENT PERIOD		MIDDLE PERIOD			
			NORTH		SOUTH	
	Sing.	**Pl.**	**Sing.**	**Pl.**	**Sing.**	**Pl.**
LANDS	33 **100%**	0 **0%**	2 **3%**	77 **97%**	12 **67%**	6 **33%**
BUILDINGS	23 **96%**	1 **4%**	4 **13%**	27 **87%**	17 **63%**	10 **37%**
ALL IMMOV. PROPERTY	56 **98%**	1 **2%**	6 **5%**	104 **95%**	29 **64%**	16 **36%**

Table 53. USE OF THE POSSESSIVE SUFFIXES IN DOUBLE-AUTHOR INSCRIPTIONS

	ANCIENT PERIOD		MIDDLE PERIOD			
			NORTH		SOUTH	
	Dual	Pl.	Dual	Pl.	Dual	Pl.
LANDS	10 **91%**	1 **9%**	0 **0%**	49 **100%**	2 **33%**	4 **67%**
BUILDINGS	5 **62.5%**	3 **37.5%**	0 **0%**	20 **95%**[15]	4 **33%**	8 **67%**
ALL IMMOV. PROPERTY	15 **79%**	4 **21%**	0 **0%**	69 **99%**[16]	6 **33%**	12 **67%**

Table 54. NUMBER OF AUTHORS OF THE INSCRIPTIONS MENTIONING IMMOVABLE PROPERTY (Summary)

	ANCIENT PERIOD		MIDDLE PERIOD			
			NORTH		SOUTH	
	1 AUTHOR	2 OR MORE	1 AUTHOR	2 OR MORE	1 AUTHOR	2 OR MORE
LANDS	33 **66%**	17 **34%**	79 **38%**	128 **62%**	18 **44%**	23 **56%**
BUILDINGS	24 **65%**	13 **35%**	31 **20%**	124 **80%**	27 **47%**	30 **53%**
ALL IMMOV. PROPERTY	57 **66%**	30 **34%**	110 **30%**	252 **70%**	45 **46%**	53 **54%**

---

[15] Taking into consideration one case of the singular form (*-hw*) in Ja 619,12.

[16] Taking into consideration one case of the singular form (*-hw*) in Ja 619,12.

Table 55. FORMS OF THE POSSESSIVE PRONOMINAL SUFFIXES USED WITH THE WORDS DESIGNATING AUTHORS' IMMOVABLE PROPERTY OF VARIOUS KINDS (Summary)

	ANCIENT PERIOD		MIDDLE PERIOD			
			NORTH		SOUTH	
	Sg.+Dl.	**Pl.**	**Sg.+Dl.**	**Pl.**	**Sg.+Dl.**	**Pl.**
LANDS	48 **84%**	9 **16%**	2 **0.7%**	275 **99.3%**	14 **34%**	27 **66%**
BUILDINGS	36 **75%**	12 **25%**	5 **2%**	196 **98%**	24 **35%**	45 **65%**
ALL IMMOV. PROPERTY	84 **80%**	21 **20%**	7 **1%**	471 **99%**	38 **35%**	72 **65%**

These results can be interpreted in the following way: in the Sabaean cultural-political area of the Middle Period ("in the North") no immovable property (with very rare exceptions[17]) could be considered to belong to individual persons. Fields, plantations, vineyards, irrigation canals, dams, houses, wells, cisterns and so on were conceived as belonging to certain groups.[18]

However, the situation in the Ancient Period differed greatly from that described above: at this time immovable property was usually considered to belong to individual persons.

---

[17] As we can see above these exceptions may be interpreted as "relics" of the Ancient Period society survived in the Sabaean Lowlands which were archaized less significantly than the "Sabaean" Highlands.

[18] It does not seem possible to state the same with respect to the livestock which appears to have been considered by the Middle "Sabaeans" in most cases as belonging to individuals rather than to whole clans (see C 521, 4; 535, 8-10; 572, 6; Gl 1126, 5, 8; Ja 709, 5-6; 2956 [= YM 617], 8; NAM 230 = AM 222 = CIAS II 95.11/o8 N1, 3-4; R 4143, 3; 4144, 4-5; Ry 535, 5-6; *Shibʿānu* 1, 11-12 &c). Such a co-existence of the clan possession of land with the individual possession of the livestock does not appear surprising, as this is attested for many archaic societies (see e.g. Kradin 1991).

This evidence, I believe, is not sufficient to produce the conclusion that individual private property relations were **completely** dominant in the Ancient Period. The sources give grounds to maintain that this type of relation was dominant at that time among a certain category of persons, i.e. among the authors of the inscriptions. Yet it is evident that not all the inhabitants of the Ancient Sabaean cultural-political area authored inscriptions. It is remarkable that a very considerable proportion of the mentions of the authors' immovable property come from the construction inscriptions. However, one of the main aims of the installation of these inscriptions seems to have been simply to claim individual private property rights in the erected object. The most epigraphically active were the persons who aimed to gain certain possessions as their private property, to stand apart from their clans and communities. Yet beside this vigorously growing category of "private proprietors" (or perhaps even around it) considerable masses of the population with traditional "clan-tribal" forms of social organization and collective property seem to have always remained.

For example, inscription C 37 (the second half of then Ancient Period - approximately the first half of the 3rd century BC [v.Wissmann 1964 a, 276-279; 1968, 9]) shows a general picture of quite highly developed private property relations. Its author, the king of Sum^{c}ay (a kingdom dependent on the Sabaeans and situated in Arḥab, in the Nothern Highland) Yuha^{c}īn, mentions (lines 2-4) *qny-hw w-byt-hw Y^{c}D w-'rḍt-hw T'LQM w-kl qny-hw w-qny 'b-hw YSM^c'L [w-q]ny w-mḥmyt w-^{c}brt w-'byt w-'rḍt twrṯy 'b-hmy SMH'FQ bn SMHYF^c mlk SM^{c}Y b-ḥqlm w-hgrm w-mḥmy-h[w ḏ-]N^{c}MN*, "his property and his house Y^{c}D and his lands T'LQM and all his property and the property of his father YSM^c'L [and] his [pro]perty and irrigated fields and terraced fields and houses and lands which they both inherited from the father (i.e. ancestor) of them both SMH'FQ son of SMHYF^c, the king of Sum^{c}ay, in the countriside as well as (in) *hagar*,[19] and hi[s] irrigated field N^{c}MN"; and further, on lines 5-6: *w-^{c}br-hw ḏt-ḏ-SMH^{c}LY fnwt syr ḤDQN ḏ-qny w-^{c}sy ^{c}mn ^{c}MS^2[FQ] bn SRWM qwl YRSM w-^{c}br-hw ḏt D'Ḫ*, "and his terraced fields of ḏ-SMH^{c}LY in the

[19] *Hagar* (*hgr*) is the main type of the ancient South Arabian settlements, it cannot be rendered either as "a city", or "a village", as it was a type of undifferentiated settlement, communal centre, quite characterictic for many archaic societies (something like archaic Greek *polis* - for more detail see Beeston 1971; Korotayev 1988). Modern languages have no appropriate word to render this notion (as well as a lot of other ancient concepts), that is why it might be more reasonable to avoid doing so and to employ instead original words of the ancient languages (as for example has already been done with the above-mentioned ancient Greek notion of *polis*).

agricultural vicinity of Ḥadaqān which he acquired and bought from ^{c}MS^{2}[FQ], son of SRWM, *qayl* of Yarsum, and his terraced fields of D'H̲"; and further, on lines 8-9: *w-^{c}br-hw ḤYS^{3} [d̲-s^{2}'m] w-^{c}sy w-qny ^{c}mn...*, "and his terraced fields ḤYS^{3} [which he bought] and acquired ..." (the end of the inscription has not been preserved).

Certainly the level of individual private ownership evidenced by the inscription is impressive. The very fact of the rigid distinction between the private land possessions of the king and the private land property of his subjects is remarkable. The king virtually acts as one of the private landowners of his kingdom; he arranges the transactions with them as with his legal equals.[20] The very "civilized" forms of the acquisition of the land possessions (through direct patrilineal inheritance and purchasing[21]) are another remarkable point. It is also notable that the above-described seller is an individual person too, though not quite an ordinary one. He seems to be a high-ranking royal official.

Yet even this inscription, while providing very good evidence for the high level of the development of individual private property relations in the Ancient Sabaean cultural-political area, shows as well the conservation of the collective clan landownership forms in this period. The fact is that the seller of the above-mentioned irrigated field of N^{c}MN is described as follows (lines 3-4): *w-mḥmy-h[w d̲-]N^{c}MN d̲-^{c}sy w-s^{2}'m ^{c}mn BKRM w-HWF^{c}T̲T w-HMT^{c}T̲T w-HWTR^{c}T̲T w-^{c}mn HWTR^{c}T̲T w-^{c}MS^{2}FQ w-YH^{c}N w-[^{c}]MSM^{c} w-GN'M w-Ẓ̣RM w-'h̲-hmw bny R'BN*, "and hi[s] irrigated field [of] N^{c}MN which he acquired and bought from BKRM and HWF^{c}T̲T and HMT^{c}T̲T and HWTR^{c}T̲T and from HWTR^{c}T̲T and ^{c}MS^{2}FQ and YH^{c}N and [^{c}]MSM^{c} and GN'M and ẒRM and their brothers[22], the sons of (the clan) R'BN". Thus, Yuha^{c}īn, the king of Sum^{c}ay, had to buy the field from more than ten sellers with their clansmen. I.e. to buy this field he had to get the consent of all the competent members of the clan R'BN and to pay all of them. Hence we have sufficient grounds to suppose

[20] The situation could be compared for example with that attested in C 516 [= Haram 15] coming from another vassal kingdom of the Sabaean cultural-political area, Haram. Its author, a subject of the king of Haram Yad̲murmalik, digs a well and then grants it on lease to his own king (lines 19-21). Certainly it should be kept in mind that this inscription is much more ancient than C 37.

[21] Yet lines 6-8 of the same inscription mention some other forms of property acquisition: acquisition through mutual agreement (*'tm*), as well as getting the immovable property as a gift. Among the grantors we find an individual person, the Sabaean kings (aiming at enlisting the support of their vassal?) and (most remarkable) all the people of Sum^{c}ay, i.e. Yuha^{c}īn's subjects as a whole.

[22] In such a context *'h̲-hmw*, "their brothers", means certainly "their clansmen", and not blood brothers.

that the whole of this clan was considered as the possessor of the field d-NᶜMN. We are very likely dealing here with a vivid example of the realization of collective clan land ownership. For similar cases (co-existence of lands belonging to individuals, very often the authors of the respective texts, and collective clan possessions of their neighbours) see also in Ancient inscriptions C 555; 615; Gl 1520/?/; Minaic R 3310 [= M 297 = Haram 42] &c.[23]

However, in general there is not much doubt that the process of the formation of individual private immovable property ownership brought really significant results in the Ancient Period when these relations reached a very high level of development. But at the end of this Period it is possible to observe the symptoms of more or less the reverse process: collective land ownership consolidates, individual private land ownership weakens.

Hence there are some grounds to suppose that the processes of "archaization" which developed in the Sabaean cultural-political area at the end of the Ancient Period brought the most significant results in one of the most fundamental fields, in the field of property relations. Yet the "archaization" of property relations in the Southern (Himyarite-Radmanite) part of the area of the Middle Sabaic epigraphy was not so total. The idea that immovable property could belong to individuals and not only to collective bodies was quite widespread here; this leads one to the supposition that the Ancient "individualistic" tradition was preserved in this area much better than in the "North".

e. "We" and "I" in the Sabaean cultural-political area

It is quite evident that in the "Middle North" all the main types of immovable property were considered to belong to certain groups, and not to individuals. It is quite evident that behind any possessive pronominal suffix *-hmw*, "their", we have the personal pronoun *hmw*, "they". And it was those *hmw*, "they" (usually not defined), who were considered as the real possessors of all the main kinds of immovable property. It is quite evident that these groups played an extremely important role in the Middle Period, and especially in the "Northern", Sabaean, cultural-political area.

[23] Certainly it does not mean that in the Ancient Period the private lands of the individual persons were always surrounded by the collective clan possessions. Some cases are known when the private lands of individual persons bordered on the private lands of other individuals without mention of any collective clan possessions in the area: Gl 1138; 1664; &c.

Another important point should certainly be kept in mind. According to a stable South Arabian epigraphic tradition, all the inscriptions should be written in the third person. So one would not write something like "I, **X**, son of **Y**, of (the clan) **Z**, **have** built **my** house". Instead one would write: "**X**, son of **Y**, of (the clan) **Z**, **has** built **his** house"[24]. Thus any *-hw*, "his", in such a context implies "my" (and conseqently "I"), as well as any *-hmw*, "their", would imply "our" (and consequently "We"). "I" and "We" seem to have been also implicated in the singular or plural forms of the Middle Sabaean titles. It is "We" who are the *qayl*s of a certain tribe **Z**, this title is "Our" and not "My" property, and that is why I would not call myself "**X**, son of (the clan) **Y**, the *qayl* of the tribe **Z**", but I would call myself "**X**, son of (the clan) **Y**, (who are) the *qayl***s** of the tribe **Z**". And that is why such an "abstract" variable as the relative proportion of some singular and plural forms turns out to be an important indicator of the character of certain social relations.

A large proportion of some singular forms is an evident indicator of "strong I", whereas a large percentage of plural forms (in certain positions and contexts) is a good indicator of "strong We" and "weak I". In these terms the Ancient epoch turns out to be a period of emancipation of "I" from "We". This process seems not to have been completed, but it yielded some significant results. At the same time the end of the Ancient epoch can be considered as a period when "We" began absorbing "I", when "We" appreciably marginalized "I" in some important spheres of social life, and when "We" almost completely forced out "I" from some other spheres (first of all from the sphere of immovable property relations).

On the other hand, it is quite evident that, for example, *'rḍ-hmw*, "their land", of the Middle Sabaic inscriptions is usually just "our land"; it is the land of We-group and as it is usually evident who We are (at least for Us), this does not need any clarification. It is not surprising that such clarifications occur rarely, but due to the really large number of all the cases it is possible to find at least several clarifications of this kind, which make it possible to find the answer to the question of who those powerful "We-groups" are. For example, the authors of Er 19 from the clan Gurat (line 1) mention certain construction works undertaken by them *b-byt-hmw b-byt GRT*, "in their *bayt*, in the *bayt* of (the clan) Gurat" (line 24). *-hmw*, "their", turns out to be

[24] See for example C 368 [= MAFRAY/ Abū-Ṯawr 2]: ^{c}M'MR *bn* 'B'MR *ḏ*-YBRN *mwd* SMH^{c}LY *w*-YṮ^{c}'MR *bny bt-hw* MRD^{c}m--- "^{c}Ammi'amar, son of Abi'amar, of (the clan) Yabran, favorite of Sumhu^{c}alay and Yaṯa^{c}'mar, **has** built **his** house (named) Marda^{c}".

equal to "of their clan", hence, "they" (and consequently "We") must be just "their (and consequently "Our") clan". In R 4627 (the end of the Ancient Period) the authors from the clan ḤLḤLM (lines 1-2) mention on line 3 *nḫl-hmw*, "their palm grove", after which we find a clarification, *nḫl bn ḤLḤLM*, "the palm grove of the clan ḤLḤLM". And every time when we have such an opportunity, it practically always turns out (not surprisingly) that "We" is just "My clan" (C 457, 7 /?/; Ja 560, 6-7; 591, 10; 603, 6-7; 615, 11-12, 21; Ga 29, 3; NAM 2659 [CIAS II 39.11/o6 N 6], 5-6; &c).[25] Thus there are certain grounds to suppose that the above-mentioned influential "We-groups", the collective bodies which were considered to be real possessors of all the main kinds of immovable property in the Middle Sabaean cultural-political area, were simply the clan groups. Hence, there is another good piece of evidence to suppose the significant consolidation of the clan organization in the "North" at the end of the Ancient Period and the rise in its importance.

The quantitative analysis of the Sabaic epigraphy undertaken above has resulted in conclusions some of which cannot be considered as universally recognized. That is why it is necessary to study how these conclusions fit into the general picture of the evolution of the Sabaean cultural-political area.

NOTES TO THE TABLES OF CHAPTER 3

Note to table 28: this table (as well as all the other tables in this chapter) considers only the application of the pronominal suffixes related to the authors of the inscriptions and the groups which include them. E.g. number X in the square 1 AUTHOR - **Singular** indicates that in Sabaic single author inscriptions "land property words" occur in combination with the singular possessive pronominal suffix (*-hw*) related to the author X times. The similar description is applicable to all the numbers (except the percentages) of all the tables of this chapter. The tables count cases, not inscriptions. The author's personal name used in the place of the pronominal suffix is considered to be equal to *-hw*, "his". The clan name used in this position is considered to be equal to *-hmw*, "their" (anyhow the number of such cases is not large).

Description of cases:

1 AUTHOR - **Singular:** Be 10 [= Ja 1093 = Q 611], 1-2, 2-3; C 37, 2, 5, 6, 8; 356, the top edge;

---

[25] Only very rarely does *-hmw* in this position mean anything else. The only important exception is -*hmw* meaning "of his clan and tribe". For example, the author of Er 22, of the clan dhū-Ghaymān, the *qayl*s of the tribe Ghaymān, asks (part 2) the deity for the well-being of *'byt-hmw*, "their houses" (certainly in such a context "house" denotes first of all a "house community" or clan community, and not simply a house building). Immediately after that a clarification follows : *'byt ḏ-Ġymn w-s^{2c}b-hmw Ġymn*, "the houses of (the clan) dhū-Ghaymān and of their tribe Ghaymān". In this case "We" has embraced both the author's clan and their tribe. It is not surprising at all, because the area of the concerns and responsibilities of the heads of the qaylite clans must have been much broader than that of the heads of the ordinary clans. The former seem to have been responsible for the well-being both of their own clans and of all the other clans of their tribes, thus they must have been thinking in broader categories than the latter. What is really surprising is the fact that the *qayl*s did so quite rarely. In general while reading the *qayl*s' inscriptions it is difficult to avoid an impression that usually they were concerned with the well-being of their own clans much more than with the well-being of the tribes which they headed.

399, 3; 403, 3; 414, 2; 516 [= Haram 15], 13-14; 518 [= Haram 49], 3; 584, 2-3; 657, 1, 2, 2; 658, 3; 939, 3-4; 982, 2; Fa 61, 3; 70, 2; Ga 27 [NIS 1], 2; Gl 1100, 2, 2; 1742; Ist 7632, 3; Ja 541, 4, 10 /?/; 550 [= C 375], 1; 555, 2, 3, 3, 3, 3; Lu 26, 4; MAFRAY/ d̲ī-Ḥadīd 2, 4-5; / Sāri^c 6, 3; 7, 3-4; R 3902 bis N 131, 3; 3913, 3; 3946, 6; 4100, 3, 4; YM 453 [CIAS I 39.11/r9/P12 N4], 2-3; YMN 3, 3; 4, 4; 7, 3;

1 AUTHOR - **Plural:** C 282, 13, 14; 342, 7, 11; 378, 4-5; 392, 4-6; 395, 3; 605 bis, 3; Er 5 §6, 6; 10 §1; 22 §1, 1, 1, 1, 1, 1, 1, 1, 2, 2, 2, 2; 24 §2, 2; 28 §2, 2; 29 §2, 2; 36, 6, 12, 12; Ghul/ Ḥūt̲ 1, 5; 2, 2-3; Gl 1218, 16; Ja 562, 13, 13; 564, 20-21, 21, 21, 21; 567, 11; 601, 17; 602 [= Na NAG 17], 17; 610, 6; 613, 22; 627 [= Na NAG 6], 5, 7, 11, 22, 22, 23; 628, 23, 23; 630, 17-18; 631, 40, 40, 40-41; 645 [= Na NAG 9], 24, 24-25, 25; 650, 13, 13-14, 14, 14, 14, 16, 16; 651, 48-49; 657, 11; 2897, 8; MAFRAY/ d̲ī-Ḥadīd 1, 5-6, 6; MAFY/ aṣ-Ṣawla^c 1A, 3; Na NAG 2, 8; R 3958, 3; 3967, 2; 4057 d, 4; 4196, 2; Ry 394, 6-7; YM 392, 6, 12, 12; YMN 9, 3;

2 AUTHORS - **Dual:** C 652, 2; 655, 2; Fa 32 [= Gl 928], 2; Ghul/ al-Masāǧid 2, 2, 2; Gl 1093, 2; 1355, 2; R 3902 bis N 130, 2-3; 4793 - 4806; 4907 [= Gl 1563], 3-4;

2 AUTHORS - **Plural:** C 308, 5, 5; 343, 5, 6, 12, 12; 544, 10; 630, 4; Er 17 §4, 4, 4; 18, 22; 19, 31; 26 §2, 2, 2, 2, 2, 2; 27 §2, 2; 37, 30-31, 31; Gl 1320/ I, 8, 10 ≈ II, 8, 9, 10; Ja 618, 23, 24, 24; 670, 27, 27-28, 29, 30; 704, 6, 6; 746, 5; 2115 (= AM 857 = NAM 1627 [CIAS II 39.11/o8 N7]), 7; MAFRAY/ al-Maktūba 1, 3; NAM 2659 [CIAS II 39.11/ o6 N6], 5; Na NAG 11 [= Er 25], 15, 15, 16, 16, 16-17, 17; R 4194, 3; 4626 [= Gl 1352 + 1354], 1; 4938, 19; Ry 404, 2, 2;

3 OR MORE - **Plural:** ^cAbadān 1, 32, 33, 35, 35, 36; C 2, 13-14, 14, 15-16, 16; 24, 4; 67, 18; 74, 5-6; 75, 7, 7; 77, 8, 8-9; 160, 11, 11-12, 12; 240, 6-7; 333, 11, 11; 348, 11-12, 12; 353, 18; 546 [= Haram 8], 10-11, 11, 11; 611, 2, 4, 6, 8; Er 4 §2, 2; 6 §2; 7 §2, 4; Fa 53a + 54 + 53b [= Ja 532]; 124, 7; Gl 1438, 6; 1537, 6, 6, 7, 7; 1725, 7; Gr 15, 16-17, 17; Ist 7630, 5, 5; Ja 561 bis, 21, 21; 563, 13; 565, 15; 567, 24; 615, 10, 10, 10-11, 20, 20, 20-21, 21; 620, 12, 12; 656, 18, 24-25; 669, 19; 703, 6, 6, 7; 735, 2; 851, 5; 1819, 7, 8, 9, 10; 2356a, 8; MAFRAY/ ad-Dimn 1, 4; Na NAG 8, 18, 18-19, 19; R 3915, 2; 3966, 6-7, 9-10; 4096, 6, 11; 4188, 6-7; 4190, 10-11, 11; 4356, 3; 4627, 3; 4636, 6; 4815, 2, 3, 6, 7; 5085, 6; Robin/ Kāniṭ 7, 11; /Umm Layla 1, 6; Ry 538, 39; YMN 5 [= MAFRAY/ Mah̲liq 1A], 4.

Note to table 29: description of cases:

1 AUTHOR - **Singular:** C 584, 2-3 /?/; Fa 61, 3;

1 AUTHOR - **Plural:** C 282, 13, 14; 342, 7, 11; 378, 4-5; 392, 4-6; 395, 3; 605 bis, 3; Er 5 §6, 6; 10 §1; 22 §1, 1, 1, 1, 1, 1, 1, 1, 2, 2, 2, 2; 24 §2, 2; 28 §2, 2; 29 §2, 2; 36, 6, 12, 12; Ghul/ Ḥūt̲ 1, 5; 2, 2-3; Gl 1218, 16; Ja 562, 13, 13; 564, 20-21, 21, 21, 21; 567, 11; 601, 17; 602 [= Na NAG 17], 17; 610, 6; 613, 22; 627 [= Na NAG 6], 5, 7, 11, 22, 22, 23; 628, 23, 23; 630, 17-18; 631, 40, 40, 40-41; 645 [= Na NAG 9], 24, 24-25, 25; 650, 13, 13-14, 14, 14, 14, 16, 16; 651, 48-49; 657, 11; 2897, 8; Na NAG 2, 8; R 3967, 2; Ry 394, 6-7; YM 392 [CIAS I 39.11/ o6 N1], 6, 12, 12;

2 AUTHORS - **Plural:** C 308, 5, 5; 343, 5, 6, 12, 12; 544, 10; 630, 4; Er 17 §4, 4, 4; 18, 22; 19, 31; 26 §2, 2, 2, 2, 2, 2; 27 §2, 2; 37, 30-31, 31; Gl 1320/ I, 8, 10 ≈ II, 8, 9, 10; Ja 618, 23, 24, 24; 670, 27, 27-28, 29, 30; 704, 6, 6; 746, 5; 2115 (= AM 857 = NAM 1627 [CIAS II 39.11/ o8 N1]), 7; NAM 2659 [CIAS II 39.11/ o6 N6], 5; Na NAG 11 [= Er 25], 15, 15, 16, 16, 16-17, 17; R 4938, 19; Ry 404, 2, 2;

3 OR MORE - **Plural:** C 2, 13-14, 14, 15-16, 16; 24, 4; 67, 18; 74, 5-6; 75, 7, 7; 77, 8, 8-9; 160, 11, 11-12, 12; 240, 6-7; 333, 11, 11; 348, 11-12, 12; 353, 18; 546 [= Haram 8], 10-11, 11, 11; Er 4 §2, 2; 6 §2; 7 §2, 4; Gl 1438, 6; 1725, 7; Gr 15, 16-17, 17; Ja 561 bis, 21, 21; 563, 13; 565, 15; 567, 24; 615, 10, 10, 10-11, 20, 20, 20-21, 21; 620, 12, 12; 656, 18, 24-25; 669, 19; 703, 6, 6, 7; 735, 2; 851, 5; Na NAG 8, 18, 18-19, 19; R 4188, 6-7; 4190, 10-11, 11; 4636, 6; Robin/ Kāniṭ 7, 11; /Umm Layla 1, 6; Ry 538, 39.

Note to table 30: practically all the Ancient Sabaic inscriptions come from the Sabaean cultural-political area.

Description of cases:

1 AUTHOR - **Singular:** C 37, 2, 5, 6, 8; 356, the top edge; 399, 3; 403, 3 /?/; 414, 2; 516 [= Haram 15], 13-14 /?/; 518 [= Haram 49], 3; 657, 1, 2, 2; 939, 3-4; 982, 2; Fa 70, 2; Ga 27 [NIS 1], 2; Gl 1100, 2, 2; 1742; Ist 7632, 3; Ja 541, 4, 10 /?/; 550 [= C 375], 1; 555, 2, 3, 3, 3, 3; R 3902 bis N 131, 3; 3913, 3; 3946, 6; YM 453 [CIAS I 39.11/r9/P12 N 14], 2-3;

2 AUTHORS - **Dual:** C 652, 2; 655, 2; Fa 32 [= Gl 928], 2; Ghul/ al-Masāǧid 2, 2, 2; Gl 1093, 2; 1355, 2; R 3902 bis N 130, 2-3; 4793-4806; 4907 [= Gl 1563], 3-4;

2 AUTHORS - **Plural:** R 4626 [= Gl 1352 + 1354], 1;

3 AUTHORS - **Plural:** Fa 53A + 54 + 53B [= Ja 532]; 124, 7; R 3915, 2; 4627, 3.

Note to table 31: description of cases:

1 AUTHOR - **Singular:** Be 10 [= Ja 1093 = Q 611], 1-2, 2-3; C 658, 3; Lu 26, 4; MAFRAY/ d̲ī-Ḥadīd 2, 4-5;/ Sāriᶜ 6, 3; 7, 3-4; R 4100, 3, 4; YMN 3, 3; 4, 4; 7, 3;

1 AUTHOR - **Plural:** MAFRAY/ d̲ī-Ḥadīd 1, 5-6, 6; MAFY/ aṣ-Ṣawlaᶜ 1A, 3; R 3958, 3; 4196, 2 /?/; YMN 9, 3;

2 AUTHORS - **Dual:** R 4194, 4, 4;

2 AUTHORS - **Plural:** MAFRAY/ al-Maktūba 1, 3; R 4194, 3, 3, 4;

3 AUTHORS - **Plural:** Gl 1537, 6, 6, 7, 7; Ja 1819, 7, 8, 9, 10; 2356 a, 8; MAFRAY/ ad-Dimn 1, 4; R 3966, 6-7, 9-10; YMN 5 [= MAFRAY/ Mah̲liq 1A], 4.

Note to table 33: in addition to the inscriptions covered by tables 29-31, these tables take into consideration the inscriptions about which we only know that they were authored by two or more persons without knowing the precise number of the authors due to the lacunae at the beginning of such inscriptions, or their ambiguity. They could not be taken into consideration in tables 29-31, but it is quite possible to cover them in these tables:
ANCIENT PERIOD: see table 30 + for "**2 or more**" - R 3911, 3, 4;
MIDDLE PERIOD, "**NORTH**": see table 29 + for "**2 or more**" - C 104, 13, 13-14; 567, 4, 7, 7-8; Ga 10 [Ga AY II/7], 2; Gl 1441, 3, 3, 5, 6; Ja 664, 16; 730, 7, 7; Na NAG 19 (= Lu 17 = YM 363 [CIAS I 95.41/ p6]), 4; YM 368 [CIAS I 39.11/ o5], 9;
MIDDLE PERIOD, "**SOUTH**": see table 31 + for "**2 or more**" - YMN 13, 6, 6, 7, 7-8.
As all the other tables of this monograph the present table counts cases and not inscriptions. E.g. the number X in the square "**1 author** - ANCIENT PERIOD" means that the combinations of the "land property words" with possessive pronominal suffixes related to the authors occur X times in the Ancient single-author inscriptions; it does **not** indicate the existence of X Ancient inscriptions containing such combinations.

Note to table 34: the table is prepared first of all on the basis of tables 29-31. Inscriptions with unknown exact number of authors have been used as well:

ANCIENT PERIOD - **Singular:** C 271; 372, 3; 576;

Dual: Gl 1069; R 3893, 2;

Plural: Gl 1694, 1; Ja 2834, 3; R 3911, 3, 4;

MIDDLE PERIOD, "NORTH" - **Plural:** Alfieri 1 [CIAS I 28.11/ P7], 4; Bron IAS 2, 3; C 11, 2; 28, 9, 9-10; 66, 3; 104, 13, 13-14; 191, 2; 228, 2; 298, 6; 323, 5, 6; 326, 5; 334, 28, 28; 350, 17-18, 18; 398, 13-14; 567, 4, 7, 7-8; DJE 15, 3; Fa 123, 11-12; Ga 10 [Ga AY II/7], 2; Ga NES II/10a [R 4006 + C 170 + R 4002]; Gl 1213, 6, 6; 1219, 8; 1437, 3; 1439, 8; 1441, 3, 3, 5, 6; Gr 3, 2, 2; Ja 514; 599, 8-9; 617, 5, 5, 8, 8-9, 9, 9; 623, 16, 16, 17, 17, 17, 18; 661, 8, 8; 664, 16; 730, 7, 7; 799, 6; 821 A, 4; Na NAG 17, 3, 3, 3-4; 19 (= Lu 17 = YM 363 [CIAS I 95.41/p6]), 4; Na NNSQ 24, 9, 9; 37, 1, 1; 65, 2, 2; R 4013, 4, 4, 4; 4138, 14, 14; 4372; 4727, 9; 4995 [= Na NNSQ 30 = Gr 8], 1; Robin/ Kānit 8, 9, 9-10; 9, 6; Ry 533, 26, 26; 541, 13, 13, 13; YM 368 [CIAS I 39.11/o5], 9;

MIDDLE PERIOD, "SOUTH" - **Plural:** Av. Būsān 4, 2; YMN 13, 6, 6, 7. Inscription Av. Būsān 4 is royal; and if the well-known Himyarite king Shamir Yuharᶜish is its only author (which apparently cannot be finally proved due to the lacuna at the beginning), *-hmw*, "their", of *wyn-hmw*, "their vineyard" (line 2), could well be the "royal plural" (completely normal in the Himyarite [but not Sabaean] royal inscriptions).

Note to table 36: this table (as well as all the other tables in this chapter) considers only the application of the pronominal suffixes related to the authors of the inscriptions and the groups which included them. The author's personal name used in the place of the pronominal suffix is considered to be equal to *-hw*, "his". The clan name used in this position is considered to be equal *-hmw*, "their" (anyhow the number of such cases is not large).

Description of cases:

1 AUTHOR - **Singular:** BF-BT 2, 3-4; C 37, 2; 368 [= MAFRAY/ Abū T̲awr 2]; 399, 2-3; 414, 2-3; 584, 2 /?/; 657, 1, 2-3, 3; 658, 3-4; 939, 3-4; 982, 1-2; Doe 6, 1-2; 7, 2; Ga 2 (= Ga 3 = Bait-al-Ashwāl 1), 1; Gl 1100, 1; 1519, 8; Ja 400 [= YM 262]B, 12; 552, 3; 555, 2, 3, 3; 832; Lu 26, 3; MAFRAY/ al-Ḥijla 1, 1; / Sāriᶜ 6, 3; 7, 3; R 3902 bis N 131, 2; 3946, 5; 4107, 2; 4108, 3; 4109, 5; 4553, 2; 4700, 3; Y.81.C.0/ 2, 2-3; YM 452 [CIAS I 39.11/ r9/ P12 N 2], 2; 544 [CIAS I 95.41/ b4], 1-2; YMN 1, 6-7; 3, 4, 4, 4, 5; 4, 4-5, 5, 5, 5-6; 11, 2; 12, 2;

1 AUTHOR - **Plural:** C 41, 2, 2; 81, 7; 86, 8; 194, 3; 429, 10; 530 [= Haram 32], 7; 531, 7; 532 [= Haram 33], 4; 534, 6; 569, 3; 581, 8; Er 22 §2; 24 §1; Ga 1A [Ga ŠY 1A], 3; Ghul/ Ḥūt̲ 2, 2; Gl 1367; Gr 29, 2; Ja 627 [= Na NAG 6], 10-11; 628, 5, 12; 630, 16; 689, 5; 2867, 9, 9, 9, 10; Lu 21 [= DJE 12],

2; MAFY/ d̲ī-aṣ-Ṣawla^c 1A, 2; Na NAG 2, 6; 3, 5; R 3967, 1; 4108, 3; 4196, 2; Robin/ Kāniṭ 5, 2; /Ṣirwāḥ 7, 6; Robin - Viallard 1, 2; Ry 501 [= Ja 2139], 3; 540, 1; YMN 9, 3; 10, 2, 4, 7;

2 AUTHORS - **Singular:** Ja 619, 12;

2 AUTHORS - **Dual:** BF-BT 1, 2-3; Ghul/ al-Masāǧid 3, 2; Gl 1720 [MAFRAY/ al-Balaq-al-Ǧanūbī 9], 4; R 3902 N 130, 4, 4; 4194, 3, 3; 4626 [= Gl 929 + 930], 1;

2 AUTHORS - **Plural:** C 40, 2, 2; 630, 3; Er 19, 24; 37, 30; Fa 79-85; Ga IS 4, 2 (the feminine form); Gl 1320 I ≈ II, 7; ^cInān 28; Ja 618, 6, 8, 16; 1818, 2-3, 3; NAM 2659 [CIAS II 39.11/ o6 N6], 17; Na NNSQ 22, 2-3; 26, 2, 4; R 3968 [+ 3979 + Ga 21], 2; 4194, 1, 1, 2; 4198, 1-2, 2, 5; 4775, 2; RB/ Ḥaṣī 1, 6-7; Ry 404, 1, 4;

3 AUTHORS - **Plural:** ^cAbadān 1, 32, 33, 33; Av. Aqmar 1, 2; 2, 2; Av. No^cḍ 9, 2, 3; BF-BT 4, 2, 4; C 1, 4; 6, 3; 17, 4; 24, 5; 26, 5; 88, 6; 102, 6; 153 [= DJE 11], 1-2, 2-3; 154, 2; 224, 3-4, 4; 241, 2; 242, 2; 276, 1, 3; 339, 2, 2, 4; 339 bis, 2, 5; 357, 17; 416, 2; 517, 2; 547 [= Haram 10], 9; 565, 2; 585, 2; 648, 3, 4; 649, 2; 650, 2; 660 + 587 [= Ja 411 A], 2, 2, 3, 3, 4; DJE 18 [= Sh 107], 2; Fa 77; 124, 6; Ga 3 [Bayt al-Ashwāl 2], 2; 29 [NIS 3], 3; 30 [NIS 4], 6; 36 [FES II/8], 7; Ga NES II/ 10b (C 176 + 201 + R 4003 + Ga 8b [AY II/5b]); Gl 1537, 5; 1592, 3; 1658, 4; Gr 27, 3; 33, 2; 34, 3; 41, 2; Ist 7630, 3; Ja 560, 6; 603, 6; 615, 11, 21; 716, 8; 1819 [= Doe/ W.Shirjān 19], 6; 2223, 3-4; 2839 [= Schreyer 1], 22; 2852, 2; 2859 [= R 4979 = Fa 128 = Sa 2], 2; 2871, 3; Lu 10 [= Ja 520], 5; MAFRAY/ ad-Dimn 1, 4; Müller/ Ṣirwāḥ 2, 2; Na NNSQ 28, 5; R 3966, 4-5, 9; 3975 (+ Ga 32 [Ga FES II/4]), 4; 3977, 3; 3991, 21-22; 4031, 3; 4033, 2; 4190, 7; 4193, 10; 4649, 2, 5; 4712, 4; 4919, 4; 4994 [= Gr 6], 2; 5085, 5-6; Robin-Bron/ Banī Bakr 1 [= BF-BT 5], 2, 5; Robin/ Ḥabāba 2; / al-H̲adara 7, 2, 3; 9, 4, 4-5, 5; / al-Hagarī 1, 3, 4, 4; / H̲amīr 1, 2-3;/ Rayda 1, 3; / Ruwā' 4; Ry 599, 2; YM 367 [CIAS I 95.41/ b6], 4.

Note to table 37: description of cases:

1 AUTHOR - **Singular:** C 37, 2; 368 [= MAFRAY/ Abū T̲awr 2]; 399, 2-3; 414, 2-3; 657, 1, 2-3, 3; Doe 6, 1-2; 7, 2; Gl 1100, 1; 1519, 8; Ja 400 [= YM 262] B, 12; 552, 3; 555, 2, 3, 3; 832; R 3902 bis N 131, 2; 3946, 5; 4553, 2; 4700, 3; Y.81.C.0/ 2, 2-3; YM 452 [CIAS I 39.11/ r9/ P12 N 2], 2;

1 AUTHOR - **Plural:** Robin/ Ṣirwāḥ 7, 6;

2 AUTHORS - **Dual:** Ghul/ al-Masāǧid 3, 2; Gl 1720 [MAFRAY/ al-Balaq-al-Ǧanūbī 9], 4; R 3902 N 130, 4, 4; 4626 [= Gl 929 + 930], 1;

2 AUTHORS - **Plural:** R 4198, 1-2, 2, 5;

3 AUTHORS - **Plural:** Fa 124, 6; Gl 1592, 3.

Note to table 38: description of cases:

1 AUTHOR - **Singular:** C 584, 2 /?/; 939, 3-4 /?/; 982, 1-2 /?/; YM 544 [CIAS I 95.41/ b4], 1-2 /?/;

1 AUTHOR - **Plural:** C 81, 7; 86, 8; 194, 3; 429, 10; 530 [= Haram 32], 7; 531, 7; 532 [= Haram 33], 4; 534, 6; Er 22 §2; 24 §1; Ghul/ Hūt̲ 2, 2; Gl 1367; Ja 627 [= Na NAG 6], 10-11; 628, 5, 12; 630, 16; 689, 5; 2867, 9, 9, 10; Lu 21 [= DJE 12], 2; Na NAG 2, 6; 3, 5; R 3967, 1; Robin/ Kāniṭ 5, 2; Ry 501 [= Ja 2139], 3; 540, 1;

2 AUTHORS - **Singular:** Ja 619, 12;

2 AUTHORS - **Plural:** C 581, 8; 630, 3; Er 19, 24; 37, 30; Fa 79-85; Ga IS 4, 2 (feminine pronominal suffix); Gl 1320 I ≈ II, 7; ^cInān 28; Ja 618, 6, 8, 16; NAM 2659 [CIAS II 39.11/ o6 N6], 17; Na NNSQ 22, 2-3; 26, 2, 4; R 3968 + 3979 [+ Ga 21], 2; 4775, 2; Ry 404, 1, 4;

3 AUTHORS - **Plural:** Av. No^cḍ 9, 2, 3; C 1, 4; 17, 4; 24, 5; 26, 5; 88, 6; 102, 6; 153 [= DJE 11], 1-2, 2-3; 154, 2; 224, 3-4, 4; 241, 2; 242, 2; 276, 1, 3; 339, 2, 2, 4; 339 bis, 2, 5; 357, 17; 416, 2; 517, 2; 547 [= Haram 10], 9; 585, 2; 650, 2; 660 + 587 [= Ja 411 A], 2, 2, 3, 3, 4; DJE 18 [= Sh 107], 2; Fa 77; Ga NES II/10b (C 176 + 201 + 213 + R 4003 + Ga 8b [AY II/ 5b]); Ja 560, 6; 603, 6; 615, 11, 21; 716, 8; 2223, 3-4; 2839 [= Schreyer 1], 22; 2852, 2; 2869 [= R 4979 = Fa 128 = Sa 2], 2; 2871, 3; Müller/ Ṣirwāḥ 2, 2; Na NNSQ 28, 5; R 3975 (+ Ga 32 [Ga FeS II/4]), 4; 3977, 3; 3991, 21-22; 4031, 3; 4033, 2; 4190, 7; 4193, 10; 4649, 2, 5; 4712, 4; 4994 [= Gr 6], 2; Robin/ Ḥabāba 2; /al-H̲adara 7, 2, 3; 9, 4, 4-5, 5; /al-Hagarī 1, 3, 4, 4; H̲amīr 1, 2-3; /Rayda 1, 3; /Ruwā' 4; Ry 599, 2; YM 367 [CIAS I 95.41/ b6], 4 /?/.

Note to table 39: description of cases:

1 AUTHOR - **Singular:** BF-BT 2, 3-4; C 658, 3-4; Lu 26, 3; MAFRAY/ al-Ḥijla 1, 1; /Sāri^c 6, 3; 7, 3; YMN 1, 6-7; 3, 4, 4, 4, 5; 4, 4-5, 5, 5, 5-6; 11, 2; 12, 2;

1 AUTHOR - **Plural:** C 41, 2, 2; 569, 3; Gr 29, 2; MAFY/ d̲ī-aṣ-Ṣawla^c 1A, 2; R 4196, 2; YMN 9, 3; 10, 2, 4, 7;

2 AUTHORS - **Dual:** BF-BT 1, 2-3; R 4194, 2, 3, 3;

2 AUTHORS - **Plural:** C 40, 2, 2; Ja 1818, 2-3, 3; R 4194, 1, 1, 2 /?/; RB/ Ḥaṣī 1, 6-7;

3 AUTHORS - **Plural:** Av. Aqmar 1, 2; 2, 2; BF-BT 4, 2, 4; C 648, 3, 4; Gl 1537, 5; 1658, 4; Gr 33, 2; 34, 3; 41, 2; Ja 1819 [= Doe/ W.Shirjān 19], 6; MAFRAY/ ad-Dimn 1, 4; R 3966, 4-5, 9; Robin-Bron/ Banī Bakr 1 [= BF-BT 5], 2, 5.

Note to table 41: in addition to the inscriptions covered by tables 37-39, this table takes into consideration the inscriptions about which we only know that they were authored by two or more persons without knowing the precise number of the authors due to the lacunae at the beginning of such inscriptions, or their ambiguity; e.g. Ga 10 [Ga AY II/7], 1: *HWFᶜṮT w-bn-hw bnw GHYFM* which is very likely to mean "HWFᶜṮT and his sons, the sons of [the clan] GHYFM" (see e.g. Bauer 1966, 58; Beeston 1984 b, 29 [§ 12:6]), consequently implying 3 or more authors; however, the possibility of *bn-hw* denoting simply "his son" [sing.] cannot be finally excluded (see e.g. part **g.** of Chapter 1 of the present monograph). Hence, there is no other way, but to identify such an inscription as having "2 or more" authors. Such inscriptions could not be taken into consideration in tables 37-39, but it is quite possible to cover them in this table:

ANCIENT PERIOD: R 3911, 2, 3; Y.81.C.0/ 1, 3;

MIDDLE PERIOD, "NORTH": C 4, 2 /?/; 29, 4 /?/; 196, 2; 457, 7, 14; 567, 2 /?/; 910, 2; DAI Bar'ān 1990-2, 2, 2; Ga 10 [Ga AY II/7], 2; Gl 1197, 2, 2; Ja 730, 8-9; Na NAG 15, 8, 25, 28; 19 (= Lu 17 = YM 363 [CIAS I 95.41/ p6]), 4; R 4030, 2; 4648, 2, 3, 3; 4655, 3; 4706, 4; 4725 [+ 3972], 1, 3; Robin/ al-Ḫadara 8, 2; Ry 615, 2; Sa 2 [= R 4979 = Fa 128], 2; 40, 2; YM 368 [CIAS I 39.11/ o5], 7;

MIDDLE PERIOD, "SOUTH": YMN 13, 9.

Note to table 42: this table has been prepared first of all on the basis of tables 36-38. Inscriptions with unknown number of authors have been used as well:

ANCIENT PERIOD - **Singular:** C 358, 2; Lu 15, 2; Müller/ Ṣirwāḥ 4; R 4552, 1-2; R 4730 [= Ja 414 = Haram 51], 1 (the very end of the Ancient Period);

Dual: R 4529, 2, 3, 3;

Plural: C 128, 1, 2; 952, 2; R 3911, 2, 3; Y.81.C.0/ 1, 3;

MIDDLE PERIOD, "NORTH" - **Plural:** C 4, 2 /?/; 29, 4 /?/; 53 [= Ja 493]; 132, 1; 174, 2-3; 182 + 183, 3; 186, 1; 191, 2; 196, 2; 216 [= Gr 20]; 228, 3; 229; 266; 281, 2; 304, 1; 365, 9-10; 457, 7, 14; 520 [= Haram 29], 1; 567, 2; 643, 1; Chelhod 14, 5; DAI Bar'ān 1990-2, 2, 2; DJE 19; Ga 6, 1; 10 [Ga AY II/7], 2; Ga NES II/ 10a [R 4006 + C 170 + R 4002]; Gl 1197, 2, 2; 1200, 2; Gl A 707, 5; Gr 3, 5; 7; Gullen 2, 3; Ja 511, 2, 2, 4; 730, 8-9; 734, 5 [feminine possessive]; 2858, 1; Lu 6 [= Sa 30], 1; MAFRAY/ Ṣanᶜā' 1, 1; Na NAG 15, 8, 25, 28; 19 (= Lu 17 = YM 363 [CIAS I 95.41/ p6]), 4; Na NNSQ 35, 2; 44; 59, 2; R 3970, 1; 3987, 1; 4013, 1-2; 4030, 2; 4040, 4; 4048, 1, 3; 4648, 2, 3, 3; 4655, 3; 4706, 4; 4724, 6; 4725 + 3972, 1, 3, 3; 4986, 3; Robin/ al-Ḫadara 8, 2; / Kānit 13 + 14, 3, 3; 20, 1; 23, 2; Ry 615, 2; Sa 2 [= R 4979 = Fa 128], 2; 13 [= Na NNSQ 62]; YM 368 [CIAS I 39.11/ o5], 7;

MIDDLE PERIOD, "SOUTH" - **Singular:** Gl 1656 (= AM 221 [CIAS I 43.31/ j9]), 3; R 4197 bis, 2;

Dual: C 569 [CIAS I 42.11/ b4], 2;

Plural: C 46, 4; 569 [CIAS I 42.11/ b4], 3; DJE 25, 2; Gl 1593, 3; Gr 40, 1; Moretti 1, 2, 3; R 4046, 2; 4169, 5 /?/; YMN 13, 9.

Note to tables 43-54: tables 43-54 are prepared on the basis of the inscriptions described in the notes to tables 28-42.

CHAPTER IV

SOME GENERAL TRENDS AND FACTORS OF EVOLUTION OF THE SABAEAN CULTURAL-POLITICAL AREA

a. Geographical conditions of Yemen and the origins of the South Arabian civilization

The evolution of the ancient Yemeni civilization was greatly influenced by the geographical conditions of Yemen. Due to these conditions at least two more or less different types of ancient Yemeni culture appeared. One of them arose in the area of the Yemeni Highlands (Jabal), and the other one in the area of the arid lowlands of the interior (Mashriq), along the edge of the Ṣayhad desert (= modern Ramlat as-Sab^{c}atayn).[1]

The main mass of accessible water resources comes to the area of the Interior Lowlands in the form of *suyūl*, floods. These floods reach this area through the wadis during the rainy monsoon seasons when it rains in the Highlands.[2] For their effective utilization (and thus for the creation of effective agricultural production) it is necessary to erect at the wadi outlets large-scale irrigation installations (Bowen 1958 b, 45-55, 63-64, 70-82; Dayton 1979; 1981; Wade 1979; Brunner 1983; Schmidt 1988 b, 55; Sauer *et al.* 1988, 101-102; Hehmeyer 1989, 33).[3] As is well known, such a necessity

---

1 The difference in the social organization of the ancient inhabitants of the Highlands and the Lowlands as well as the relation between this difference and the difference in the geographic conditions of the respective areas have already been noticed by some scholars (see for example Robin 1979, 11; 1982 b, 19-25; Chelhod 1985, 45). These scholars relate the difference in the ancient social organization of the Highlands and Lowlands to the rugged terrain of the former and the open one of the latter. Certainly this factor is important, but it seems impossible to explain the influence of the geographic conditions on the social evolution of the respective communities only by this factor.

2 The amount of direct natural precipitation in the Lowlands is very low: for example in the areas of Mārib and Timna^{c} at present it constitutes on average approximately less than 100 mm a year (Grolier, Tibbitts, Ibrahim 1984, 15, fig.5; Dresch 1989, 10, fig 1.5 &c), though in ancient times it might have been slightly higher (see for example Wade 1979, 115).

3 It is remarkable that due to the extremely low level of the ground waters ("In the highlands and Mashriq the underground reserves of water are much poorer /than in Tihāmah - A.K./ and they are situated at a depth of about 100 m" /Kotlov 1971, 13/) the use of the wells for irrigation would have been really effective together with the large-scale *sayl* irrigation raising the level of these waters (Bowen 1958 b, 63-64; Sauer *et al.* 1988, 102).

is one of the strongest factors in early state formation. And this factor was present in Mashriq.[4]

But there was one more factor in early state formation in this region. The famous Incense Route passed just along the edge of the Ṣayhad desert (Bowen 1958 a, 39, 42; Bāfaqīh 1973, 181-188; Groom 1981, 165-188) and, as is well known, long-distance trade could be quite an important factor in this process. In general, the development of long-distance trade through the edge of the Ṣayhad desert and the formation of statehood and civilization in this region must be considered as two interrelated processes.[5] From the "technical" point of view, as the way through the edge of the Ṣayhad desert was evidently more convenient than any other ways (including those through the Highlands),[6] it must have been a factor leading to the

---

[4] With respect to the irrigation system of the Mārib oasis, there are some grounds to maintain that in the first half of the Ancient Period the creation and the maintenance of this system was one of the main functions of the Sabaean state organization and personally its heads, *mukarrib*s (C 622; 623; R 3943,5; 3945,2-3; 3946,5-6; Fa 70 &c; Bauer 1964, 11-12; Lundin 1971, 154-155; 160). It is not surprising as the erection of the large-scale irrigation installations was most necessary just in the region of Mārib which is situated at the outlet of wadi Aḏanat with the largest catchment area in Mashriq (Grolier, Tibbitts, Ibrahim 1984, 38; Schmidt 1988 b, 58).

[5] The majority of scholars date the beginning of the Transarabian incense trade to the end of the second millennium BC (Bowen 1958 a, 35; Bulliet 1975, 65-67; von Wissmann 1975, 53-54; 1982, 16, 21-26, 43; Bāfaqīh 1985, 14; Sauer *et al.* 1988, 100-101; 106) or by the beginning of the first millennium BC (Robin 1984, 211) that concurs with the beginning of the formation of South Arabian statehood and civilization (Lundin 1971, 98-103; von Wissmann 1982, 16-60; de Maigret, Robin 1989, 278-291). The only important exception seems to be Groom, who denies the existence of the Transarabian incense trade in the beginning of the first millennium BC. Yet his research is based on the "short" chronology of South Arabian history (Pirenne 1955; 1956), thus according to Groom the beginning of the Transarabian incense trade also concurs with the beginning of South Arabian civilization according to this chronology, the 6th century BC (Groom 1981, 38-54). At present "the short chronology" seems to be outdated after the radiocarbon datings obtained by the Italian, Russian, French and American archaeologists (Sauer *et al.* 1988, 91, 100; de Maigret, Robin 1989, 278-291; Breton 1991; Robin 1990, 143; 1991 c, 51; 1991 d, 128; Sedov 1992). These datings together with the data of Suḫu texts (Cavigneux, Ismail 1990, 351f.; Liverani 1991), the Assyrian royal inscriptions (Pritchard 1950, 284-286; Lundin 1971, 99; Liverani 1991, 1, 4-5 &c), the Old Testament (I Kings 10, 1-13; II Chronicles 9, 1-12; Jeremiah 6, 20; Ezekiel 27, 22-24; 38, 13; Isaiah 45, 14; 60, 2, 6) &c make look very plausible the hypothesis that both early South Arabian civilization (dominated by the Sabaeans) and early Transarabian trade (dominated at that time by the same community?) already existed in the beginning of the first millennium BC.

[6] A much more realistic alternative is either the way North from the Ṣayhad, through the wide passage between this desert and the sands of the Rubᶜ-al-Khālī (Wadi Ḥaḍramawt - Ḥuṣn-al-ᶜAbr - Mushayniqah well - Najrān), or the way through the narrow gravel corridor in the Ṣayhad sand-desert surveyed by Philby (Philby 1939, 358-409; Bowen 1958 a, 39; Beeston 1979 b, 7; 1988 b, 161; 1991 a). This alternative has one evident advantage over the Southern way: both of the above-mentioned ways are much shorter. Yet the Southern way has its own very important advantage: it goes through populated areas with good water, food and forage supplies, whereas the Northern routes pass through the waterless desert regions. Hamilton, who studied the routes of the South Arabian caravan trade in the forties of this century, noticed that the traders going through the Northern (but not Southern) way used only lightly loaded small caravans (Hamilton 1942, 110). Hamilton directly states that the Southern way is preferable to the Northern ones: "Camel caravans bearing merchandise are cumbrous things. They prefer the long, easy way around to the difficult short cut, and a comfortable place to rest where you pay your road dues and sleep without anxiety" (Hamilton 1942,

Incense Route beginning to pass through the edge of the Ṣayhad. Such a situation in its turn must have been a factor in the early state formation in this region.[7]

The main mass of the water resources comes to the Highlands in the form of the natural precipitation which is brought by monsoons (Kotlov 1971, 11-12; Krahmalov 1977, 4-5; Grolier, Tibbitts, Ibrahim 1984, 14; Dresch 1989, 8-9 &c).[8] Effective agricultural production could be established here without the erecting of large-scale irrigation installations (Piotrovskiy 1985, 37; Varisco 1983, 27-31, 33-34). The terracing of the fields and the construction of small-scale irrigation works (which first of all provide the optimal utilization of rain water) could be done by extended families, clan groups and local communities (for details see Korotayev 1995 b), and there was (and there is) no need for the state organization in this respect.[9] It is also quite an important factor that the Highlands were situated quite far from both the main centres of incense production and the main incense trade routes.

b. Lowlands and Highlands in the Ancient Period

Thus, it is not surprising at all that the first South Arabian states arose in the area of the Interior Lowlands. At the beginning, the main area of the South Arabian

---

111; see also Stark 1936, 201-202). It seems that only in the second half of the Ancient Period, after the final disintegration of the early Commonwealth of the Sabaean *mukarribs*, with the rising tension between different South Arabian kingdoms and growing political instability along the edge of Ṣayhad desert, the Hadrami and Minaean traders began widely using the Northern routes to avoid the passage through the territories of the hostile kingdoms (Beeston 1991).

[7] It has been repeatedly stated that the long-distance trade in certain circumstances could be a powerful factor in early state formation (Gluckman 1965, 143; Kubbel 1974, 9-10, 96-103; Kozlova, Sedov, Tyurin 1968, 520-523; Büttner 1981, 42 &c).

[8] The amount of precipitation in the Yemeni Highlands varies from the average 1000 mm a year in the area of Ibb to less than 500 mm a year in the area of ᶜAmrān (Kotlov 1971, 11-12; Krahmalov 1977, 4-5; Dresch 1989, 10, fig. 1.5 &c). In antiquity the climate of Southern Arabia might have been more humid, and the natural precipitation might have been more even by the years (Dayton 1975; Wade 1979, 115; Piotrovskiy, Piotrovskaya 1984, 106 &c).

[9] The example of Ifugao (Luson island, Philippines) shows most distinctly that communities based on terraced agriculture in the mountains could develop for millennia very successfully, reaching high levels of agricultural skill, social differentiation &c without any distinct forms of statehood (Meshkov 1982, 183-197). It is remarkable that Varisco, undertaking his field research in modern Yemen, comes to the conclusion that the tribal organization is very effective in the conditions of the Yemeni Highlands (Varisco 1983, 33-34). For detail see Korotayev 1995 b, part **a**.

civilization looked like a bow-like strip along the edge of the Ṣayhad desert (with the main centres in the areas of Mārib, Timna^{c}, Shabwah and the wadis al-Jawf and Markhah).[10] Civilization penetrated into the Yemeni Highlands sometime later, and this process seems to have often been connected to the subjugation of the considerable territories of the Highlands by the Lowland states, first of all by the Sabaean and Qatabanian "commonwealths". It was also connected to the cultural influence of the Lowland communities, colonization &c. For example, it is necessary to point out the fact that the majority of the Earliest Highland inscriptions come from the area of Bakīl (*s^{2c}bn BKLM*) confederation (von Wissmann 1964 a, 361-362; Robin 1982 a, I, 67, 95), whereas there are some grounds to suppose that originally *bakīl* (*bkl*) were the Sabaean (or "Sabaean"?) settlers. In 1964 Bauer, while studying the use in the inscriptions of the term *bkl*, "settlers", came to the conclusion that the consonance of this term with the name of one of the largest pre-Islamic[11] Yemeni tribal confederations, Bakīl, is not fortuitous. The members of this confederation were indeed the descendants of the Sabaean settlers in the respective area of the Highlands (Bauer 1964, 23; 1965 a, 317).[12] This conclusion has found its confirmation in Robin's study of the tribal geography of the Yemen Highlands (Robin 1982 a).

While studying the spatial distribution of the temples of the main Sabaean deity, Almaqah, in the Yemeni Highlands, Robin showed that the area of these temples appears as a strip stretched from Shibām-Aqyān in the south to Bayt-Kulāb in the north (Robin 1982 a, I, 54, 61). This strip turns out to have been separated from the main territory of Almaqah sanctuaries in the Lowlands by a vast Highland area

---

[10] This fact has been repeatedly stated by different scholars. "The vast majority of archaic Sabaic-language texts emanate from the areas around Mārib and Khawlanite Ṣirwāḥ, from the W. Jawf, and from the string of oases on the edge of the desert between Mārib and the Jawf. These are all low-lying in relation to the great Yemeni massif with its high-level plateaux of the Qā^{c} Ṣan^{c}ā', Qā^{c} al-Bawn and Arḥāb. Archaic inscriptions in this highland area are very sparse indeed" (Beeston 1975 a, 5; see also Beeston 1975 b, 28; Bāfaqīh 1985, 20-21; Robin 1984, 198; 1991 c, 52; e, 63 &c).

[11] It might be reasonable to mention that Bakīl remains one of the most important Yemeni tribal confederations up to the present, though it lacks any considerable integrity (The same is as true for the situation at the beginning of the Christian Era).

[12] Bauer makes the following comment to this conclusion: "The settling of the representatives of different tribes in one town led in the circumstances of ancient South Arabia to the establishment of new very strong tribal links, to the reconstruction of the communal-tribal relations in these towns occupied by the members of different tribes, whereas such a congregation was perceived by the authorities as a certain tribe-community" (Bauer 1965 a, 317; see also 1964, 23). It is remarkable that up to the present Bakīl remains one of the largest and most important confederations of the Yemeni tribes, though its territory considerably (but not completely) differs from that of the ancient Bakīl (see for example Chelhod 1985, 12, 46-47).

without the temples of Almaqah, but with numerous shrines of a non-Sabaean deity, Ta'lab (pp. 54, 62, 63-65). It is very important that the Highland area of Almaqah temples has turned out to be practically identical with the territory of the ancient confederation Bakīl (pp. 47, 54, 61, 63-67). All those[13] have independently led Robin to the supposition that the area where the Bakīl confederation originated was colonized by the Sabaeans in the Most Ancient Sub-Period of their history (p. 67). Thus the Most Ancient inscriptions of the Highlands seem to have originated mainly in the zone of the early Sabaean colonization.[14]

In general, there are some grounds to say that in the Ancient Period a considerable part of the Yemeni Highlands was something like a "semi-barbarian" tribal periphery of the Lowland civilization; for quite a considerable part of this Period the above-mentioned "periphery" was subjugated by the Lowland centres of the South Arabian civilization[15] both politically (Beeston 1975 b, 28; Robin 1982 a, I, 95-96; II, 18; von Wissmann 1964 a, 277 f., 362; 1968) and culturally.[16] During this Period the Highland communities seem to have remained more archaic than the Lowland ones.

c. Lowlands and Highlands in the Middle Period. Problem of "archaization"

In the Middle Period we see the Highlands politically dominating in Yemen

---

[13] Together with the facts that almost all the Sabaic inscriptions of the Most Ancient Subperiod (the Subperiod of *mukarribs* of Saba') in the Highlands were found on the territory of this confederation, that another Sabaean deity, SM^{c}, was venerated in the territory of the same confederation, and that the tribe Fayshān very closely associated with the Sabaeans since the beginning of their history was present in this territory in the Ancient Period (p.67).

[14] The Most Ancient inscriptions from the other areas of the Highlands are very sparse and appear to come from a very small number of centres, first of all from Itwah-Riyām (Lundin 1973 b, 35). I would suppose that in the Most Ancient Sub-Period only a few "civilization hotbeds" existed in the Highlands outside the zone of the Sabaean colonization.

[15] The main role was played by the Sabaean centre, yet the role of the Qatabanian centre (especially in Ancient Sub-period 2) was also very important (see for example von Wissmann 1968). The Minaean-Madhabian centre might have also exerted some cultural influence on certain Highland Areas (cp. C 609; von Wissmann 1964 a, 319, 343-344, 355; Robin 1982 a, I, 48-49; Bāfaqīh 1988 &c).

[16] One of the clearest pieces of evidence is Ta'lab's decree (R 4176) where Ta'lab, the tutelary deity of the largest Highland tribal confederation, Sum^{c}ay, orders the Sum^{c}ayites not to fail to go on pilgrimage to Almaqah, the most important **Sabaean** deity (line 1; for the latest interpretations of the text see Ghul 1984; Müller 1988; see also Robin 1982 a, I, 95-96 &c).

(Beeston 1975 a, 5; b, 29; Rhodokanakis 1927, 113; Robin 1976 a, 3; 1982 b, 17; 1984, 212; 1991 c, 52; e, 63, 67 &c).[17] Perhaps it is even possible to speak here about an "internal barbarian conquest", but it should not be understood literally: the process of the transition of politically dominance from the centre of the civilization to the semi-barbaric periphery was quite prolonged. Some role in this process was certainly played by the transfer of the main incense trade routes from land to sea. That must have caused a considerable decline in the economic importance of the edge of the Ṣayhad desert (J.Ryckmans 1951, 331; Bowen 1958 a, 35; Irvine 1973, 301; von Wissmann 1981, 66; Robin 1982 a, I, 98; b, 17; 1984, 212; Crone 1987, 23-36; Audouin, Breton, Robin 1988, 74).[18] Quite a significant role may have also been played by the processes of Arabian aridization (see for example Fedele 1988, 36; Robin 1991 e, 63; f, 88). But the most important factor seems to have been the silting of the irrigation systems.[19] As a result, the situation in the Lowlands became similar to an ecological catastrophe (Serjeant 1960, 583; Piotrovskiy, Piotrovskaya 1984, 107; Robin 1984, 220-221; 1991 f, 88; Sauer *et al.* 1988, 102).[20]

It seems that here we could observe a process that occurs quite frequently in history: **the cultural-political expansion of civilization to its barbarian periphery → barbarian conquest of the centre of the civilization → the barbarian**

[17] Both in the Sabaean area and in what was the Qatabanian cultural-political area in the Ancient Period (and became the Himyarite one in the Middle Period - see e.g. Robin 1991 c, 53). With respect to the Sabaean cultural-political area it is very remarkable that after the end of the "traditional" dynasty of the kings of Saba' and dhū-Raydān (the Sabaean origins of which appear to be quite hypothetical, but not completely improbable - see Korotayev 1994 e) at the end of the 1st century AD (Robin 1991 a) all the Middle Northern "kings of Saba' (and dhū-Raydān)" whose clan affiliation we can trace turn out to come from the Highlands and be of non-Sabaean origin (see for example von Wissmann 1964 a, genealogische Tafel IIIa; 1964 b, 498; 1968, 13; 1976, abb. 22; Bāfaqīh 1990, 339-360). The only evidenced attempt of the Sabaean aristocracy (in alliance with certain qaylite clans of the Highlands) to come to power in Mārib seems to have been the revolt of Nimrān Awkān, yet this attempt was completely unsuccessful (C 429; Ja 594, 684, 711, 739, 758; see also Jamme 1962, 327-328; Bāfaqīh 1990, 339-360). For some more evidence see Korotayev 1995 b, part **c**.

[18] In the second half of the 1st millennium BC the main part of the Lowlands must have been also affected by the Hadramis and Minaeans who seem to have widely begun to use the direct way through the gravel corridor in the Ṣayhad desert (or through al-ᶜAbr ?) bypassing such important ancient South Arabian centres as Wadi Markhah, Timnaᶜ or Mārib (Beeston 1991 a).

[19] It seems to be partly caused by the degradation of the natural plant cover of the Western slopes of the Yemeni Mountains due both to the anthropogenic factors and the probable climatic change (e.g. Robin 1991 f, 88). The other probable cause is "an increase in the saline content of the soils and clays due to centuries of intensive irrigation" comparable to the well-known Mesopotamian case (Sauer *et al.* 1988, 107).

[20] In addition, it might be reasonable to mention as one of its likely causes "an increase in the saline content of the soils and clays due to centuries of intensive irrigation" comparable to the well-known Mesopotamian case (Sauer *et al.* 1988, 107).

periphery becoming "civilized" . Considerable territorial expansion of the territory of the civilization in such cases is usually accompanied by the decline in some respects in the "level" of civilization in its centre.[21]

The situation can be also described in the following words: several factors mentioned above caused a significant decline of the Sabaean state and civilization by the end of the 1st millennium BC.[22] The weakening state organization seems to have become incapable of providing guarantees of life and property to individuals, and it was the clan organization that took on these functions to a considerable extent.[23]

Though the "Sabaean" state, which seems to have found itself on the brink of complete collapse at the end of the Ancient Period, considerably reconsolidated during the Middle Period, it remained rather weak, especially in comparison with the Ancient Sabaean state. Indeed, the inscriptions witness the existence of quite a strong state organization in the centre of the early Sabaean Commonwealth. For example, this relatively developed state apparatus let the Sabaean *mukarrib*s erect dozens of various buildings (irrigation structures, temples, city walls &c) in many parts of the Commonwealth.[24] We know relatively much about the Ancient Sabaean civil officials who could be appointed ($s^{2}ym$) to organize certain constructions or to be in charge of a certain city &c.[25]

In a sharp contrast with the relatively scanty Ancient epigraphy, the numerous

---

[21] These facts make me avoid applying the term "Archaic Period" (see for example Beeston *et al.* 1982) to the first millennium of the Sabaean history. The Middle "Sabaean" society seems to be more "archaic" than the Ancient one in many respects. I would rather prefer to consider the Ancient Period as a "classical" epoch of the Sabaean history. These considerations seem to be supported by some data on the cultural development of the Sabaean civilization (Robin 1984, 208-209; Schmidt 1988 b, 86).

[22] For example, direct evidence for the tremendous decline of the Sabaean state at the end of the Ancient Period has been recently found by Robin in the materials of the German Archaeological Expedition in Mārib (Robin 1989 b, 222); see also Pirenne 1956, 174-178; von Wissmann 1968, 10 &c.

[23] It is almost a rule that in agrarian societies the weakening of the state organization causes the consolidation of the clan structures (for more detail see Korotayev, Obolonkov 1989; 1990).

[24] C 366 a; b; 367 + Lu 16; 490; 622; 623; 627; 629; 631; 632 a; b; 634; 636; 957; Ga 46 [Ga MM]; Gl 1122 + 1116 + 1120; 1558 [= MAFRAY-al-Asāḥil 6]; 1560 [= MAFRAY-al-Asāḥil 5]; 1561; 1567 [= MAFRAY-ad-Durayb 3]; A 710; 775 [MAFRAY-Ḫirbat Sa^{c}ūd 4]; 776 [= MAFRAY Ḫirbat Sa^{c}ūd 2]; 777 [= MAFRAY-Ḫirbat Sa^{c}ūd 8]; MAFRAY-al-Asāḥil 2; 3; 7; -Ḫirbat Sa^{c}ūd 6; 10; Ph 133 [= MAFRAY-al-Asāḥil 1]; R 3943; 3945; 3946; 3948 [= Gl 1550 = MAFRAY-ad-Durayb 4]; 3949; 3950; 4399; 4401; 4429; 4494; 4844 [= MAFRAY-Ḫirbat Sa^{c}ūd 1]; 4850 [= MAFRAY-Ḫirbat Sa^{c}ūd 3]; 4904 [= Gl 1559 = MAFRAY-al-Asāḥil 4]; 4906; 5096 &c.

[25] C 375 [= Ja 550]; 439; 494; 496 [= MAFRAY-Ḫirbat Sa^{c}ūd 13]; 566; Ja 552; 555; 557; MAFRAY-al-Balaq-al-Ǧanūbī 1 [= Gl 1719 + 1717 + 1718]; R 4428; 4635; 4845 bis; Ry 584; Sh 20 &c; see also J.Ryckmans 1951, 62-64, 83, 85, 88-90, 92; Audouin, Breton, Robin 1989, 74-76 &c.

Middle "Sabaean" inscriptions give us almost no information of this kind.[26] In general, the Middle "Sabaean" inscriptions do not witness to the existence of almost any specific features of the regular state in the Middle Sabaean cultural-political area, neither a regular civil administration[27] nor a regular system of taxation[28] nor an artificial administrative-territorial division. The silence of the sources does not seem to be fortuitous, as the Middle Sabaean political system did not really need these institutions. This system appears to have consisted of the weak state in its centre and

---

[26] This fact has been already noticed by J.Ryckmans (1951, 62-64, 175-176).

[27] See e.g. Korotayev 1993 b; 1995 a, part **III.5.**; 1995 b, part **c.** For example, there are no grounds to suppose the Middle "Sabaean" royal power exercised any actual governing through its agents on the level of the "tribes", *shaᶜb*s. There is no doubt that the *qayl* were **not** the agents of the royal power. The stability of the qaylite dynasties really impresses in comparison with the relative instability of the Middle "Sabaean" royal dynasties. In the 2nd - 3rd centuries AD almost a dozen royal dynasties superseded each other on the Mārib throne, whereas we always find the same clans as the *qayl*s of the main "Sabaean" tribes from the beginning of the Middle Period (and often earlier) to its end (and often later). We have sufficient evidence that *qayl*s needed certain consent (*tqnᶜ*) of the other *qayl*s (as well as the Sabaeans and the royal army, *ḫms*) to become the "Sabaean" kings (Ja 562, 4-8; 564, 4-6; Loundine 1973 a, 190; Lundin 1984, 46; see also al-Hamdānī 1980, 121 /?/) whereas certain clans were *qayl*s of corresponding tribes irrespective of the will of any Middle "Sabaean" kings. The "Sabaean" royal power interfered in the internal affairs of the *shaᶜb*s extremely rarely (see for example Gl 1628) and most likely as a certain mediator. The only significant evidence of serious interference of this kind is attested on the part of the Himyarite royal power after it finally subjugated the Sabaean cultural-political area, when certain traces of regular state administration could be attested here (Er 37, 10-23; Ja 647, 25-30; 651; 671+788, 10-14; R 3910; Shibᶜanu 1, 15-18 &c). It is not surprising at all, taking into consideration the much higher degree of political centralization of the Himyarite kingdom (see part **f.** of this Chapter), the above-mentioned inscriptions seem to witness the attempts to establish a similar system of the regular state administration in the "North".

[28] See below part **d.1.** of this chapter. Though, if Kitchen's interpretation of line 16 of Shibᶜanu 1 (Kitchen 1995) is correct, this inscription may be considered as evidence for existence of some kind of regular taxation in some parts of the Sabaean cultural area after its final subjugation by the Himyarite kings in the late 3rd century AD. It does not appear completely unlikely, taking into consideration the much higher degree of the political centralization of the Himyarite kingdom (see part **f.** of this Chapter) and the fact that the Himyarite kings tried to establish some kind of a similar centralized regular state administration in the Sabaean cultural-political area (see the previous note). It should be also maintained that the Middle "Sabaean" inscriptions seem to tend to portray a society which is likely to appear more archaic than it was in reality. For example, these inscriptions never mention craftsmen (as well as crafts) and traders (as well as long-distance trade), though both quite developed crafts and long-distance trade were no doubt present in Pre-Islamic Yemen (see for example Piotrovskiy 1985, 138-140). It is not surprising at all, taking into consideration the well-known fact that such occupations were regarded as somehow unworthy in many pre-industrial societies (Crone 1989, 19, 70-71, 103; Kullanda 1992; Lapina 1985, 72-86 &c) including tribal areas of Modern Yemen (e.g. Dresch 1989, 118-123). The inscriptions seem to mention only "worthy" types of the human activities: warfare, religion, agriculture &c; the collecting (or payment) of taxes is most unlikely to be in such a list (cp. e.g. *Luke* 18, 9-4; 19, 1-10; it is not relevant for the temple tithe the payment of which must have been considered as something quite "worthy" - see below, part *d.1.* of this chapter). Thus the Middle "Sabaean" inscriptions seem to portray the society as it **must** have been from the point of view of the "Sabaeans" (some "pure" society of warriors and agriculturalists without such "indecent" things as, for example, crafts). Hence I would not be completely surprised if the recently discovered documents on wood (which have a much less solemn, more everyday, nature - see for example ᶜAbdallāh 1986 b; Bauer, Akopyan, Lundin 1990; Beeston 1989; Robin 1991 d; Ryckmans 1986; 1993; Ryckmans *et al.* 1994 &c) provided evidence for the existence of certain state taxation in the Middle Sabaean cultural-political area, though I would insist that this is not inevitable, as the Middle "Sabaean" political system could do without any regular state taxation at all.

strong autonomous "tribes" (chiefdoms, *sha*^{c}*b*s2) on its periphery (see e.g. Korotayev 1993 a). The only really well-attested obligation of these tribes was to provide military service (*s*^{2}*w*^{c}) to their kings. However, this apparently very loose system turned out to work very effectively (see below).

In any case, there are serious grounds to suppose that by the end of the Ancient Period the Sabaean state had significantly weakened and notwithstanding its partial reconsolidation during the Middle Period it had never regained the strength it had in the Earliest Sub-Period. As a result we can see by the Middle Period the consolidation of the clan organization which acted as a partial substitute for the weak state and remained really strong during the whole of the Middle Period.

d. Some "nontribal" elements of the Middle "Sabaean" socio-political system

Of course, the general level of development of the Sabaean cultural-political area always remained quite high and the clan-tribal organization was not sufficient for the effective regulation of this relatively complex social system. Thus the clan and communal institutions were inevitably supplemented by some other institutions which stood to a significant extent outside clans and communities and above them. Among the most important ones I would list the following:

d.1. The sub-system of the temple centres

The "internal barbarian conquest" took place in the area with a certain set of universally recognized values, such as the authority of the "king of Saba'" or the deity Almaqah (let alone ^{c}Athtar, whose celestial authority seems to have been universally recognized by all the "civilized" pre-monotheistic South Arabians), or the highly unified epigraphic tradition. In the turbulent processes of the end of the Ancient Period cultural continuity was preserved to a very high extent. The religious structure changed surprisingly insignificantly.[29] The authority of the temples also seems to have been preserved. On the one hand, in the numerous Middle Sabaic texts we have practically no mentions of the vast land possessions of the temples of Almaqah, which

[29] The religious changes within the Middle Period appear to have been much more considerable.

must have been considerable in the Ancient Period judging by C 376.[30] But that is completely compensated for by the following.

As has been mentioned above, the inscriptions keep persistently silent about the existence of anything like a regular system of state taxation in the Middle Sabaean cultural-political area and to my mind it is not completely fortuitous, because the political organization of this area (as we can reconstruct it) did not need such a system. But the same inscriptions provide a lot of the data about the existence in the same area, in the same time, of the temple tithe (Gl 1438,5; Er 22 §1; Ja 656, 17; Na NAG 11 [= Er 25], 9 &c). There are some grounds to suppose that it was simply a **temple** tithe and not a hidden form of state taxation. For example, it was possible to submit the tithe in the form of a statue dedicated to the temple (C 342, 5-6; 567, 3-4; Er 26 §1; Ja 615, 9; 617, 4; 650, 4-5 &c). It is evident that such a tithe could be used by the temple only.

It might also be reasonable to mention that there are certain grounds to suppose that the Middle Sabaean temples (at least some of them) acted in effect as "insurance companies" which would provide assistance (to build, say, a house after it had been destroyed). By paying their tithe (*$^{c}s^{2}r$*) to the temples, the worshippers paid a sort of "premium" to this "insurance company", whereby they could expect to get their "compensation" when they needed it (Korotayev 1994 b).

I would also stress that the overwhelming majority of the mentions of the temple tithe come from the Middle Period. Thus it is difficult to avoid the impression that against the background of the general weakening of the state organization at the end of the Ancient Period the temples reinforced their authority, providing another substitute (in addition to the consolidating clan organization) for the weakening state.[31]

Within the political system of the Middle Sabaean cultural area an especially important role was played by the "federal" temples of Almaqah (first of all, of course,

---

[30] Almost the only attested Middle "Sabaean" land possessions of the temples are Ta'lab's pastures in Sum^{c}ay - Gl 1142 and 1143; Robin/Kānit̩ 4. Fragmentary Fa 63, 2 mentions *$^{c}s^{2}t$ 'LMQH $b^{c}l$ 'WM*, "cornland /?/ of Almaqah, the lord of Awwām"; yet the context of the inscription is not sufficient to establish definitely that this means true land possessions of the main "federal" temple of the Sabaean cultural-political area.

[31] Incidentally, these two points (the high level of the cultural continuity and the consolidation of the authority of the temples) seem to be able to explain another important phenomenon, the growth of the epigraphic activity with the transition from the Ancient to the Middle Period (for details see Korotayev 1995 b, part **g.**).

Awwām, but also Bar'ān and Ḥirwān) which constituted truly supra-tribal institutions (see e.g. Korotayev 1995 a, Chapter 5). Originally Almaqah was the chief tribal deity of the Sabaeans, and naturally the Fayshanites closely allied with them.[32] Yet the formation and evolution of the Sabaean Commonwealth led to the situation when Almaqah began to be venerated by the non-Sabaean tribes of the Sabaean cultural-political area as well. Originally, in many Southern Arabian tribes the cult of Almaqah was introduced by the Sabaeans literally by force (see e.g. R 3945, 16). Naturally, the disintegration of the early Sabaean Commonwealth must have led to the disappearance of this cult in the territories of most tribes which went outside Sabaean political control (see e.g. Bauer 1989, 155).

However, as has been already mentioned above, what remained of the early Sabaean Commonwealth turned out to be a rather stable cultural-political entity. A dozen tribes, mainly situated not far from the Sabaean heartland, the Mārib oasis, retained their loyalty to the terrestrial authority of the Sabaean kings and the celestial authority of Almaqah,[33] thus forming the Sabaean cultural-political area; and the integrating role of the latter within the Sabaean cultural-political area seems to be as important as that of the former. The inscriptions provide considerable material proving the existence of the following four main channels of the integrating function of the above mentioned "federal Sabaean" temples: /a./ eponyms, /b./ pilgrimage; /c./ tithe; /d./ dedications and other rituals (Korotayev 1995 a, Chapter 5).

It might be also worth mentioning that the "federal Sabaean" temples of Almaqah seem to have started the process of the legal integration of the Sabaean cultural-political area creating a few legal norms which were valid for the Sabaean area as a whole, whereas the Middle "Sabaean" norms issued by kings, *sha*ᶜ*b*s and their rulers were valid for the respective tribes and communities only (for details see Korotayev 1994 a).

---

32 See e.g. R 3945 and 3946.

33 Similarly the Sabaeans seem to have introduced rather artificially the cult of another Sabaean deity, D̲T-BᶜDNM, among the Amirites (*'MRM*) having built a temple of this deity in the main settlement of this tribal confederation, ḤNN (R 3943, 4). Yet several centuries later the Amirites appear to venerate this Sabaean deity quite voluntarily (e.g. C 517; 534 &c). Naturally, the presence of the common deities venerated by both the Sabaeans and the Amirites must have strengthened their affiliation to the Sabaean cultural-political area, providing additional integrative links for this cultural-political system.

d.2. Royal power

Royal power, notwithstanding its relative weakness, seems to have played an important and useful role in the functioning of the Middle Sabaean cultural-political system. Royal power concentrated the military potential of the "Sabaean" semi-independent chiefdoms, *sha^{c}bs2,* and directed it outside the area. The tribal levies, instead of fighting each other, thus destroying the area, provided more or less successful defence of it. Thus at least two tasks were solved simultaneously: /1/ the intertribal conflicts were effectively prevented[34] and /2/ a high level of concentration of the forces to counteract external enemies was provided. Tribes + royal power turned out to be many times stronger than a mechanical sum of the tribes; as a result the advantages of the existence of royal power seem to have been so evident that it was permanently preserved in some form, notwithstanding the weakness of the power of many individual kings. In general, it is necessary to state that in the Middle Sabaean cultural area we can observe the formation of a political system which was simple, effective and perfectly adapted to the conditions of the Northern Highlands. Without any significant limitation of the autonomy of the tribes it effectively managed to solve its external tasks quite successfully, counteracting its considerably stronger enemies who often had much higher economic potential and much more political centralization.[35]

Hence the process of the significant socio-political transformation of the Sabaean cultural area at the end of the Ancient and the beginning of the Middle Period can be also considered as a quite adequate social adaptation to the new situation which appeared in the Sabaean cultural-political area by the end of the 1st millennium BC, with the relative decline of the Sabaean Lowlands (caused by the above-mentioned factors) and the rise in the importance of the "Sabaean" Highlands. Indeed, the Middle "Sabaean" political system, which was much less like a regular state than the Ancient one which included strong clan and tribal structures as its

[34] In any case such conflicts seems to have been extremely rare (see for example Er 6 §1 ?) in the Middle Period especially in comparison with the later epochs of the Yemeni history.

[35] I.e. the politically centralized and economically strong Himyarite kingdom in the South, the gigantic Hadrami kingdom in the East, the militarily strong Arab tribes and the Kindite kingdom in the North, and the Axumite kingdom, with its allies, in the West, which in the 2nd-3rd centuries AD reached one of the peaks of its might.

integral elements, turned out to be a really effective form for the socio-political organization of a complex society in the Northern Highlands. Most political entities which have appeared in this region from that time till the present have shown evident similarities to the Middle "Sabaean" socio-political organization (Dresch 1984; 1989; Gerasimov 1987, 45-55; Abū Ghānim 1990).[36]

Royal power seems to have occupied a position which was emphatically outside the clan system. The Middle "Sabaean" kings never mentioned their clan affiliation after their accession to the throne, as if they kept aloof from this affiliation. The very important extra-clan state institute seems to be also represented by the professional royal army (*ẖms*) which served as the backbone of the "Sabaean" military force (Beeston 1976 b, 7-9).

d.3. *Maqtawīs*

Maqtawīs (see Chapter 1) usually served individual persons (individual kings and not royal power as a whole, individual members of the clans and not whole clans) and always individually. We always find an individual person and never a whole clan as a *maqtawī*. Thus their dependence stands in a sharp contrast to the collective dependence of *'dm*, "clients", which appears to have been much less individualized, much more stable and steady. As a result, the institution of *maqtawīs* turned out to be very flexible and "untraditional". It supplemented well the traditional clan and communal structures.[37] The royal *maqtawīs* could be well considered as a germ of the state administrative personnel, the "central officialdom", though according to the inscriptions almost all of them performed only military (and sometimes diplomatic) functions. It does not look surprising, taking into consideration the nature of the Middle "Sabaean" royal power. *Maqtawīs* of the *qayls* may be considered as a germ of the local, "provincial" officialdom. These are the *maqtawīs* (especially royal ones not of noble origins) among whom we seem to observe the highest level of the individualization of the social relations attested in Middle "Sabaean" epigraphy.

---

[36] Whereas the Ancient Sabaean socio-political system seems to be very suitable for the conditions of the 1st millennium BC Lowlands.

[37] In other words the institution of *'dm* seems to have secured the stability and continuity of the Middle "Sabaean" socio-political system, whereas the institution of the *maqtawīs* ensured its flexibility.

e. The Sabaean Lowlands in the Middle Period

However, as has been shown in Chapter 3, the "archaization" of the Sabaean Lowlands was not so total as that of the "Sabaean" Highlands. The Lowlands went on playing the role of the cultural centre of the civilization. Their general cultural prestige remained very high.

Thus the Awwām temple near the original Sabaean capital Mārib continued being the main religious centre of the Sabaean cultural-political area (Ryckmans 1964 b, 13-15; 1973 b; 1980 b, 204; Höfner 1970, 261 &c). Mārib itself went on performing the functions of the capital of the whole area, though quite logically in the Highlands Ṣanᶜā' appeared as the second capital in the Middle Period - see e.g. Lundin 1988; Bāfaqīh 1990, 149-156.

In the Ancient Period *mlk*, "the king" was a rather ordinary title for political leaders of autonomous territorial communities, *shaᶜb*s.[38] In the Middle Period the most stable and solid suzerainty over an autonomous Highland community or tribe did not give one any grounds to proclaim oneself the king of this community. During this period the only legitimate royal titles were those combining *mlk*, "the king of" with a name of an old Lowland community (either Saba' or Qatabān or Ḥaḍramawt[39]), though it was possible to add something after this name. In the Middle Sabaean cultural-political area the only legitimate royal title was "the king of Saba'"[40], though the basic meaning of Saba' in this period was still "the civil community of Mārib and the vicinities".[41] Even the Himyarite "kings of Saba' and dhū-Raydān" (who very often had no suzerainty over Saba' at all) would never call themselves simply "kings of dhū-Raydān"[42]. Such a combination (king + a name of any Highland community) seems to have been completely unthinkable in the Middle Period.

---

[38] See for example R 3945, 7, 15, 17, 18; Beeston 1972 a, 260; 1975 c, 191; Lundin 1971, 217; 1973 a, 166; 1979 b, 152; Bāfaqīh 1988, 27 &c.

[39] Naturally till the final collapse of the latter two states.

[40] With a possible variant "the king of Saba' and dhū-Raydān".

[41] Er 24 §2; Ja 647, 23; 660, 14; 662, 3-4, 13-14; 690, 10-11; 703, 8; 735, 8; 740 A, 7, 13-14; Na NAG 12 [= Er 11], 22; R 4624, 5; 4775, 4 &c.

[42] Which would have very often been much closer to reality. It is remarkable that a considerable number of the Middle Northern kings called themselves "kings of Saba'" (without "dhū-Raydān").

The palace of Salḥīn (*SLḤN*) in Mārib played the role of the symbol of Middle "Sabaean royalty" (Bāfaqīh 1990, 81-98 &c), though quite logically another symbol of "Sabaean royalty", the palace of Ghumdān (*ĠMDN*) appears in the Highlands, in Ṣanᶜā' (Bāfaqīh 1990, 152-155 &c).

In the Middle Period, notwithstanding the existence of the very stable Sabaean cultural-political area which contained a considerable part of both the Highlands and the Lowlands, a significant difference between these two sub-areas remained. For example, there is a considerable difference between the relatively democratic constitution of the civil community of Mārib (the same might be true as well with respect to such Lowland towns as Nashq and Nashān[43]) and the "aristocratic" political organization of the Highland tribes dominated by the qaylite clans.[44]

The Lowlands finally lost their central position in the system of Yemeni civilization only at the very end of the Late ("Monotheistic") Period,[45] though even in the middle of the 6th century AD Mārib still played an important role - see e.g. C 541.

f. The Himyarite-Radmanite cultural-political area in the Middle Period

The decline of the Ancient Qatabanian state took place significantly later than that of the Ancient Sabaean one.[46] As a result the social continuity between the Ancient and the Middle Period in the Qatabanian cultural-political area was stronger, and the social transformation in the "South" turned out to be less dramatic. In the

---

[43] Lowland Ṣirwāḥ in the Middle Period shows both "Highland" and "Lowland" features in its political organization. On the one hand, we find here the politically dominant qaylite clan Dhū-Ḥabāb (*ḏ-ḤBB*: Er 23; 28; Fa 3; Ja 617; 649; Höfner 1973, 10-52 &c), yet in general the internal organization of this community remains quite democratic (see e.g. Ja 2856).

[44] This difference has already been noticed by Beeston (1975 c, 190-191; 1976 b, 4; 1979 a, 120) and Lundin (1969 a, 56-57; Loundine 1973 b, 27-28); see also Korotayev 1993 a; b; 1994 f.

[45] The cause of it might have been that the ecological catastrophe on the brink of which the Lowlands found themselves at the end of the Ancient Period seems to have taken place by the 7th century AD (Robin 1984, 220-221). Only really strong state (or civil communal) organization could provide any solution to the growing problems of the Lowland oases, but there was a complete lack of such an organization in the Yemeni Lowlands at the end of the 6th century AD (Dayton 1979, 127). The final decline of the Lowland civilization might have been somehow related to the processes of the "bedouinization" of South Arabia which began in more or less significant form by the end of the 1st millennium BC and were significantly accelerated in the 3rd century (von Wissmann 1964 b, 493; Robin 1984, 213, 221; 1991 f).

[46] In the 2nd-1st centuries BC, when the Sabaean state was in a deep decline, the Qatabanian kingdom appears to have been flourishing.

Middle Period the state organization of the Himyarite South appears to be significantly stronger than that of the Sabaean North (C 448 + Ga 16 [Hakir 1]; R 4230; Bāfaqīh, Robin 1980, 15; Robin 1981 b, 338), so it is not surprising to find that the clan-tribal organization in the Middle South was weaker than that of the North and that it played a less significant social, economic and political role.

Quite an impressive feature of Yemeni history is that we find a more or less similar picture in 20th century Yemen: very strong clan-tribal structures and very weak state ones in the Yemeni Uplands to the North of Naqīl Yiṣliḥ (in the "Sabaean Highlands") and relatively weak clan-tribal structures and relatively strong state ones to the South of it, in the "Himyarite Highlands" (Burrowes 1987, 9; Dresch 1989, 8-15 &c; Obermeyer 1982, 31-32; Weir 1991, 87-88; Wenner 1967, 38 &c). Thus the above described picture appears almost invariable in Yemeni history since the first centuries AD.[47]

This fact leads one to the supposition that there must be some fundamental basis for such a stable difference between the "North" and the "South". Its main objective factor is evident: the significant difference in the geographical conditions. It is really remarkable to find that the Highland territories of the two Middle Period cultural-political areas are practically identical with the two main ecological zones of the Yemeni uplands (Gochenour 1984, 3; see also Obermeyer 1982, 31-32; Dresch 1989, 8-15).[48] The much more fertile and humid[49] Southern Highlands can bear much denser population, providing much more surplus (which is necessary to maintain state structures) than the "North", thus representing much better conditions for a stable and relatively strong politically centralized state organization.[50]

---

[47] Quite impressively, at present the line between the tribal North and non-tribal South is often drawn precisely at the same place (the Yislaḥ Pass) where the border between the Northern and Southern Kingdoms of the kings of Saba' and dhū-Raydān ran 1800 years ago (cf. Dresch 1989, 14; Bāfaqīh 1990).

[48] Incidentally the third ecological zone of the Uplands ("Western Highlands") is virtually identical to the area of the Highlands which in Pre-Islamic times most effectively resisted subjugation (in any form, both politically and culturally) by any of the centres of the ancient South Arabian civilization (notwithstanding its extreme proximity to the zone of the Earliest Sabaean colonization).

[49] The amount of natural precipitation falling in the Southern Highlands must have always been considerably higher in the historical epoch, simply because almost all of this amount is brought to Yemen by monsoons coming from the Indian Ocean, and most of the moisture they contain must almost inevitably fall in the area of the Southern Highlands before they reach the North.

[50] A similar idea has been already expressed by Dresch with respect to the North: "The land of Hashid and Bakil would provide a poor economic basis for any elaborate exploitative class" (Dresch 1984, 156; see also 1989, 8-15). The relatively meagre natural environment of the "North" could not support the high

g. General characterization of the Middle Sabaean political system

As has been mentioned above, the Middle Sabaean political system may be characterized as consisting of a weak state in its centre and strong chiefdoms on its periphery.[51] However, there is no doubt that this was a real *system*, i.e. it had properties which could not be reduced to the characteristics of its elements.[52] It should be also taken into consideration that the state and chiefdoms were not the *only* elements of this political system. It included as well, for example, a sub-system of temple centres[53] and the civil community of Mārib,[54] as well as some true tribes (not chiefdoms) in the area of the Sabaean Lowlands (primarily the tribes of the Amirite confederation).[55] With the transition from the Ancient to the Middle Period the Sabaean political system was essentially transformed, becoming as a whole very different from the "state", but remaining, however, on basically the same level of political complexity. Without losing any political complexity and sophistication, the Middle "Sabaeans" managed to solve in quite different ways the problems which are normally solved by states, such as the mobilization of resources for the functioning of the governing sub-system, territorial organization of a vast space and the provision of guarantees of life and property.

---

density of the population which is necessary to secure the solidity and stability of state structures in such a rugged terrain which we find in the "Sabaean Highlands" (for more detail see Korotayev 1989; 1991).

[51] Incidentally, a significant transformation appears to have occurred in the area in the Early Islamic Period (see e.g. Robin 1982 a; b; Piotrovskiy 1985), and by the late Middle Ages the political system of the former "Sabaean" region seems to have consisted mainly of a stronger state in its centre and true tribes (not chiefdoms) on its periphery, whereas regular state structures persisted in the Southern (former Himyarite) cultural-political area (see e.g. Dresch 1989).

[52] It does not seem productive either to consider the Middle Sabaean cultural-political area as an agglomerate of political units, like an alliance of states, or tribes: the level of the political integration of this entity was rather high, quite comparable to that of an average early state. Hence, this entity must be considered as belonging to the same level of political integration as e.g. an early state rather than an alliance of early states.

[53] As has been mentioned above (part **d.1.** of this chapter), the Middle "Sabaean" temples had important political functions; however, the level of their autonomy appears to have been normally very high, and by no means could they be described as integral parts of the administrative sub-systems of the Middle "Sabaean" state and chiefdoms.

[54] It does not appear reasonable to characterize this civil community either as a "chiefdom", or as a true "tribe". There are also some grounds to suppose the existence of autonomous civil communities in Nashq and Nashān. The *shaᶜb* of Ṣirwāḥ also seems to have had some evident features of the civil community (see above part **e.** of this Chapter).

[55] See e.g. von Wissmann 1964 a; Robin 1991 f.

The Middle "Sabaean" experience seems to demonstrate that an integrated territorial entity (even when it is considerably large, complex and highly developed in comparison with e.g. an average chiefdom) need not necessarily be organized politically as a state. This appears to show that for the "early state" (in Claessen's sense of this term [see Claessen, Skalnik 1978]) the transition to the "mature state" or complete "degeneration" into "tribes" and "chiefdoms" were not the only possible ways of evolution. One of the possible alternatives was its transformation into a "political system of the Middle Sabaean type". The real processes of political evolution seem to have been actually much less "unilinear" than is sometimes supposed.

CONCLUSION

The main research subject of this book is the phenomenon of the "positive deviation" in Sabaic epigraphy, i.e. the use of the plural in the places where one would expect the singular or dual. The quantitative analysis of this phenomenon undertaken in this book leads me to the supposition that its main causes are social and not purely linguistic, though the linguistic trend towards the supplanting of the dual by the plural observed in Middle Sabaic epigraphy can partly (but only partly) explain the positive deviation from the dual. Hence, the study of this phenomenon leads me to the following suppositions with respect to the social history of ancient Yemen:

1. Clan organization seems to have played an important role in the social life of Middle Sabaean society (= the Middle Sabaean cultural-political area = the Northern part of the area of the Middle Sabaic epigraphy, the 1st century BC - the 4th century AD):

1.a. All the main types of immovable property (fields, vineyards, houses, irrigation structures, wells &c) were considered as a rule, almost without exceptions, to be the property of clan groups, not of individuals.

1.b. Clan groups (not individuals) were considered to be chiefs of the tribes.

1.c. Clan groups were often considered to be both objects of the client dependence, and the patrons of the clients (*'dm*).

1.d. Tribes were often considered to consist of clan groups (not of individuals).

2. In the Ancient Sabaean cultural-political area (the 1st millennium BC) the role of the clan organization was remarkably less important:

2.a. It is impossible to say that almost all kinds of immovable property were considered here to be in the possession of clans. In the majority of the cases individual (not clan) possessions are mentioned in the Ancient Sabaean inscriptions. Though private ownership might not have become completely universal in the Ancient Period, it is quite evident that the process of the formation and proliferation of this form of ownership went quite far in this Period.

2.b. In the Ancient Period the individual forms of cliental dependence seem to have played a much more important role than the clan ones. In the majority of the cases individual persons (not clients) were considered to be both "patrons" and "clients".

2.c. Individual persons (not clans) were usually considered to be leaders of tribes and communities in the Ancient Period.

2.d. Tribes were always considered to consist of individuals (not clans) in this period.

3. One may suppose that the process of the formation of the state and civilization in the Lowlands went far enough in the Ancient Period to cause a considerable decline of the clan organization and the ejecting of it to the periphery (both in the spatial and social senses of this word) of the social system.

4. Hence, it is possible to suppose that with the transition from the Ancient to the Middle Period the clan organisation in the "North" consolidated significantly; its social importance grew considerably.

5. The "archaization" of the social life in the Southern (Himyarite-Radmanite) part of the area of the Middle Sabaic epigraphy (most of which was a part of the Qatabanian cultural-political area in the Ancient Period) was less strong than in the Northern ("Sabaean") part. The Ancient "individualized" tradition survived in the South to some extent, and the positions of the clan organization were not so solid here as they were in the North.

6. The above-mentioned social changes fit quite well in the general picture of the Pre-Islamic Yemeni history.

6.a. Several factors described in Chapter 4 caused a significant decline of the Sabaean state and civilization by the end of the 1st millennium BC. The weakening state organization seems to have become incapable of providing guarantees of life and property to individuals, and it was the clan organization that took on these functions to a considerable extent. As a result we can see by the Middle Period the consolidation of the clan organization which acted as a partial substitute for the weak state. This process can be also considered as quite an adequate social adaptation to the new situation which appeared in the Sabaean cultural-political area by the end of the 1st millennium BC with the relative decline of the Sabaean Lowlands (caused by the above-mentioned factors) and the rise of the importance of the "Sabaean" Highlands. Indeed, the Middle "Sabaean" political system, which was much less like a regular state than the Ancient one which included strong clan and tribal structures as its integral elements, turned out to be a really effective form of socio-political organization for a complex society in the Northern Highlands. Most political entities which appeared in this region from that time till the present have shown evident similarities to the Middle "Sabaean" socio-political organization.

6.b. The Middle Sabaean political system may be also characterized as consisting of a weak state in its centre and strong chiefdoms on its periphery. However, there is no doubt that this was a real *system*, i.e. it had some integrative properties which could not be reduced to the characteristics of its elements. It should be also taken into consideration that the state and chiefdoms were not the *only* elements of this political system. It included as well e.g. a sub-system of temple centres and the civil community of Mārib, as well as some true tribes (not chiefdoms) in the area of the Sabaean Lowlands, primarily the tribes of the Amirite confederation. With the transition from the Ancient to Middle Period the Sabaean political system was essentially transformed, becoming as a whole very different from the "state", but remaining, however, on basically the same level of political complexity. Without losing any political complexity and sophistication, the Middle "Sabaeans" managed to solve in quite different ways the problems which in complex societies are normally solved by states, such as the mobilization of resources for the functioning of the governing sub-system, the territorial organization of a vast space and the provision of guarantees of life and property. The Middle "Sabaean" experience seems to demonstrate that a large, complex, highly developed (in comparison with, for example, an average chiefdom) and integrated territorial entity need not necessarily be organized politically as a state. This appears to show that for the "early state" the transition to the "mature state" or complete "degeneration" into "tribes" and "chiefdoms" were not the only ways of possible evolution. One of the possible alternatives was its transformation into a "political system of the Middle Sabaean type". The real processes of political evolution seem to have been actually much less "unilinear" than is sometimes supposed. A significant transformation appears to have occurred in the area in the Early Islamic Period, and by the late Middle Ages the political system of the former "Sabaean" region seems to have consisted mainly of a stronger state in its centre and true tribes (not chiefdoms) on its periphery, whereas regular state structures persisted in the Southern (former Himyarite) cultural-political area.

6.c. The decline of the Ancient Qatabanian state took place significantly later than that of the Ancient Sabaean one. As a result the social continuity between the Ancient and the Middle Period in the Qatabanian cultural-political area was stronger, and the social transformation in the "South" turned out to be less dramatic. As a result, in the Middle Period the state organization in the "South" appears considerably stronger than in the "North"; whereas the clan organization seems to have been much weaker. Quite an impressive feature of Yemeni history is that we find a more or less similar picture in 20th century Yemen: very strong clan-tribal structures and very weak state ones in the Yemeni Uplands to the north of Naqīl Yiṣliḥ (in the "Sabaean Highlands") and relatively weak clan-tribal structures and relatively strong state ones to the south of it, in the "Himyarite Highlands". Thus the picture described above appears as almost invariable in Yemeni history since the first centuries AD. This fact leads one to the supposition that there must be some fundamental basis for such a stable difference between the "North" and the "South". Its main objective factor is evident: the significant difference in the geographical conditions. It is really remarkable to find that the Highland territories of the two Middle Period cultural-political areas are practically identical with two main ecological zones of the Yemeni uplands.

7. The clan organization was not universal, even in the Middle Sabaean cultural-political area. The dense network of the clan relations was considerably weaker near the king and, perhaps, the most important temple centres, as they stood outside the clan organization and above it. In spatial dimensions, the zone of the weaker clan relations could be localized in the area of Mārib and, perhaps, Nashq, Nashān and Ṣanᶜā'.

MAPS

Map 1. ECOLOGICAL ZONES OF YEMEN

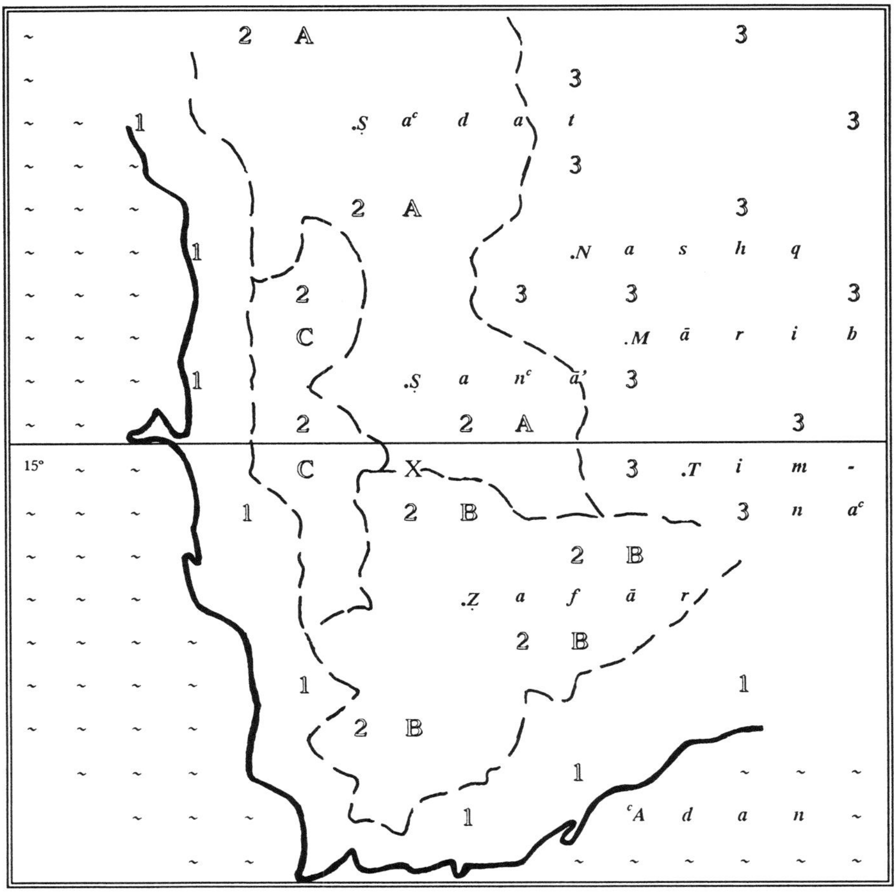

Ecological zones:

1 - Tihāmah

2 - Highlands (*al-Jabal*)

2 A - Northern Highlands
2 B - Southern Highlands
2 C - Western Highlands

X - Naqīl Yiṣliḥ

3 - Mashriq

Map 2. **SABAEAN AND HIMYARITE-RADMANITE CULTURAL-POLITICAL AREAS IN THE MIDDLE PERIOD**

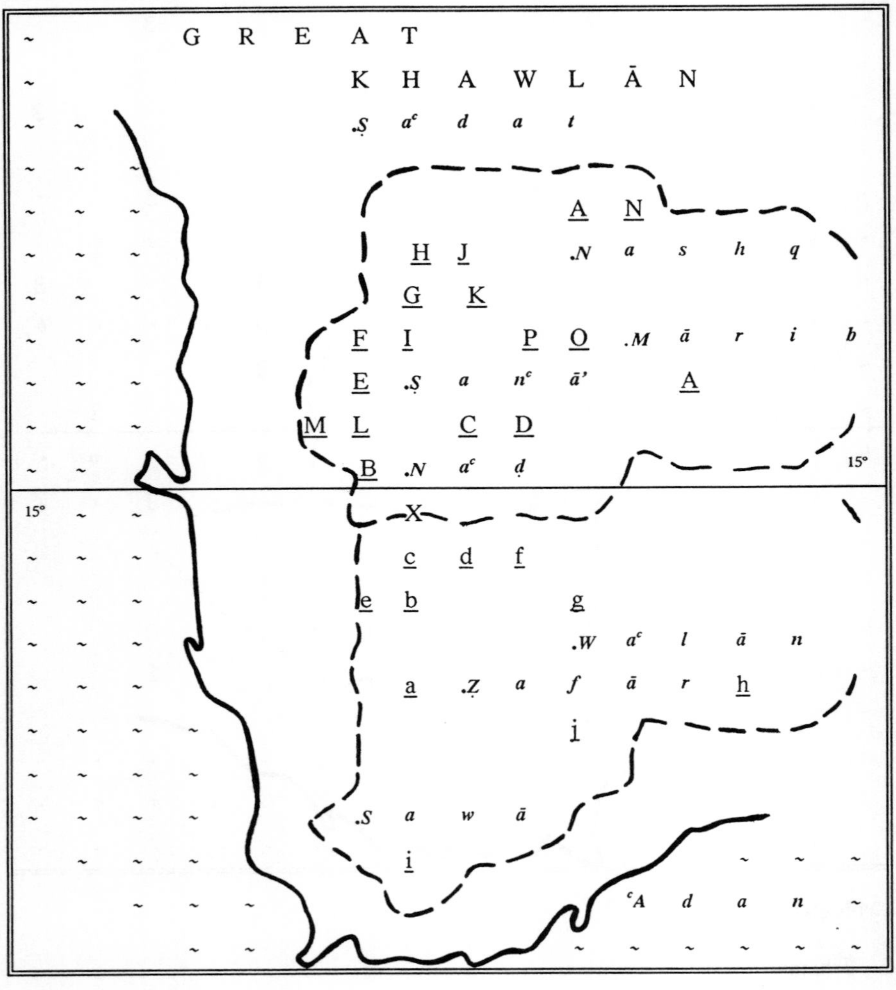

I - SABAEAN CULTURAL-POLITICAL AREA (main tribes):

A - Saba'
B - Samhar ("confederation" Dhimrī)
C - Ghaymān
D - Tan^{c}īm and Tan^{c}īmat
E - Ma'dhin

L - Sihmān
M - Yaqna^{c} /?/
N - Amīr
O - Ṣirwāḥ
P - Khawlān (Northern)

"Confederation" Bakīl:

F - dhū-Shibām
G - dhū-^{c}Amrān
H - dhū-Raydat

Northern periphery of the Middle Sabaean cultural-political system:

Great Khawlān

"Confederation" Sum^{c}ay

I - Ḥumlān
J - Ḥāshid   K - Yarsum

X - Naqīl Yiṣliḥ

II - HIMYARITE-RADMANITE CULTURAL-POLITICAL AREA (main tribes):

a - Ḥimyar
b - Muqra'
c - Muha'nif
d - Qasham ("confederation" Dhimrī)
e - Alhān

f - Shadad
g - Radmān and (Southern) Khawlān
h - Maḏḥā
i - Ma^{c}āfir (under the Ethiopian control most of the 3rd century AD)
j - Haṣbaḥ

Map 3. ANCIENT SOUTH ARABIA

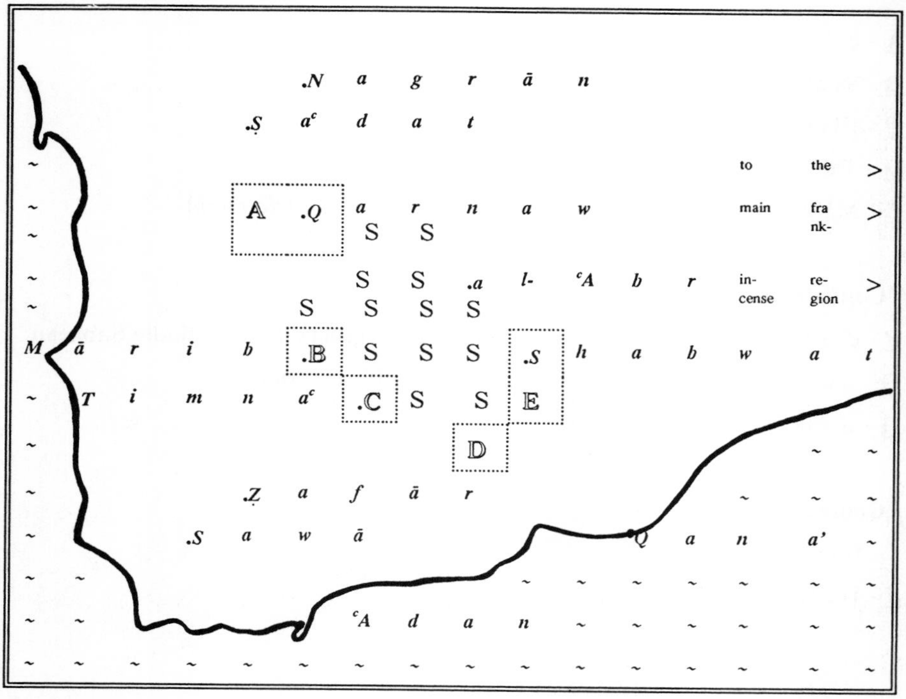

The main centres of the Most Ancient South Arabian civilization:

A - "Madhabian" centre (Nashān, Kamināhū, Haram, Ma^cīn, Inabba')

B - Sabaean centre

C - Qatabanian centre

D - Awsanian centre (Wadi Markha)

E - Hadrami centre

SSSSS
SSSSS - the Ṣayhad desert
SSSSS

BIBLIOGRAPHY

LIST OF ABBREVIATIONS

ABADY	- *Archäologische Berichte aus dem Yemen*. Mainz am Rhein
AfO	- *Archiv für Orientforschung*. Graz
AION	- *Annali dell'Istituto Orientale di Napoli*. Napoli
BiOr	- *Bibliotheca Orientalis*. Leiden
BSOAS	- *Bulletin of the School of Oriental and African Studies*. London.
CRAIBL	- *Académie des inscriptions & belles-lettres. Comptes rendus...*. Paris
EI	- *The Encyclopaedia of Islam. New Edition*. Leiden.
EV	- *Epigrafika Vostoka*. Moskva
JAOS	- *Journal of the American Oriental Society*. New Haven
JRAS	- *Journal of the Royal Asiatic Society*. London
JSS	- *Journal of Semitic Studies*. Manchester
KSINA	- *Kratkiye soobsheniya Instituta narodov Azii*. Moskva
NESE	- Degen, R., Müller, W.W., Röllig, W., *Neue Ephemeris für Semitische Epigraphik*. Wiesbaden
OA	- *Oriens Antiquus*. Roma
PPPIK	- *Pismennyye pamyatniki i problemy istorii kultury narodov Vostoka*. Leningrad
PS	- *Palestinskiy Sbornik*. Moskva - Leningrad
PSAS	- *Proceedings of the Seminar for Arabian Studies*. London
RSO	- *Rivista degli Studi Orientali*. Roma
SBAW	- *Sitsungsberichte der Akademie der Wissenschaften in Wien. Philosophisch-historische Klasse*. Wien
SEG	- *Sammlung Eduard Glaser*. Wien
VDI	- *Vestnik Drevney Istorii*. Moskva
WZKM	- *Wiener Zeitschrift für die Kunde des Morgenlandes*. Wien
ZDMG	- *Zeitschrift der Deutschen Morgenländischen Gesellschaft*. Wiesbaden

ᶜABDALLĀH 1979 - ᶜAbdallāh, Y.M., "Mudawwanāt al-nuqūsh al-Yamaniyyah al-qadīmah. Nuqūsh jadīdah", *Dirāsāt Yamaniyyah*. 1979, N2, 47-64; N 3, 29-50.

ᶜABDALLĀH 1986 a - ᶜAbdallāh, Y.M., ed., *Al-Hamdānī, a Great Yemenī Scholar. Studies on the Occasion of his Millennial Anniversary*. Ṣanᶜā', 1986.

ᶜABDALLĀH 1986 b - ᶜAbdallāh, Y.M., "Khaṭṭ al-musnad wa-al-nuqūsh al-yamaniyyah al-qadīmah. Dirāsah li-kitābah yamaniyyah qadīmah manqūshah ᶜalā al-khashab", *Al-Yaman al-Jadīd*. 15/5 (1986), 10-26; 15/6 (1986), 10-28.

ᶜABDALLĀH 1988 - ᶜAbdallāh, Y.M., "Madīnat al-Siwā fī 'Kitāb al-Ṭawāf ḥawla al-baḥr al-Aritri", *Raydān*. 5 (1988), 101-114.

ᶜABDALLĀH *ET AL.* 1979 - ᶜAbdallāh, A.M., *et al.*, eds., *Studies in the History of Arabia*. Vol.I. *Sources for the History of Arabia*. Pt.1. Riyadh, 1979.

ABŪ GHĀNIM 1990 - Abū Ghānim, F.ᶜA.A., *Al-qabīlah wa-al-dawlah fī-al-Yaman*. al-Qāhira, 1990.

AFANASYEV 1975 - Afanasyev, V.G., *Sotsialnaya informatsiya i upravleniye obshchestvom*. Moskva, 1975.

AUDOUIN, BRETON, ROBIN 1988 - Audouin, R., Breton, J.-F., and Robin, C., "Towns and Temples - the Emergence of South Arabian Civilization", Daum 1988, 63-77.

AVANZINI 1977, 1980 - Avanzini, A., *Glossaire des inscriptions de l'Arabie du Sud*. 2 volumes. Firenze, 1977, 1980 (Quaderni di Semitistica, 3).

AVANZINI 1985 - Avanzini, A., "Problemi storici della regione di al-Hadā' nel periodo preislamico e nuove iscrizioni", *Studi yemeniti*, 1 (1985) [Quaderni di semitistica, vol.14], 53-115 and t.1-34.

AVANZINI 1991 - Avanzini, A., "L'anthroponymie en Arabie du Sud comme source pour l'histoire", Robin, C., ed., *Études sud-arabes, recueil offert à J.Ryckmans*. Louvain, 1991 (Publications de l'institut orientaliste de Louvain, 39), 19-30.

BĀFAQĪH 1973 - Bāfaqīh, M.ᶜA., *Ta'rīkh al-Yaman al-qadīm*. Bayrūt, 1973.

BĀFAQĪH 1985 - Bāfaqīh, M.ᶜA., "Mūjaz ta'rīkh al-Yaman qabl al-Islām", Bāfaqīh, M.ᶜA., *et al.*, eds., *Mukhtārāt min al-nuqūsh al-Yamaniyyah al-qadīmah*. Tūnis, 1985, 14-65.

BĀFAQĪH 1988 - Bāfaqīh, M.ᶜA., "Mamlakat Ma'dhin: Shawāhid wa-fardiyyāt", *Dirāsāt Yamaniyyah*. 34 (1988), 20-29.

BĀFAQĪH 1990 - Bāfaqīh, M.ᶜA., *L'unification du Yémen antique. La lutte entre Saba', Ḥimyar et le Ḥaḍramawt du Ier au IIIème siècle de l'ère chrétienne*. Paris, 1990 (Bibliothèque de Raydān, 1).

BĀFAQĪH, BĀṬĀYIᶜ 1988 - Bāfaqīh, M.ᶜA., and Bāṭāyiᶜ, A., "Nuqūsh min al-Ḥadd", *Raydān*. 5 (1988), 61-80.

BĀFAQĪH, ROBIN 1978 - Bāfaqīh, M.ᶜA., and Robin, C., "Min nuqūsh Maḥram Bilqīs", *Raydān*. 1 (1978), 11-56.

BĀFAQĪH, ROBIN 1979 a - Bāfaqīh, M.ᶜA., and Robin, C., "Inscriptions inédites de Yanbuq (Yémen Démocratique)", *Raydān*. 2 (1979), 15-76.

BĀFAQĪH, ROBIN 1979 b - Bāfaqīh, M.ᶜA., and Robin, C., "Naqsh Aṣbaḥī min Ḥaṣī", *Raydān*. 2 (1979), 11-23 (the Arabic part of the journal).

BĀFAQĪH, ROBIN 1980 - Bāfaqīh, M.ᶜA., and Robin, C., "Ahammiyyat nuqūsh Jabal al-Miᶜsāl", *Raydān*. 3 (1980), 9-29.

BAUER 1964 - Bauer, G.M., *Sabeyskiye nadpisi kak istochnik dlya issledovaniya pozemelnyh otnosheniy v Sabe "epohi mukarribov"*. Moskva, 1964.

BAUER 1965 a - Bauer, G.M., "Nekotoryye sotsialnyye terminy v drevneyemenskih tekstah", *Semitskiye yazyki*. 2/1 (1965), 313-335.

BAUER 1965 b - Bauer, G.M., "Termin *gwlm* v yuzhnoaraviyskoy epigrafike", *KSINA*. 66 (1965), 205-219.

BAUER 1966 - Bauer, G.M., *Yazyk yuzhnoaraviyskoy pismennosti*. Moskva, 1966.

BAUER 1989 - Bauer, G.M., "Gorodishe Raybun po dannym epigrafiki", *VDI* 1989, N2, 153-157.

BAUER, AKOPYAN, LUNDIN 1990 - Bauer, G.M., Akopyan, A.M., and Lundin, A.G., "Novyye epigraficheskiye pamyatniki iz Hadramauta", *VDI*. 1990 N 2, 168-174.

VAN BEEK 1969 - van Beek, G.W., *Hajar bin Ḥumeid, Investigations at a Pre-Islamic Site in South Arabia*. Baltimore, 1969 (Publications of the American Foundation for the Study of Man, V).

BEESTON 1937 - Beeston, A.F.L., *Sabaean Inscriptions*. Oxford, 1937.

BEESTON 1949 - Beeston, A.F.L., "A Sabaean Boundary Formula", *BSOAS*. 13 (1949), 1-3.

BEESTON 1952 - Beeston, A.F.L., "Four Sabaean Texts of the Istanbul Archaeological Museum", *Le Muséon*. 65 (1952), 271-283.

BEESTON 1954 - Beeston, A.F.L., "Notes on Old South Arabian Lexicography VI", *Le Muséon*. 67 (1954), 311-322.

BEESTON 1956 - Beeston, A.F.L., *Epigraphic South Arabian Calendars and Datings*. London, 1956.

BEESTON 1959 - Beeston, A.F.L., "Two Middle Sabaean Votive Texts", *BO*, 16 (1959), 17-18.

BEESTON 1962 a - Beeston, A.F.L., "Arabian Sibilants", *JSS*. 7 (1962), 222-233.

BEESTON 1962 b - Beeston, A.F.L., *A Descriptive Grammar of Epigraphic South Arabian*. London, 1962.

BEESTON 1962 c - Beeston, A.F.L., "Epigraphic and Archaeological Gleanings from South Arabia", *Oriens Antiquus*. 1 (1962), 41-52.

BEESTON 1969 - Beeston, A.F.L., "A Sabaean Trader's Misfortunes", *JSS*. 14 (1969), 227-230.

BEESTON 1971 - Beeston, A.F.L., "Functional Significance of the Old South Arabian "Town"", *PSAS*. 1 (1971), 26-28.

BEESTON 1972 a - Beeston, A.F.L., "Kingship in Ancient South Arabia", *Journal of the Economic and Social History of the Orient*. 15/1-3 (1972), 256-268.

BEESTON 1972 b - Beeston, A.F.L., "Notes on Old South Arabian Lexicography VII", *Le Muséon*. 85 (1972), 535-544.

BEESTON 1972 c - Beeston, A.F.L., "Pliny's Gebbanitae", *PSAS*. 2 (1972), 4-8.

BEESTON 1973 - Beeston, A.F.L., "Notes on Old South Arabian Lexicography VIII", *Le Muséon*. 86 (1973),

BEESTON 1975 a - Beeston, A.F.L., "The Himyarite Problem", *PSAS*. 5 (1975), 1-7.

BEESTON 1975 b - Beeston, A.F.L., "Mashākil al-nuqūsh", *al-Ḥikmah*. 38 (1975), 24-29.

BEESTON 1975 c - Beeston, A.F.L., "Notes on Old South Arabian Lexicography IX", *Le Muséon*. 88 (1975), 187-198.

BEESTON 1976 a - Beeston, A.F.L., "Notes on Old South Arabian Lexicography X", *Le Muséon*. 89 (1976), 407-423.

BEESTON 1976 b - Beeston, A.F.L., *Warefare in Ancient South Arabia (2nd - 3rd centuries A.D.)*. London, 1976 (Qahtan: Studies in old South Arabian Epigraphy. Fasc.3).

BEESTON 1978 a - Beeston, A.F.L., "Epigraphic South Arabian Nomenclature", *Raydān*. 1 (1978), 13-21.

BEESTON 1978 b - Beeston, A.F.L., "Notes on Old South Arabian Lexicography XI", *Le Muséon*. 91 (1978), 195-206.

BEESTON 1978 c - Beeston, A.F.L., "Temporary Marriage in Pre-Islamic South Arabia", *Arabian Studies*. 4 (1978), 21-25.

BEESTON 1979 a - Beeston, A.F.L., "Some Features of Social Structure in Saba'", Abdallāh *et al.* 1979, 115-123.

BEESTON 1979 b - Beeston, A.F.L., "Some Observations on Greek and Latin Data Relating to South Arabia", *BSOAS*. 42 (1979), 7-12.

BEESTON 1981 - Beeston, A.F.L., "Notes on Old South Arabian Lexicography XII", *Le Muséon*. 94 (1981), 55-73.

BEESTON 1982 - Beeston, A.F.L., "Languages of pre-Islamic Arabia", *Etudes de Linguistique arabe*. Leiden, 1982, 178-186.

BEESTON 1983 - Beeston, A.F.L., "Women in Saba'", Bidwell, R.L., and Smith, G.R., eds., *Arabian and Islamic Studies. Articles Presented to R.B. Serjeant*. London - New York, 1983, 7-13.

BEESTON 1984 a - Beeston, A.F.L., "The Religions of Pre-Islamic Yemen", Chelhod *et al.* 1984, 259-269.

BEESTON 1984 b - Beeston, A.F.L., *Sabaic Grammar*. Manchester, 1984 (Journal of Semitic Studies Monograph No.6).

BEESTON 1986 - Beeston, A.F.L., "Free and Unfree: The Sayhadic case", *PSAS*. 16 (1986), 1-6.

BEESTON 1987 a - Beeston, A.F.L., "An Autobiography", Robin, Bāfaqīh 1987, XV-XX.

BEESTON 1987 b - Beeston, A.F.L., "Apologia for 'Sayhadic'", *PSAS*. 17 (1987), 13-14.

BEESTON 1987 c - Beeston, A.F.L., "Habashat and Aḥābīsh", *PSAS*. 17 (1987), 5-12.

BEESTON 1988 a - Beeston, A.F.L., "Miscellaneous Epigraphic Notes II", *Raydān*. 5 (1988), 5-32.

BEESTON 1988 b - Beeston, A.F.L., "Pre-Islamic Yemen in a Recent Publication", *JRAS*. (1988), 160-164.

BEESTON 1988 c - Beeston, A.F.L., "Two Sabaic Texts", *Raydān*. 5 (1988), 33-38.

BEESTON 1989 - Beeston, A.F.L., "Mahmoud ᶜAli Ghul and the Sabaean Cursive Script", *Arabian Studies in Honour of Mahmoud Ghul: Symposium at Yarmouk Univ., December 8-11, 1984*. Irbid - Wiesbaden, 1989 (Yarmouk University Publications, Institute of Archaeology and Anthropology Series, 2), 15-19.

BEESTON 1991 a - Beeston, A.F.L., "The Arabian Aromatics Trade in Antiquity". Paper presented at the "Arabia Antiqua" International Conference (Rome, May 1991).

BEESTON 1991 b - Beeston, A.F.L., "The Sayhadic Hunt at Šiᶜb al-ᶜAql", Robin, C., ed., *Etudes sud-arabes, recueil offert a J.Ryckmans*. Louvain, 1991 (Publications de l'institut orientaliste de Louvain, 39), 49-57.

BEESTON *ET AL.* 1982 - Beeston, A.F.L., Ghul, M.A., Müller, W.W., and Ryckmans, J., *Sabaic Dictionary (English-French-Arabic)*. Louvain-la-Neuve, Beyrouth, 1982.

BIELLA 1982 - Biella, J.C., *Dictionary of Old South Arabic, Sabaean Dialect*. Cambridge, Mass., 1982 (Harvard Semitic Studies no.25).

BORODKIN 1986 - Borodkin, L.I., *Mnogomernyy statisticheskiy analiz v istoricheskih issledovaniyah*. Moskva, 1986.

BOTTERWECK 1950 - Botterweck, G.J., "Altsüdarabische Glaser-Inschriften", *Orientalia*. 19 (1950), 435-444.

BOWEN 1958 a - Bowen, R.L., "Ancient Trade Routes in South Arabia", Bowen, Albright 1958, 35-42.

BOWEN 1958 b - Bowen, R.L., "Irrigation in Ancient Qataban (Bayḥān)", Bowen, Albright 1958, 43-136.

BOWEN, ALBRIGHT 1958 - Bowen, R.L., and Albright, F.P., *Archaeological Discoveries in South Arabia*. Baltimore, 1958 (Publications of the American Foundation for the Study of Man, II).

BRETON 1988 - Breton, J.-F, "Ancient Shabwa, the Capital of Haḍramawt", *Daum 1988*, 111-115.

BRETON 1989 - Breton, J.-F, "Rabota frantsuzskoy arheologicheskoy missii v Yuzhnom Yemene", *VDI*. 1989 N3, 148-155.

BRETON 1991 - Breton, J.-F., "Quelques dates pour les debuts de la civilization "Sudarabique"", summary of paper presented at the "Arabia Antiqua" Conference (Rome, May 1991).

BRON 1970 - Bron, F., "Antiquités sud-arabes dans les collections suisses", *AION*. 30 (1970), 549-554, pl.I-IV.

BRON 1979 - Bron, F., "Inscriptions et antiquités sudarabiques", *Semitica*. 29 (1979), 131-135, pl. VI-VII.

BRON 1981 - Bron, F., "Inscriptions de Ṣirwāḥ", *Raydān*. 4 (1981), 29-34, pl.I-X.

BRON 1988 - Bron, F., "Inscriptions du Maḥram Bilqīs (Mārib), au Musée de Bayḥān", *Raydān*. 5 (1988), 39-51.

BRON 1992 - Bron, F., *Mémorial Mahmud al-Ghul. Inscriptions sudarabiques*. Paris, 1992 (L'Arabie préislamique, 2).

BRUNNER 1983 - Brunner, U., *Die Erforschung der antiken Oase von Mārib mit Hilfe geomorphologischer Untersuchunsmethoden*. Mainz am Rhein, 1983 (ABADY, 2).

BULLIET 1975 - Bulliet, R.W., *The Camel and the Wheel*. Cambridge, 1975.

BURCKHARDT 1830 - Burckhardt, J.L., *Notes on the Bedouins and the Wahabys*. London, 1830.

BURROWES 1987 - Burrowes, R.D., *The Yemen Arab Republic: the Politics of Development, 1962-1986*. Boulder, London, Sydney, 1987.

BÜTTNER 1981 - Büttner, T., *Istoriya Afriki s drevneyshih vremen*. Moskva, 1981.

CAQUOT, NAUTIN 1970 - Caquot, A., and Nautin, R., "Une nouvelle inscription grecque d'Ezana, roi d'Axoum", *Journal des savants*. 1970, octobre - decembre, 265-273.

CAVIGNEAUX, ISMAIL 1990 - Cavigneaux, A., and Ismail, B.Kh., "Die Statthalter von Suḫu und Mari im 8. Jh. v. Chr.", *Baghdader Mitteilungen*. 21 (1990), 321-456.

CHELHOD *ET AL*. 1984 - Chelhod, J., et un groupe d'auteurs, *L'Arabie du Sud, histoire et civilisation*. Vol.1. *Le peuple yéménite et ses racines*. Paris, 1984 (Islam d'hier et d'aujourd'hui, 21).

CHELHOD 1985 - Chelhod, J., "Les structures sociales et familiales", *Chelhod et al. 1985*, 15-123.

CHELHOD *ET AL*. 1985 - Chelhod, J., et un groupe d'auteurs, *L'Arabie du Sud: histoire et civilization. 3. Culture et institutions du Yémen*. Paris, 1985 (Islam d'hier et d'aujourd'hui, 25).

CLAESSEN, SKALNIK 1978 - Claessen, H.J.M., and Skalnik, P., eds., *The Early State*. The Hague - Paris - New York, 1978.

Corpus 1889-1908, 1911, 1929 - *Corpus Inscriptionum Semiticarum. Pars quarta. Inscriptiones himyariticas et sabaeas continens*. Tomus 1, 2, 3. Paris, 1889-1908, 1911, 1929.

Corpus 1977, 1986 - *Corpus des inscriptions et antiquites Sud-Arabes*. TT.1,2. Louvain, 1977, 1986.

CRONE 1980 - Crone, P., *Slaves on Horses. The Evolution of the Islamic Polity*. Cambridge &c, 1980.

CRONE 1987 - Crone, P., *Meccan Trade and the Rise of Islam*. Oxford, 1987.

CRONE 1989 - Crone, P., *Pre-Industrial Societies*. Oxford - Cambridge, MA, 1989.

CRONE 1991 - Crone, P., "*Mawlā*", *EI*. 6 (1991), 874-882.

DAE 1913 - *Deutsche Aksum-Expedition*. Bd. 4. Berlin, 1913.

DANILOV 1963 - Danilov, A.I., "Marksistsko-leninskaya teoriya otrazheniya i istoricheskaya nauka", *Sredniye veka*. 24 (1963), 24-36.

DANILOVA 1968 - Danilova, L.V., ed., *Problemy istorii dokapitalisticheskih obshchestv*. Moskva, 1968.

DAUM 1988 - Daum, W., ed., *Yemen: 3000 Years of Art and Civilization in Arabia Felix*. Innsbruck - Frankfurt/Main, 1988.

DAYTON 1975 - Dayton, J.E., "The Problem of Climatic Change in the Arabian

Peninsula", *PSAS*. 5 (1975), 33-60.

DAYTON 1979 - Dayton, J.E., "A Discussions of the Hydrology of Mārib", *PSAS*. 9 (1979), 124-129.

DAYTON 1981 - Dayton, J.E., "Mārib Visited, 1979", *PSAS*. 11 (1981), 7-26D.

DEGEN, MÜLLER 1974 - Degen, R., Müller, W.W., "Eine hebräisch-sabäische Bilinguis aus Bait al-Ašwal", *NESE*. 2 (1974), 117-123.

DEOPIK 1986 - Deopik, D.V., "Sotsialno-ekonomicheskaya struktura gosudarstva Tyampa i yeyo evolutsiya po dannym kolichestvennogo analiza vidov nadpisey i ih prostranstvenno-vremennogo raspredeleniya", Volkov, S.V., ed., *Kolichestvennyye metody v izuchenii stran Vostoka*. Moskva, 1986, 80-107.

DIAKONOFF 1969 - Diakonoff, I.M., "The Rise of the Despotic State in Ancient Mesopotamia", Diakonoff, I.M., ed., *Ancient Mesopotamia. Socio-Economic History*. Moscow, 1969, 173-203.

DIAKONOFF 1983 - Diakonoff, I.M., "Pervyi etap Rannedinasticheskogo perioda", Diakonoff, I.M., ed., *Istoriya drevnego Vostoka. Pt.1. Mesopotamiya*. Moskva, 1983, 167-170.

DIAZ ESTEBAN 1969 - Diaz Esteban, F., "Inscripcion sudarabiga en Madrid", *Trabajos de Prehistoria*. 26 (1969), 360-363.

DOE 1963 - Doe, D.B., *The Site of Am ᶜAdiya near Mukeiras on the Audhali Plateau, South West Arabia*. Aden, 1963 (Department of Antiquities Publication, 2).

DOE 1964 - Doe, D.B., *The Wadi Shirjān*. Aden, 1964 (Department of Antiquities Publication, 4).

DOE, JAMME 1968 - Doe, D.B., Jamme, A., "New Sabaean Inscriptions from South Arabia", *Journal of the Royal Asiatic Society* (1968), 2-28, pl.I-V.

DRESCH 1984 - Dresch, P., "Tribal Relations and Political History in Upper Yemen", Pridham 1984, 154-174.

DRESCH 1989 - Dresch, P., *Tribes, Government, and History in Yemen*. Oxford, 1989.

DREWES 1980 - Drewes, A.J., "The Lexicon of Ethiopian Sabaean", *Raydān*. 3 (1980), 35-54.

EARLE 1987 - Earle, T.K., "Chiefdoms in Archaeological and Ethnohistorical Perspective", *Annual Review of Anthropology*. 16 (1987), 279-308.

EARLE 1991 - Earle, T.K., "The Evolution of Chiefdoms", Earle, T.K., ed., *Chiefdoms: Power, Economy, and Ideology*. Cambridge &c., 1991, 1-15.

ENGELS [1884] 1990 - Engels, F., *Der Ursprung der Familie, des Privateigentums und des Staats*. Berlin, 1990 (Karl Marx Friedrich Engels Gesamtausgabe [MEGA]. Bd. I/29).

EPHᶜAL 1982 - Ephᶜal, I., *The Ancient Arabs. Nomads on the Borders of the Fertile Crescent 9th-5th Centuries B.C.* Jerusalem - Leiden, 1982.

ERYĀNĪ 1973 - al-Eryānī, M.ᶜA., *Fī ta'rīkh al-Yaman. Sharḥ wa-taᶜlīq ᶜalā nuqūsh lam tunshar, 34 naqshᵃⁿ min majmūᶜat al-qāḍī ᶜAlī ᶜAbdallāh al-Kahālī*. al-Qāhirah, 1973.

ERYĀNĪ 1988 - al-Eryānī, M.ᶜA., "Al-Eryānī 69", *Raydān*. 5 (1988), 9-18.

ERYĀNĪ 1990 - al-Eryānī, M.ᶜA., *Fī ta'rīkh al-Yaman. Nuqūsh musnadiyyah wa-taᶜlīqāt*. Ṣanᶜā', 1990.

EVANS-PRITCHARD 1940 [1967] - Evans-Pritchard, E.E., *The Nuer: a Description of the Modes of Livelihood and Political Institutions of a Nilotic People*. Oxford, 1940 [1967].

FAKHRY, RYCKMANS 1952 - Fakhry, A., *An Archaeological Jorney to Yemen*. Vol.3. *Epigraphical Texts* by G.Ryckmans. Cairo, 1952.

FEDELE 1988 - Fedele, F.G., "North Yemen: The Neolithic", Daum 1988, 34-37.

FERGUSON [1767] 1966 - Ferguson, A., *An Essay on the History of Civil Society*. Edinburgh, 1966 /1st published 1767/.

FERGUSON 1792 - Ferguson, A., *Principles of Moral and Political Science*. Edinburgh, 1792.

GARBINI 1969 - Garbini, G., "Una nuova iscrizione di Sarahbi'il Yacfur", *AION*. 29 (1969), 559-566, tav. II-IV.

GARBINI 1970 a - Garbini, G., "Antichità yemenite", *AION*. 30 (1970), 400-404, 537-548, tav I-XXXIX.

GARBINI 1970 b - Garbini, G., "Una bilingue sabeo-ebraica di Ẓafār", *AION*. 30 (1970), 153-165, tav. I-II.

GARBINI 1971 a - Garbini, G., "Frammenti epigrafici sabei [I]", *AION*. 31 (1971), 538-542, tav.I-II.

GARBINI 1971 b - Garbini, G., "Iscrizioni sabee da Hakir", *AION*. 31 (1971), 303-311, tav.I-III.

GARBINI 1973 a - Garbini, G., "Frammenti epigrafici sabei II", *AION*. 33 (1973), 587-593.

GARBINI 1973 b - Garbini, G., "Nuove iscrizioni sabee", *AION*. 33 (1973), 31-46.

GARBINI 1973 c - Garbini, G., "Un nuovo documento per la storia dell'antico Yemen", *OA*. 12 (1973), 143-163.

GARBINI 1973 d - Garbini, G., "Note di epigrafia sabea I", *AION*. 33 (1973), 431-438.

GARBINI 1974 a - Garbini, G., ed., *Iscrizioni sudarabiche*. Vol.1: *Iscrizioni minee*. Napoli, 1974.

GARBINI 1974 b - Garbini, G., "Note di epigrafia sabea II", *AION*. 34 (1974), 291-299.

GARBINI 1976 - Garbini, G., "Iscrizioni sudarabiche"", *AION*. 36 (1976), 293-315, tav. I-V.

GARBINI 1978 - Garbini, G., "Sabaean Fragments", *Raydān*. 1 (1978), 33-35.

GERASIMOV 1987 - Gerasimov, O.G., *Yemenskiye dokumenty*. Moskva, 1987.

GHUL 1959 - Ghul, M.A., "New Qatabani Inscriptions", *BSOAS*. 22 (1959), 1-22, 419-438.

GHUL 1984 - Ghul, M.A., "The Pilgrimage at Itwat" (ed. by A.F.L. Beeston), *PSAS*. 14 (1984), 33-39.

GLUCKMAN 1965 - Gluckman, M., *Politics, Law and Ritual in Tribal Society*. Oxford, 1965.

GOCHENOUR 1984 - Gochenour, D.T., "Towards a Sociology of the Islamization of Yemen", Pridham 1984, 1-20.

GROHMANN 1963 - Grohmann, A., *Arabien*. München, 1963 (Kulturgeschichte des Alten Orients. 3. Abschn., 4. Unterabschn. [Handbuch der Altertumswissenschaft. 3. Abt., 1. Teil, 3. Bd.]).

GROLIER, TIBBITTS, IBRAHIM 1984 - Grolier, M.J., Tibbitts, G.C., Ibrahim, M.M., *A Qualitative Appraisal of the Hydrology of the Yemen Arab Republic from Landsat Images*. Washington, 1984 (Geological Survey Water-Supply, paper 1757-P).

GROMYKO 1968 - Gromyko, M.M., "O 'neposredstvennyh' i 'kosvennyh' istoricheskih istochnikah", *Izvestiya Sibirckogo otdeleniya AN SSSR*. 1968 N 6/2, 84-90.

GROOM 1981 - Groom, N., *Frankincense and Myrrh. A Study of the Arabian Incense Trade*. London - New York, 1981.

GUREVICH 1968 - Gurevich, A.Ya., "Individ i obshchestvo v varvarskih gosudarstvah", Danilova 1968, 384-424.

AL-ḤADĪTHĪ 1978 - al-Ḥadīthī, N., *Ahl al-Yamān fī ṣadr al-Islām*. Bayrūt, 1978.

AL-HAMDĀNĪ 1980 - al-Hamdānī, al-Ḥasan, *Kitāb al-Īklīl*. II. Taḥqīq Muḥammad al-Akwa[c]. Baghdād, 1980.

HAMILTON 1942 - Hamilton, R.A.B., "Six Weeks in Shabwa", *Geographical Journal*. 100 (1942), 107-123.

HARTMANN 1978 /1909/ - Hartmann, M., *Der Islamische Orient*. II. *Die Arabische Frage (mit einem Versuche der Archäologie Jemens)*. Amsterdam, 1978 /1st ed. - 1909/.

HEHMEYER 1989 - Hehmeyer, I., "Irrigation Farming in the Ancient Oasis of Mārib", *PSAS*. 19 (1989), 33-44.

HÖFNER 1954 - Höfner, M., "Ta'lab als Patron der Kleinviehhirten", *Serta Cantabrigiensia*. Aquis Mattiacis /Wiesbaden/, 1954, 29-36.

HÖFNER 1970 - Höfner, M., "Die vorislamischen Religionen Arabiens", in: Gese, H., Höfner, M., and Rudolph, K., *Religionen Altsyriens, Altarabiens und der Mandäer*. Stuttgart, 1970 (Religionen der Menschheit, 10,2).

HÖFNER 1973 - Höfner, M., *Inschriften aus Sirwāh, Haulān (I. Teil)*. Wien, 1973 (SEG VIII. - SBAW. 291/1).

HÖFNER 1976 - Höfner, M., *Inschriften aus Sirwāh, Haulān (II. Teil)*. Wien, 1976 (SEG XII. - SBAW. 304/5).

HÖFNER 1981 - Höfner, M., *Sabäische Inschriften (Letzte Folge)*. Wien, 1981 (SEG XIV. - SBAW 378).

HÖFNER 1987 - Höfner, M., "Neuinterpretation zweiter altsüdarabischer Inschriften", Robin, Bāfaqīh 1987, 37-48.

HÖFNER, SOLÁ SOLÉ 1961 - Höfner, M., and Solá Solé, J.M., *Inschriften aus dem Gebiet zwischen Mārib and Gôf*. Wien, 1961 (SEG, II; SBAW, 238/3).

[c]INĀN 1396 H - [c]Inān, Z., *Ḥaḍārat al-Yaman al-qadīmah*. Ṣan[c]ā', 1396 H.

IRVINE 1973 - Irvine, A.K., "The Arabs and the Ethiopians", Wiseman, D.J., ed., *Peoples of the Old Testament Times*. Oxford, 1973, 287-311.

IRYĀNĪ, GARBINI 1970 - Iryāni, M.[c]A., and Garbini, G., "A Sabaean Rock-Engraved Inscription at Mosna[c]", *AION*. 30 (1970), 405-408 and pl. I-III.

JAMME 1947 - Jamme, A., "Le panthéon sud-Arabe d'après les sources épigraphiques", *Le Muséon*. 60 (1947), 57-147.

JAMME 1954 - Jamme, A., "Trois plaques épigraphiques sabéennes du Musée de Ṣan[c]ā'", *BO*. 11 (1954), 42-43.

JAMME 1955 a - Jamme, A., "Inscriptions de al-[c]Amāyid à Māreb", *Le Muséon*. 68 (1955), 313-324.

JAMME 1955 b - Jamme, A., "Inscriptions des alentours de Māreb (Yémen)", *Cahiers de Byrsa*. 5 (1955), 265-281, pl. I-II.

JAMME 1955 c - Jamme, A., "Inscriptions sud-arabes de la collection Ettore Rossi", *RSO*. 30 (1955), 103-130.

JAMME 1956 - Jamme, A., "Les antiquités sud-arabes du Museo Nazionale Romano", *Monumenti Antichi*. 43 (1956), 1-120 and pl.I-XII.

JAMME 1957 - Jamme, A., "Sabaean Inscriptions on Two Bronze Statues from Mārib (Yemen)", *JAOS*. 77 (1957), 32-36.

JAMME 1958 - Jamme, A., "Inscriptions Related to the House Yafash in Timna[c]", Bowen, Albright 1958, 183-193.

JAMME 1962 - Jamme, A., *Sabaean Inscriptions From Maḥram Bilqīs (Mārib)*. Baltimore, 1962 (Publications of the American Foundation for the Study of Man, 3).

JAMME 1966 - Jamme, A., *Sabaean and Ḥasaean Inscriptions from Saudi Arabia*. Roma, 1966 (Studi Semitici, 23).

JAMME 1970 a - Jamme, A., "Liḥyanite, Sabaean and Thamudic Inscriptions from Western Saudi Arabia", *RSO*. 45 (1970), 91-113, pl.I-X.

JAMME 1970 b - Jamme, A., "The Pre-Islamic Inscriptions of Riyadh Museum", *OA*. 9 (1970), 115-139.

JAMME 1971 - Jamme, A., *Miscellanées d'ancient arabe*. Vol. 2, Washington, 1971.

JAMME 1972 - Jamme, A., *Miscellanées d'ancient arabe*. Vol. 3, Washington, 1972.

JAMME 1976 - Jamme, A., *Carnegie Museum 1974/1975 Yemen Expedition*. Pittsburgh, 1976.

JAMME 1980 - Jamme, A., *Miscellanées d'ancient arabe*. Vol. 11, Washington, D.C., 1980.

JAMME 1981 - Jamme, A., "Pre-Islamic Arabian Miscellanea", *Stiegner 1981*, 95-110.

JAMME 1982 - Jamme, A., *Miscellanées d'ancient arabe*. Vol. 12, Washington, D.C., 1982.

JAMME 1986 - Jamme, A., "Some Inscribed Antiquities of the Yemen Museum in Ṣanᶜā'", ᶜbdallāh 1986 a, 61-84.

JAUSSEN 1948 - Jaussen, A., *Coutumes des Arabes au pays de Moab*. Paris, 1948.

KENSDALE 1953 - Kensdale, W.E., "Ḥaywᶜṯtr Yaḍaᶜ and the Nāᶜiṭ Inscription", *Le Muséon*. 66 (1953), 371-372.

KITCHEN 1995 - Kitchen, K.A., "A Qatabanian Governor of Nashqum and Najran under the Himyarite King Shammar Yuharᶜish, c.290 AD", *PSAS*. 25 (1995) - in press.

KNAUF 1989 - Knauf, E.A., "The Migration of the Script, and the Formation of the State in South Arabia", *PSAS*. 19 (1989), 79-91.

KOROTAYEV 1988 - Korotayev, A.V., "K stanovleniyu gorodskih struktur v Yuzhnoy Aravii (nachalo 1 tys. do n.e. - 6 v. n.e.): termin *hgr* v drevneyemenskoy epigrafike", Ashrafyan, K.Z., Habayeva, R.V., eds., *Gorod na traditsionnom Vostoke*. Moskva, 1988, 37-41.

KOROTAYEV 1989 - Korotayev, A.V., "O nekotoryh ekonomicheskih predposylkah klassoobrazovaniya i politogeneza", Blümchen, S.I., *et al.*, eds., *Linguisticheskaya rekonstruktsiya i drevneyshaya istoriya Vostoka*. Part 1. Moskva, 1989, 75-95.

KOROTAYEV 1990 a - Korotayev, A.V., "Rodovaya organizatsiya v sotsialno-ekonomicheskoy strukture sabeyskogo obshchestva", *Kandidat istoricheskih nauk* thesis (University of Moscow - Institute of Oriental Studies, Soviet Academy of Sciences). Moskva, 1990.

KOROTAYEV 1990 b - Korotayev, A.V., *Rodovaya organizatsiya v sotsialno-ekonomicheskoy strukture sabeyskogo obshchestva*. Official summary of the thesis. Moskva, 1990.

KOROTAYEV 1991 - Korotayev, A.V., "Nekotorye ekonomicheskiye predposylki klassoobrazovaniya i politogeneza", Korotayev, A.V., and Chubarov, V.V., eds., *Arhaicheskoye obshchestvo*. Moskva, 1991, 136-191.

KOROTAYEV 1993 a - Korotayev, A., "Middle Sabaean Cultural-Political Area: Material Sources of Qaylite Political Power", *Abr-Nahrain*. 31 (1993), 93-105.

KOROTAYEV 1993 b - Korotayev, A., "Middle Sabaean Cultural-Political Area: *Qayl*s, their *Bayt* and *Shaᶜb*", *Aula Orientalis*. 11 (1993) - in press.

KOROTAYEV 1994 a - Korotayev, A., "Legal System of the Middle Sabaean Cultural-Political Area", *Acta Orientalia*. 55 (1994) - in press.

KOROTAYEV 1994 b - Korotayev, A., "Middle Sabaean Cultural-Political Area: Problem of Local Taxation and Temple Tithe", *Le Muséon*. 107 (1994) - in press.

KOROTAYEV 1994 c - Korotayev, A., "Middle Sabaic *bn Z*: Clan Group, or Head of Clan ?", *JSS*. 39 (1994), 207-220.

KOROTAYEV 1994 d - Korotayev, A., "Some Trends of Evolution of Sabaean Cultural-Political Area: From Clan Titles to Clan Names?", *New Arabian Studies*. 2 (1994), 153-165.

KOROTAYEV 1994 e - Korotayev, A., "Was the "Traditional Sabaean Dynasty" of the 1st Century A.D. Really Sabaean", *Archiv Orientálni*. 62 (1994), 27-31.

KOROTAYEV 1994 f - Korotayev, A., "The Sabaean Community (*SB'*; *'SB'N*) in the Political Structure of the Middle Sabaean Cultural Area", *Orientalia*. 63 (1994) - in press.

KOROTAYEV 1995 a - Korotayev, A., *Pre-Islamic Yemen: Socio-Political Organization of the Sabaean Cultural Area in the 2nd and 3rd Centuries A.D.* Wiesbaden, 1995 (in press).

KOROTAYEV 1995 b - Korotayev, A., "Some General Trends and Factors of Evolution of the Sabaean Civilization", *Journal of the Economic and Social History of the Orient*. 38 (1995) - in press.

KOROTAYEV, OBOLONKOV 1989 - Korotayev, A.V., Obolonkov, A.A., "Rodovaya organizatsiya v sotsialno-ekonomicheskoy strukture klassovyh obshchestv", *Sovetskaya etnografiya*. 1989, N2, 36-45.

KOROTAYEV, OBOLONKOV 1990 - Korotayev, A.V., Obolonkov, A.A., "Rod kak forma sotsialnoy organizatsii v rabotah dorevolutsionnyh russkih i sovetskih issledovateley", Kim, G.F., and Ashrafyan, K.Z., eds., *Uzlovyye problemy istorii dokapitalisticheskih obshchestv Vostoka*. Moskva, 1990, 3-52.

KOTLOV 1971 - Kotlov, L.I., *Yemenskaya Arabskaya Respublika*. Moskva, 1971.

KOVALCHENKO 1969 - Kovalchenko, I.D., "O primenenii matematiko-statisticheskih metodov v istoricheskih issledovaniyah", Schmidt 1969, 115-133.

KOVALCHENKO 1979 - Kovalchenko, I.D., "Istoricheskiy istochnik v svete ucheniya ob informatsii", Kovalchenko, I.D., ed., *Aktualnyye problemy istochnikovedeniya istorii SSSR, spetsialnyh istoricheskih distsiplin i ih prepodovaniya v vuzah*. Vol.1. Novorossiysk, 1979, 31-46.

KOVALCHENKO 1982 - Kovalchenko, I.D., "Istoricheskiy istochnik v svete ucheniya ob informatsii", *Istoriya SSSR*. 1982, N 3, 129-148.

KOVALCHENKO 1984 - Kovalchenko, I.D., "Vvedeniye", Kovalchenko, I.D., ed., *Kolichestvennyye metody v istoricheskih issledovaniyah*. Moskva, 1984, 3-14.

KOVALCHENKO 1987 - Kovalchenko, I.D., *Metody istoricheskogo issledovaniya*. Moskva, 1987.

KOVALCHENKO, BORODKIN 1987 - Kovalchenko, I.D., and Borodkin, L.I., *Sovremennyye metody izucheniya istochnikov s ispolzovaniyem EVM*. Moskva, 1987.

KOVALCHENKO, VORONKOVA, MURAVYOV 1981 - Kovalchenko, I.D., Voronkova, S.V., and Muravyov, A.V., "Predmet i zadachi isctochnikovedeniya", in Kovalchenko, I.D., ed., *Istochnikovedeniye istorii SSSR*. Moskva, 1981.

KOZLOVA, SEDOV, TYURIN 1968 - Kozlova, M.G., Sedov, L.A., and Tyurin, V.A., "Tipy ranneklassovyh obshchestv v Yugo-Vostochnoy Azii", *Danilova 1968*, 516-545.

KRADIN 1991 - Kradin, N.N., "Osobennosti klassoobrazovaniya i politogeneza u kochevnikov", Korotayev, A.V., and Chubarov, V.V., eds., *Arhaicheskoye obshchestvo*. Moskva, 1991, 301-324.

KRAHMALOV 1977 - Krahmalov, S.P., *Yemenskaya Arabskaya Respublika i yeyo vooruzhennyye sily*. Moskva, 1977.

KUBBEL 1974 - Kubbel, L.E., *Songayskaya derzhava*. Moskva, 1974.

KULLANDA 1992 - Kullanda, S.V., *Drevnyaya Yava*. Moskva, 1992.

KUZISHCHIN 1984 - Kuzishchin, V.I., "Vvedeniye. Nekotoryye problemy istochnikovedeniya istorii Drevnego Vostoka", in Kuzishin, V.I., ed., *Istochnikovedeniye istorii grevnego Vostoka*. Moskva, 1984, 4-19.

LAPINA 1985 - Lapina, Z.G., *Ucheniye ob upravlenii gosudarstvom v srednevekovom Kitaye*. Moskva, 1985.

LITTMANN 1950 - Littmann, A., "Äthiopische Inschriften", *Miscellanea academica berolinensia*. II/2. Berlin, 1950, 97-127.

LITVAK 1969 - Litvak, B.G., "O putyah razvitiya istochnikovedeniya massovyh istochnikov", Schmidt 1969, 102-114.

LIVERANI 1991 - Liverani, M., "Early Caravan Trade between South-Arabia and Mesopotamia", paper presented at the "Arabia Antiqua" Conference (Rome, May 1991).

LOUNDINE 1973 a - Loundine, A.G., "Deux inscriptions sabéennes de Mārib", *Le Muséon*. 86 (1973), 179-192.

LOUNDINE 1973 b - Loundine, A.G., " Le regime citadin de l'Arabie du Sud aux IIe - IIIe siècles de notre ère", *PSAS*. 3 (1973), 26-28.

LUNDIN 1961 - Lundin, A.G., "Yuzhnaya Araviya v VI veke", *PS*. 8 (1961), 1-159.

LUNDIN 1963 - Lundin, A.G., "Novyye yuzhnoarabskiye nadpisi muzeya v Ṣan^{c}a'", *Epigrafika Vostoka*. 15 (1963), 37-50.

LUNDIN 1964 - Lundin, A.G., "O prave na vodu v sabeyskom gosudarstve epohi mukarribov", *PS*. 11 (1964), 45-57.

LUNDIN 1965 a - Lundin, A.G., *Eponymenliste von Saba (aus dem Stamme Ḫalil)*. Wien, 1965 (SEG V - SBAW 248/1).

LUNDIN 1965 b - Lundin, A.G., "Nekotoryye voprosy zemelnyh otnosheniy v drevney Yuzhnoy Aravii". *KSINA*. 86 (1965), 148-154.

LUNDIN 1966 - Lundin, A.G., "Novyi fragment sabeyskoy nadpisi perioda mukarribov", *PS*. 15 (1966), 47-53.

LUNDIN 1968 - Lundin, A.G., "Novaya sabeyskaya nadpis s formuloy *ḏ-ṣry-hw*", *PPPIK*. 4 (1968), 28-30.

LUNDIN 1969 a - Lundin, A.G., "Gorodskoy stroy Yuzhnoy Aravii vo II-IV vv. n.e.", *PPPIK*. 5 (1969), 55-57.

LUNDIN 1969 b - Lundin, A.G., "Novyye Yuzhnoarabskiye nadpisi muzeya v Ṣan^{c}ā'. II", *Epigrafika Vostoka*. 19 (1969), p.14-20.

LUNDIN 1971 - Lundin, A.G., *Gosudarstvo mukarribov Saba' (sabeyskiy eponimat)*. Moskva, 1971.

LUNDIN 1972 - Lundin, A.G., "Sabeyskiye nadpisi muzeya v Ta^{c}izze", *Epigrafika Vostoka*. 21 (1972), 10-18.

LUNDIN 1973 a - Lundin, A.G., "Gorod i gosudarstvo v Yuzhnoy Aravii I tys. do n.e.", *Drevniy Vostok. Goroda i torgovlya (III-I tys. do n.e.)*. Vol.1, Yerevan, 1973, 162-177.

LUNDIN 1973 b - Lundin, A.G., "Novyye nadpisi iz Arḥaba", *PPPIK*. 9 (1973), 32-44.

LUNDIN 1973 c - Lundin, A.G., "Novyye yuzhnoarabskiye nadpisi iz vadi Ḫirr", *PPPIK*. 9 (1973), 81-89.

LUNDIN 1974 a - Lundin, A.G., "Novyye materialy o yuzhnoaraviyskom eponimate", *VDI*. 1974, N4, 95-105.

LUNDIN 1974 b - Lundin, A.G., "Sabeyskiy chinovnik i diplomat III v. n.e.", *PS*. 25 (1974), 95-104.

LUNDIN 1979 a - Lundin, A.G., "Irrigatsiya v drevnem Yemene", *VDI*. 1979, N 3,

179-184.
LUNDIN 1979 b - Lundin, A.G., "Gorodskaya organizatsiya v drevnem Yemene", *Problemy antichnoy istorii i kultury*. Yerevan, 1979, 149-155.
LUNDIN 1984 - Lundin, A.G., "Dve sabeyskiye nadpisi iz Mariba", *EV*. 22 (1984), 41-47.
LUNDIN 1987 a - Lundin, A.G., "Katabanskiy dekret o zemlepolzovanii RES 3854", *VDI*. 1987, N 3, 43-61.
LUNDIN 1987 b - Lundin, A.G., "Sabeyskiy dekret o zemlepolzovanii iz Ḥadaqāna", *PS*. 29 (1987), 91-100.
LUNDIN 1988 - Lundin, A.G., "Sabaean City Ṣanᶜā' in the 1st to 6th Centuries AD", Berzina, S.Ya., ed., *Ancient and Mediaeval Monuments of Civilization of Southern Arabia. Investigation and Conservation Problems*. Moscow, 1988, 39-48.
DE MAIGRET 1981 - de Maigret, A., "Two Prehistoric Cultures and a New Sabaean Site in the Eastern Highlands of North Yemen", *Raydān*. 4 (1981), 191-204, pl.I-XIII.
DE MAIGRET 1988 - de Maigret, A., ed., *The Sabaean Archaeological Complex in the Wādī Yalā (Eastern Ḫawlān aṭ-Ṭiyāl, Yemen Arab Republic. A Preliminary Report*. Roma, 1988 (Istituto Italiano per il Medio ed Estremo Oriente, Reports and Memoirs, 21).
DE MAIGRET, ROBIN 1989 - de Maigret, A., and Robin, C., "Les fouilles italiennes de Yalā (Yémen du Nord): Nouvelles données sur la chronologie de l'Arabie du Sud préislamique", *CRAIBL*. 1989, 255-291.
MALINOWSKI 1947 - Malinowski, B., *Freedom and Civilization*. London, 1947.
MARX 1976 - Marx, K., *Ökonomische Manuskripte 1857/58*. Berlin, 1976 (Karl Marx Friedrich Engels Gesamtausgabe [MEGA]. Bd.II/1.1).
MEDUSHEVSKAYA 1964 - Medushevskaya, O.M., "Razvitiye teorii sovetskogo istochnikovedeniya", *Trudy Moskovskogo Gosudarstvennogo istoriko-arhivnogo instituta*. 24/2 (1964), 3-16.
MEDUSHEVSKAYA 1968 - Medushevskaya, O.M., "Sbornik, podgotovlennyi istorikami GDR, i voprosy istochnikovedeniya", *Sovetskiye arhivy*. 1968, N 4, 116-121.
MESHKOV 1982 - Meshkov, K.Yu., "Filippiny", in: *Malye narody Indonezii, Malayzii i Filippin*. Moskva, 1982, 175-226.
MIRONOV 1984 - Mironov, B.N., *Istorik i sotsiologiya*. Leningrad, 1984.
MORETTI 1971 - Moretti, P., "Iscrizioni sabee a Mariya", *AION*. 31 (1971), 119-122, tav.I-II.
MORGAN [1877] 1963 - Morgan, L.H., *Ancient Society, or Researches in the Lines of Human Progress from Savagery through Barbarism to Civilization*. Cleveland - New York, 1963 /1st published 1877/.
MÜLLER 1972 a - Müller, W.W., "Epigraphische Nachlese aus Ḥāz", *NESE*. 1 (1972), 75-85.
MÜLLER 1972 b - Müller, W.W., "Neuentdeckte sabäische Inschriften aus al-Ḥuqqa", *NESE*. 1 (1972), 103-121.
MÜLLER 1972 c - Müller, W.W., "Sabäische Inschriften aus dem Museum in Taᶜizz", *NESE*. 1 (1972), 87-101.
MÜLLER 1974 a - Müller, W.W., "Eine sabäische Gesandschaft in Ktesiphon und Seleukeia", *NESE*. 2 (1974), 155-165.
MÜLLER 1974 b - Müller, W.W., "Eine sabäische Inschrift aus dem Jahre 566 der ḥimjarischen Aera", *NESE*. 2 (1974), 139-144, fig. 37, pl. XI.
MÜLLER 1974 c - Müller, W.W., "Sabäische Texte zur Polyandrie", *NESE*. 2 (1974),

125-138.
MÜLLER 1974 d - Müller, W.W., "CIH 140. Eine Neuinterpretation auf der Grundlage eines gesicherteren Textes", *AION*. 34 (1974), 413-420.
MÜLLER 1976 - Müller, W.W., "Anhang", Höfner 1976, 41-45.
MÜLLER 1978 a - Müller, W.W., "Sabäische Felsinschriften von der jemenitischen Grenze zur Rub^c al-Ḫālī", *NESE*. 3 (1978), 113-136, Taf.V-VIII.
MÜLLER 1978 b - Müller, W.W., "Sabäische Felsinschrift von Masna^cat Māriya", *NESE*. 3 (1978), 137-148, Taf.IX.
MÜLLER 1982 a - Müller, W.W., "Die Inschriften vom Tempel des Waddum ḏu-Masma^cim", *ABADY*. 1 (1982), 101-106.
MÜLLER 1982 b - Müller, W.W., "Sabäische Felsinschriften von Gabal Balaq al-Ausaṭ", *ABADY*. 1 (1982), 67-72.
MÜLLER 1986 a - Müller, W.W., "Eine Gebührenordnung vom Mariber Stadttempel Ḥarūnum", *ABADY*. 3 (1986), 66-70.
MÜLLER 1986 b - Müller, W.W., "KRWM im Lichte einer neuentdeckten sabäischen Jagdinschrift aus der Oase von Mārib", *ABADY*. 3 (1986), 101-107.
MÜLLER 1986 c - Müller, W.W., "Die sabäische Gedenkstele des Herrn von Yakrub", *ABADY*. 3 (1986), 71-73.
MÜLLER 1986 d - Müller, W.W., "Ein sabäisches Urkundenfragment aus Ḫuraibat Raḥāba", *ABADY*. 3 (1986), 97-100.
MÜLLER 1986 e - Müller, W.W., "Zu der vierzeiligen Bustrophedon-Inschrift am Wadi al-Gufaina", *ABADY*. 3 (1986), 59-60.
MÜLLER 1987 a - Müller, W.W., "Eine altsabäische Landeigentumsurkunde vom Wadi Aḏana", *ABADY*. 4 (1987), 191-194.
MÜLLER 1987 b - Müller, W.W., "Weitere alt sabäische Inschriften vom Tempel des Waddum ḏu-Masma^cim", *ABADY*. 4 (1987), 185-189.
MÜLLER 1988 - Müller, W.W., "Altsüdarabische Rituale und Beschwörungen", Kaiser, O., ed., *Texte aus der Umwelt des Alten Testaments*. Band II. *Religiöse Texte*. Lieferung 3. *Rituale und Beschwörungen II*. Gütersloh, 1988, 438-452.
MUSIL 1928 - Musil, A., *The manners and customs of the Rwala Bedouins*. New York, 1928.
NĀMĪ 1943 - Nāmī, Kh.Y., *Nashr nuqūsh sāmiyyah qadīmah min janūb bilād al-^cArab wa-sharḥu-hā*. Al-Qāhirah, 1943.
NĀMĪ 1947 - Nāmī, Kh.Y., "Nuqūsh ^carabiyyah janūbiyyah", *Majallat Kulliyyat al-Ādāb li-Jāmi^cat Fu'ād al-awwal*. 9/1 (1947), 15-27, pl.1-4.
NĀMĪ 1954 - Nāmī, Kh.Y., "Nuqūsh ^carabiyyah janūbiyyah II", *Majallat Kulliyyat al-Ādāb li-Jāmi^cat al-Qāhirah*. 16/2 (1954), 21-43, pl.1-4.
NĀMĪ 1957 - Nāmī, Kh.Y., "Nuqūsh Khirbat Barāqish IV", *Majallat Kulliyyat al-Ādāb li-Jāmi^cat al-Qāhirah*. 19/2 (1957), 93-124.
NĀMĪ 1958 - Nāmī, Kh.Y., "Nuqūsh ^carabiyyah janūbiyyah III", *Majallat Kulliyyat al-Ādāb li-Jāmi^cat al-Qāhirah*. 20/1 (1958), 55-63.
NĀMĪ 1960 - Nāmī, Kh.Y., "Nuqūsh ^carabiyyah janūbiyyah IV", *Ḥawliyyat Kulliyyat al-Ādāb li-Jāmi^cat al-Qāhirah*. 22/2 (1960), 53-63, pl.1-4.
NĀMĪ 1961 - Nāmī, Kh.Y., "Nuqūsh ^carabiyyah janūbiyyah V", *Ḥawliyyat Kulliyyat al-Ādāb li-Jāmi^cat al-Qāhirah*. 23/1 (1961), 1-9, pl.1.
NĀMĪ 1962 - Nāmī, Kh.Y., "Nuqūsh ^carabiyyah janūbiyyah VI", *Ḥawliyyat Kulliyyat al-Ādāb li-Jāmi^cat al-Qāhirah*. 24/1 (1962), 1-8, pl. I-IV.
NEBES 1988 - Nebes, N., "The Infinitive in Sabaean and Qatabanian Inscriptions", *PSAS*. 18 (1988), 63-78.
NEBES 1992 - Nebes, N., "New Inscriptions from the Bar'ān Temple (al-^cAmā'd) in

the Oasis of Mārib", Harrak, A., ed., *Contacts between Cultures. West Asia and North Africa*. Vol.1. Lewiston - Queenston - Lampeter, 1992, 160-164.

NIELSEN 1927 - Nielsen, D., ed., *Handbuch der Altarabischen Altertumskunde*. I. *Die Altarabische Kultur*. Kopenhagen, 1927.

OBERMEYER 1982 - Obermeyer, G.J., "Le formation de l'imamt et de l'état au Yémen: Islam et culture politique", Bonnenfant, P., ed., *La péninsule Arabique d'aujourd'hui*. T.II. *Etudes par pays*. Paris, 1982, 31-48.

OPPENHEIM 1964 - Oppenheim, A.L., *Ancient Mesopotamia. Portrait of a Dead Civilization*. Chicago & London, 1964.

PHILBY 1939 - Philby, H.St.J.B., *Sheba's Daughters*. London, 1939.

PHILBY, TRITTON 1944 - Philby, H.St.J.B., and Tritton, A.S., "Najrān Inscriptions", *JRAS*. 1944, 119-129, pl.14-15.

PIOTROVSKIY 1977 - Piotrovskiy, M.B., *Predaniye o himyaritskom tsare As*ᶜ*ade al-Kāmile*. Moskva, 1977.

PIOTROVSKIY 1978 - Piotrovskiy, B.B., ed., *Yuzhnaya Araviya. Pamyatniki drevney istorii i kultury*. Vol.1. Moskva, 1978.

PIOTROVSKIY 1985 - Piotrovskiy, M.B., *Yuzhnaya Araviya v ranneye crednevekovye. Stanovleniye srednevekovogo obshchestva*. Moskva, 1985.

PIOTROVSKIY, PIOTROVSKAYA 1984 - Piotrovskiy, M.B., and Piotrovskaya, I.L., "Chelovek i priroda v Aravii: Drevnost i sovremennost", *Geografiya i razvivayushiyesya strany*. Leningrad, 1984, 106-108.

PIRENNE 1955 - Pirenne, J., "La Grèce et Saba. Une nouvelle base pour la chronologie sud-arabe", *Mémoires présentés par divers savants a l'Académie des Inscriptions et Belles-Lettres*. 15 (1955), 89-196.

PIRENNE 1956 - Pirenne, J., *Paléographie des inscriptions Sud-Arabes. Contribution a l'histoire de l'Arabie du Sud antique*. I. *Des origines jusqu'à l'époque himyarite*. Bruxelles, 1956.

PIRENNE 1966 - Pirenne, J., "Contribution à l'Epigraphie Sud-Arabique", *Semitica*. 16 (1966), 73-99, pl.I-IV.

PIRENNE 1979 - Pirenne, J., "Recently Discovered Inscriptions and Archaeology as Sources for Ancient South Arabians Kingdoms", *Abdallāh et al. 1979*, 45-56.

PIRENNE 1980 - Pirenne, J., "Prospection historique dans la region du royame de Awsān", *Raydān*. 3 (1980), 213-255, pl.I-XIV.

PIRENNE 1981 - Pirenne, J., "Deux prospections historiques au Sud-Yémen (Novembre - Décembre 1981)", *Raydān*. 4 (1981), 204-240, pl.I-XIV.

PIRENNE 1987 - Pirenne, J., "Documents inédits de Baynūn", Robin, Bāfaqīh 1987, 99-112.

PIRENNE 1990 - Pirenne, J., *Les témoins écrits de la région de Shabwa et l'Histoire*. Paris, 1990 (Fouilles de Shabwa. Vol.1 - Bibliothèque Archéologique et Historique, 134).

PRIDHAM 1984 - Pridham, B.R., ed., *Contemporary Yemen: Politics and Historical Background*. London, Sydney, 1984.

PRITCHARD 1950 - Pritchard, J.B., *Ancient Near Eastern Texts Relating to the Old Testament*. Princeton, 1950.

PRONSHTEIN 1971 - Pronshtein, A.P., *Metodika istoricheskogo issledovaniya*. Rostov-na-Donu, 1971.

RATHJENS, HÖFNER 1966 - Rathjens, C., [and Höfner, M.,] *Sabaeica, Bericht über archäologischen Ergebnisse seiner zweiten, dritten und vierten Reise nach Südarabien*. III. *Bearbeitung der von Carl Rathjens in Sabaeican I und II in Abbildungen veröffentlichten altsüdarabischen Inschriften, sowie einiger sonstiger von ihm gesammelter Inschriftensteine* von Maria Höfner. Hamburg, 1966 (Mitteilungen aus dem Museum für Völkerkunde in Hamburg, XXVIII).

Répertoire 1929, 1935, 1950, 1968 - *Répertoire d'Épigraphie Sémitique* publié par la Comission du Corpus Inscriptionum Semiticarum. TT. V, VI, VII, VIII. Paris, 1929, 1935, 1950, 1968.

RHODOKANAKIS 1922 - Rhodokanakis, N., *Katabanische Texte zur Bodenwirtschaft* II. Wien, 1922 (SBAW 198/2).

RHODOKANAKIS 1927 - Rhodokanakis, N., "Das öffentliche Leben in den alten südarabischen Staaten", Nielsen 1927, 109-142.

RICKS 1989 - Ricks, S.D., *Lexicon of Inscriptional Qatabanian*. Roma, 1989 (Dissertationes Scientificae de Rebus Orientis Antiqui, 14).

ROBIN 1976 a - Robin, C., "L'Arabie du Sud antique. Le royaume de Saba", *Bible et Terre Sainte*. 177 (1976), 1-17.

ROBIN 1976 b - Robin, C., "Résultats épigraphiques et archéologiques de deux brefs séjours en République Arabe du Yémen", *Semitica*. 26 (1976), 167-188.

ROBIN 1978 a - Robin, C., "Le problème de Hamdān: des qayls aux trois tribus", *PSAS*. 8 (1978), 46-52.

ROBIN 1978 - Robin, C., "Quelques graffites préislamiques de al-Ḫazā'in (Nord-Yémen)", *Semitica*. 28 (1978), 103-128, pl.III-VI.

ROBIN 1979 - Robin, C., *La cité et l'organisation sociale a Ma^{c}īn: L'exemple de Yṯl (aujourd'hui Barāqiš)*. - The Second International Symposium on Studies in the History of Arabia. Pre-Islamic Arabia (Dept. of History and Dept. of Archaeology. Faculty of Arts, University of Riyādh). 1399 / 1979.

ROBIN 1981 a - Robin, C., "Documents de l'Arabie antique II", *Raydān*. 4 (1981), 121-134.

ROBIN 1981 b - Robin, C., "Les inscriptions d'al-Mi^{c}sāl et la chronologie de l'Arabie méridionale au IIIe siècle de l'ère chrétienne", *CRAIBL*. 1981, 315-339.

ROBIN 1981 c - Robin, C., "Les montagnes dans la religion sudarabique", Stiegner 1981 b, 263-281.

ROBIN 1982 a - Robin, C., *Les hautes terres du Nord-Yémen avant l'Islam*. Istanbul, 1982, 2 vols.

ROBIN 1982 b - Robin, C., "Esquisse d'une histoire de l'organisation tribale en Arabie du Sud antique", Bonnenfant, P., ed., *La péninsule Arabique d'aujourd'hui*. T.II. *Etudes par pays*. Paris, 1982, 17-30.

ROBIN 1984 - Robin, C., "La civilisation de l'Arabie méridionale avant l'Islam", Chelhod *et al.* 1984, 195-223.

ROBIN 1986 - Robin, C., "Du nouveau sur les Yaz'anides", *PSAS*. 16 (1986), 181-197.

ROBIN 1987 a - Robin, C., "L'inscription Ir 40 de Bayt Ḍab^{c}ān et la tribu Ḏmry", Robin, Bāfaqīh 1987, 165-180.

ROBIN 1987 b - Robin, C., "Trois inscriptions sabéennes decouvertes près de Barāqish (Republique Arabe du Yémen)", *PSAS*. 17 (1987), 165-177.

ROBIN 1989 a - Robin, C., "Aux Origines de l'Etat Himyarite: Himyar et Dhu-Raydan", *Arabian Studies in Honour of Mahmoud Ghul*. Irbid - Wiesbaden, 1989, 104-112.

ROBIN 1989 b -Robin, C., [Rev.:] ABADY 3 (1986), *Bulletin critique des annales islamologiques*. 1989, N 2, 222-224.

ROBIN 1990 - Robin, C., "Première mention de Tyr chez les Minéens d'Arabie du Sud", *Semitica*. 39 (1990), 135-147, pl. V.

ROBIN 1991 a - Robin, C., "^{c}Amdān Bayyin Yuhaqbiḍ, roi de Saba' et ḏū-Raydān", Robin, C., ed., *Etudes sud-arabes, recueil offert a J.Ryckmans*. Louvain, 1991,

167-191 (Publications de l'institut orientaliste de Louvain, 39).

ROBIN 1991 b - Robin, C., ed., *L'Arabie antique de Karib'īl à Mahomet. Novelles données sur l'histoire des Arabes grâce aux inscriptions*. Aix-en-Provence, 1991 (Revue du Monde Musulman et de la Méditerranée, 61).

ROBIN 1991 c - Robin, C., "Cités, royaumes et empires de l'Arabie avant l'Islam", Robin 1991 b, 45-53.

ROBIN 1991 d - Robin, C., "Les écritures de l'Arabie avant l'Islam", Robin 1991 b, 127-137.

ROBIN 1991 e - Robin, C., "Quelques épisodes marquants de l'histoire sudarabique", Robin 1991 b, 55-70.

ROBIN 1991 f - Robin, C., "La pénétration des Arabes nomades au Yémen", Robin 1991 b, 71-88.

ROBIN 1991 g - Robin, C., "Les langues de la Péninsule Arabique", Robin 1991 b, 89-111.

ROBIN 1992 a - Robin, C., "Guerre et épidémie dans les royaumes d'Arabie du Sud, d'après une inscription datée (IIe siècle de l'ère chrétienne)", *CRAIBL*. 1992, 215-234.

ROBIN 1992 b - Robin, C., *Inventaire des inscriptions sudarabiques*. T.1. *Inabba', Haram, al-Kāfir, Kamna et al-Ḥarāshif*. Paris - Rome, 1992.

ROBIN 1993 - Robin, C., "A propos d'une nouvelle inscription du règne de Sha^{c}r^{um} Awtar, un reéxamen de l'éponymat sabéen à l'époque des rois de Saba' et dhū-Raydān", Nebes, N., ed., *Festschrift für Walter W. Müller*. Mainz, 1993 (in press).

ROBIN, BĀFAQĪH 1980 - Robin, C., and Bāfaqīh, M., "Inscriptions inédites du Maḥram Bilqīs (Mārib) au Musée de Bayḥān", *Raydān*. 3 (1980), 83-112.

ROBIN, BĀFAQĪH 1981 - Robin, C., and Bāfaqīh, M., "Deux nouvelles inscriptions de Radmān datant du IIe siècle de l'ère chrétinne", *Raydān*. 4 (1981), 67-90.

ROBIN, BĀFAQĪH 1987 - Robin, C., and Bāfaqīh, M.A., eds., *Ṣayhadica. Recherches sur les inscriptions de l'Arabie préislamique offertes par ses collègues au professeur A.F.L.Beeston*. Paris, 1987 (L'Arabie préislamique, 1).

ROBIN, BRON 1979 - Robin, C., and Bron, F., "Deux inscriptions sudarabiques du Haut-Yāfi^{c} (Sud-Yemen)", *Semitica*. 29 (1979), 137-145, pl.VIII.

ROBIN, RYCKMANS 1978 - Robin, C., and Ryckmans, J., "L'attribution d'un bassin a une divinité en Arabie du Sud antique", *Raydān*. 1 (1978), 39-64.

ROBIN, RYCKMANS 1980 - Robin, C., and Ryckmans, J., "Les inscriptions de al-Asāḥil, ad-Durayb et Ḫirbat Sa^{c}ūd (Mission Archéologique Française en République Arabe du Yemen: prospection des antiquités préislamiques, 1980)", *Raydān*. 3 (1980), 113-181, pl.1-30.

ROBIN, RYCKMANS 1982 a - Robin, C., and Ryckmans, J., "Dédicace de bassins rupestres antiques à proximité de Bāb al-Falag (Mārib)", *ABADY*. 1 (1982), 107-115.

ROBIN, RYCKMANS 1982 b - Robin, C., and Ryckmans, J., "Inscriptions sabéennes de Sirwāḥ remployées dans la maison de ^{c}Abd Allāh az-Zā'idī", *ABADY*. 1 (1982), 117-122.

ROUX 1964 - Roux, G., *Ancient Iraq*. London, 1964.

RYCKMANS 1949 - Ryckmans, G., "Inscriptions sud-arabes, huitième série", *Le Muséon*. 62 (1949), 55-124.

J. RYCKMANS 1951 - Ryckmans, J., *L'institution monarchique en Arabie Méridionale avant L'Islam (Ma^{c}īn et Saba')*. Louvain, 1951 (Bibliotheque du Muséon, 28).

G. RYCKMANS 1951 - Ryckmans, G., *Les religions arabes préislamiques*. 2-me ed.,

Louvaine, 1951 (Bibliothèque du Muséon, 26).
RYCKMANS 1953 - Ryckmans, G., "Inscriptions sud-arabes, dixième série", *Le Muséon*. 66 (1953), 267-317.
J. RYCKMANS 1954 - Ryckmans, J., [Rev.:] von Wissmann, Höfner 1952, *BiOr*. 11 (1954), 135-137.
G. RYCKMANS 1954 - Ryckmans, G., "Inscriptions sud-arabes, onzième série", *Le Muséon*. 67 (1954), 99-119.
RYCKMANS 1955 - Ryckmans, G., "Inscriptions sud-arabes, Douzième série", *Le Muséon*. 68 (1955), 297-312, pl.I.
RYCKMANS 1956 a - Ryckmans, G., "Inscriptions sud-arabes, Trezième série", *Le Muséon*. 69 (1956), 139-163, pl.I.
RYCKMANS 1956 b - Ryckmans, G., "Inscriptions sud-arabes, Quatorzième série", *Le Muséon*. 69 (1956), 369-389.
RYCKMANS 1957 - Ryckmans, G., "Inscriptions sud-arabes, Quinsième série", *Le Muséon*. 70 (1957), 97-126, pl.I-V.
RYCKMANS 1959 - Ryckmans, G., "Inscriptions sud-arabes, dix-septième série", *Le Muséon*. 72 (1959), 159-176, pl.I-III.
RYCKMANS 1960 - Ryckmans, G., "Inscriptions sud-arabes. Dix-huitième série", *Le Muséon*. 73 (1960), 5-25, pl.I-III.
RYCKMANS 1964 a - Ryckmans, J., "Chronologie des rois de Saba' et d̲ū-Raydān", *OA*. 3 (1964), 1-24.
RYCKMANS 1964 b - Ryckmans, J., *Chronologie des rois de Saba' et dū-Raydān*. Istanbul, 1964.
RYCKMANS 1966 - Ryckmans, J., "Himyaritica (2)", *Le Muséon*. 79 (1966), 475-500.
RYCKMANS 1967 - Ryckmans, J., "Le texte Sharafaddīn, Yemen, p.44, bas, droite", *Le Muséon*. 80 (1967), 508-512, pl.I.
RYCKMANS 1973 a - Ryckmans, J., "Le repas rituel dans la religion sud-arabe", *Symbolae biblicae et mesopotamicae Francisco Mario Theodore de Liagre Böhl dedicatae*. Leiden, 1973, 327-334.
RYCKMANS 1973 b - Ryckmans, J., "Un rite d'istisqā' au temple sabéen de Mārib", *Annuaire de l'Institut de Philologie et d'Histoire Orientales et Slaves. 20 (1968-1972) = Mélanges Jackue Pirenne*. Bruxelles, 1973, 379-388.
RYCKMANS 1974 a - Ryckmans, J., "Himyaritica (3)", *Le Muséon*. 87 (1974), 237-263.
RYCKMANS 1974 b - Ryckmans, J., "Himyaritica (4)", *Le Muséon*. 87 (1974), 493-521.
RYCKMANS 1975 - Ryckmans, J., "Himyaritica (5)", *Le Muséon*. 88 (1975), 199-219.
RYCKMANS 1980 a - Ryckmans, J., "L'inscription Iryani 18", *Raydān*. 3 (1980), 183-185.
RYCKMANS 1980 b - Ryckmans, J., "ᶜUzzā et Lāt dans les inscriptions sud-arabes: à propos de deux amulettes méconnues", *JSS*. 25 (1980) 193-204.
RYCKMANS 1983 - Ryckmans, J., *A Three Generations' Matrilineal Genealogy in a Ḥasaean Inscription: Matrilineal Ancestry in Pre-Islamic Arabia*. Revised text of paper presented at the "Bahrain Through the Ages" Conference (Bahrain, 3-10 December 1983).
RYCKMANS 1986 - Ryckmans, J., "Une écriture minuscule sud-arabe antique récemment découverte", Vanstiphout, H.L.J., *et al.*, eds., *Scripta Signa Vocis: Studies about Scripts, Scriptures, Scribes and Languages*. Groningen, 1986, 185-199.
RYCKMANS 1993 - Ryckmans, J., "Inscribed Old South Arabian Sticks and Palm-Leaf Stalks: An Introduction and a Palaeographical Approach", *PSAS*. 23 (1993),

127-140.

RYCKMANS *et al.* 1994 - Ryckmans, J., Müller, W.W., and ᶜAbdallāh, Yu., *Textes du Yémen Antique inscrits sur bois*. Louvain-la-Neuve, 1994 (Publications de l'Institut Orientaliste de Louvain, 43).

SAGGS 1984 - Saggs, H.W.F., *The Might that was Assyria*. London, 1984.

SAUER *ET AL.* 1988 - Sauer, J.A., Blakely J.A., Toplyn, M.R., Glanzman, W.D., Ghaleb, A.O., Grolier, M.J., Overstreet, W.C., and Tiede, L.J., "Archaeology along the Spice Route of Yemen", Potts, D.T., ed., *Araby the Blest*. Copenhagen, 1988 (CNI Publications, 7), 91-115.

SCHAFFER 1972 - Schaffer, B., *Sabäische Inschriften aus verschiedenen Fundorten (I. Teil)*. Wien, 1972 (SEG VII. - SBAW, 282/1).

SCHAFFER 1975 - Schaffer, B., *Sabäische Inschriften aus verschiedenen Fundorten (II. Teil)*. Wien, 1975 (SEG X. - SBAW. 299/3).

SCHMIDT 1969 - Schmidt, S.O., "Sovremennyye problemy istochnikovedeniya", Schmidt 1969, 7-58.

SCHMIDT 1969 - Schmidt, S.O., ed., *Istocnnikovedeniye. Teoreticheskiye i metodicheskiye problemy*. Moskva, 1969.

SCHMIDT 1988 a - Schmidt, J., "Ancient South Arabian Sacred Buildings", Daum 1988, 78-98.

SCHMIDT 1988 b - Schmidt, J., "The Sabaean Irrigation Economy of Mārib", Daum 1988, 55-62.

SEDOV 1992 - Sedov, A., Personal communication.

SERJEANT 1960 - Serjeant, R., [Rev.:] Bowen 1958 b, *BSOAS*. 23 (1960), 582-585.

SHARAFADDĪN 1967 - Sharafaddīn, A.H., *Ta'rīkh al-Yaman al-thaqāfī. Al-juz' al-thālith*. Al-Qāhirah, 1967.

SHIFMAN 1989 - Shifman, I.Sh., "Gosudarstvo v sisteme sotsialnyh institutov v drevney Palestine (vtoraya polovina III - pervaya polovina I tysyacheletiya do n.e.)", Dandamayev, M.A., ed., *Gosudarstvo i sotsialnyye struktury na drevnem Vostoke*. Moskva, 1989, 55-89.

SOLÁ SOLÉ 1964 - Solá Solé, J.M., *Inschriften aus Riyām*. Wien, 1964 (SEG IV - SBAW, 243/4).

STARK 1936 - Stark, F., "Notes on the Southern Incense Route of Arabia", *Islamic Culture*. 10 (1936), 193-212.

STIEGNER 1981 a - Stiegner, R.G., "Altsüdarabische Fragmente: Wādi al-Sirr (N.Jemen). 1978", Stiegner 1981 b, 325-346.

STIEGNER 1981 b - Stiegner, R.G., ed., *Al-Hudhud. Festschrift Maria Höfner zum 80. Geburstag*. Graz, 1981.

TATAROVA, TOLSTOVA 1987 - Tatarova, G.G., and Tolstova, Yu.N., "Rol apriornogo znaniya pri ispolzovanii matematicheskih metodov dlya izucheniya sotsialnyh yavleniy", Kovalchenko, I.D., ed., *Kompleksnyye metody v istoricheskih issledovaniyah*. Moskva, 1987, 52-53.

TOLSTOVA 1987 - Tolstova, Yu.N., "Rol soderzhatelnyh gipotez pri ispolzovanii matematiki v obshchestvennyh naukah", Poletayev, R.E., Kornakovskiy, I.L., eds., *Kompleksnyye metody v izuchenii istoricheskih protsessov*. Moskva, 1987, 6-24.

TSCHINKOWITZ 1969 - Tschinkovitz, H., *Kleine Fragmente (I. Teil)*. Wien, 1969 (SEG VI - SBAW, 261/4).

TSCHINKOWITZ-NAGLER 1975 - Tschinkowitz-Nagler, H., *Kleine Fragmente (II. Teil)*. Wien, 1975 (SEG XI - SBAW, 301/3).

URSUL 1973 - Ursul, A.D., *Otrazheniye i informatsiya*. Moskva, 1973.

VARISCO 1983 - Varisco, D., "Irrigation in an Arabian Valley: a System of Highland Terraces in the Yemen Arab Republic", *Expedition*. 25 (1983), 27-34.

VASILYEV 1980 - Vasilyev, L.S., "Stanovleniye politicheskoy administratsii (ot lokalnoy gruppy ohotnikov i sobirateley k protogosudarstvu-chiefdom)", *Narody Azii i Afriki*. 1980, N 1, 172-186.

VEDENOV, KREMYANSKIY 1965 - Vedenov, M.F., Kremyanskiy, V.I., "O spetsifike biologicheskih struktur". *Voprosy filosofii*. 1965, N 1, 84-94.

WADE 1979 - Wade, R., Archaeological Observations around Mārib 1976", *PSAS*. 9 (1979), 114-123.

WEIR 1991 - Weir, Sh., "Trade and Tribal Structures in North West Yemen", *Cahiers du GREMAMO*. 10 (1991), 87-101.

WEIR 1994 - Weir, Sh., Letter of 31 January, 1994.

WEIR 1995 - Weir, Sh., (Forthcoming monograph on the tribes of Rāziḥ [Northern Yemen]). London: British Museum Press, 1995.

WENNER 1967 - Wenner, M.W., *Modern Yemen: 1918-1966*. Baltimore, 1967.

VON WISSMANN 1964 a - von Wissmann, H., *Zur Geschichte und Landeskunde von Alt-Südarabien*. Wien, 1964 (SEG, III. SBAW, 246).

VON WISSMANN 1964 b - von Wissmann, H., "Ḥimyar: Ancient History", *Le Muséon*. 77 (1964), 429-497.

VON WISSMANN 1968 - von Wissmann, H., Zur Archäologie und Antiken Geographie von Südarabien. Istanbul, 1968.

VON WISSMANN 1975 - von Wissmann, H., *Die Geschichte von Saba'*. I. *Frühe Geschichte*. Wien, 1975 (SBAW, 301/5).

VON WISSMANN 1976 - von Wissmann, H., "Die Geschichte des Sabäerreichs und der Feldzug des Aelius Gallus", Temporini, H., ed., *Aufstieg und Niedergang der römischen Welt. Geschichte und Kultur Roms im Spiegel der neueren Forschung*. II. *Principat*. Neunter Band (1. Halbband). Berlin, 1976, 308-544.

VON WISSMANN 1981 - von Wissmann, H., *Araviya. Materialy po istorii otkrytiya*. Moskva, 1981.

VON WISSMANN 1982 - von Wissmann, H., *Die Geschichte von Saba'*. II. *Das Grossreich der Sabäer bis zu seinem Ende im frühen 4. Jh.v.Chr.* (Herausgegeben von W.W.Müller). Wien, 1982.

VON WISSMANN, HÖFNER 1952 - von Wissmann, H., and Höfner, M., *Beiträge zur historischen Geographie des vorislamischen Südarabien*. Mainz - Wiesbaden, 1952 (Akademie der Wissenschaften und der Literatur in Mainz. Abhandlungen der Geistes- und Sozialwissenschaften Klasse, 4).

YAKOBSON 1987 - Yakobson, V.A., "Chapter 1. Drevnyaya Mesopotamiya", in *Mezhgosudarstvennyye otnosheniya i diplomatiya na drevnem Vostoke*. Moskva, 1987, 6-28.

YAKOBSON 1989 - Yakobson, V.A., "Tsari i goroda drevney Mesopotamii", Dandamayev, M.A., ed., *Gosudarstvo i sotsialnyye struktury na drevnem Vostoke*. Moskva, 1989, 17-37.

SIGLA OF THE INSCRIPTIONS CITED

The system of epigraphic sigla used in the present monograph is based on the ones proposed by Avanzini (1977) and Beeston *et al.* (1982).

^{c}Abadān - Pirenne 1981
Alfieri - Corpus 1977
AM = Aden Museum - Corpus 1977; 1986
Ashm.Mus. - Beeston 1959
Be - Beeston 1962 c
BF-BT - Bāfaqīh, Bāṭāyi^{c} 1988
BR - Bāfaqīh, Robin 1979 a; b
Bron - Bron 1970; 1979
C = CIH - Corpus 1889-1908, 1911, 1929
CIAS = Corpus 1977,1986
DAE = Deutsche Aksum-Expedition - DAE 1913; Littmann 1950
DAI - Nebes 1992
DJE = Deutsche Jemen-Expedition - Müller 1972 a; b; c; 1974 d; 1978 b
Doe - Doe 1963; 1964; Beeston 1988 a
Er - Eryānī 1973; 1988; 1990; Bron 1992; Robin 1987 a; Ryckmans 1980 a; de Maigret 1988
Fa - Inscriptions discovered by A.Fakhry - Fakhry, Ryckmans 1952
Ga - Garbini 1969; 1970 a; b; 1971 a; b; 1973 a; b; c; d; 1974 b; 1976; 1978
Ghul - Bron 1992
Gl - Inscriptions from E. Glaser's collection - Botterweck 1950; Höfner 1954; 1973; 1976; 1981; Höfner, Solá Solé 1964; Lundin 1965 a; J.Ryckmans 1954; Schaffer 1972; 1975; Solá Solé 1964; Tschinkowitz 1969; Tschinkowitz-Nagler 1975
Gr - Inscriptions discovered by P.A. Gryaznevich - Piotrovskiy 1978
Gullen - Beeston 1988 c
Haram - Robin 1992 b
HI - Van Beek 1969
I = Itwah - Lundin 1974 a
^{c}Inān - ^{c}Inān 1396 H.; Bāfaqīh, Robin 1978
Ist. - Beeston 1952
Ja - Jamme 1954; 1955 a; b; c; 1956; 1957; 1958; 1962; 1966; 1970 a; b; 1971; 1972; 1976; 1980; 1981; 1982; 1986; Doe, Jamme 1968
al-Kāfir - Robin 1992 b
Kamna - Robin 1992 b
Kensdale - Kensdale 1953
Kortler - Müller 1978 a
Lu - Lundin 1963; 1966; 1969 b; 1972; 1973 b
M - Garbini 1974 a
M. Bayḥān - Bron 1988
Madrid - Diaz Esteban 1969
MAFRAY - Robin 1991 a; g; 1992 a; b; Robin, Bāfaqīh 1981; Robin, Ryckmans 1980; 1982 a; b
MAFY - Robin 1991 a
Moretti - Moretti 1971
Mü - Müller 1974 c

Müller/ Ṣirwāḥ - Müller 1976
NAM = National Aden Museum - Corpus 1986
Na NAG - Nāmī 1947; 1954; 1958; 1960; 1961; 1962
Na NNSQ - Nāmī 1943
Ph - Philby, Tritton 1944
Pirenne - Pirenne 1980, 1987
Q - Ricks 1989
R = RÉS - Répertoire 1929; 1935; 1950
RB - Robin, Bāfaqīh, 1980
Robin - Bron 1981; Robin 1978; 1981 a; Robin 1982 a, v.2; Robin, Ryckmans 1978
Robin, Bron/ Haut Yāfi^{c} - Robin, Bron 1979
Ry - G.Ryckmans 1949; 1953; 1954; 1955; 1956 a; b; 1957; 1959; 1960
Sa - Rathjens[, Höfner] 1966
Schm = Schmidt - Müller 1982 a; b; 1986 a; b; c; d; e; 1987 b
Sh - Sharafaddīn 1967; Loundine 1973 a; Lundin 1974 b; 1984; Müller 1974 a
Shib^{c}anu - Kitchen 1995
Ta = Muḥammad Taufīq's collection - Nāmī 1957
VL = Van Lessen's collection - Bron 1992; Ghul 1959
Y. - de Maigret 1981; 1988
YM = Yemen Museum (Ṣan^{c}ā') - Corpus 1977; Jamme 1982; 1986
YMN - ^{c}Abdallāh 1979.

INDEX

T

U

V

W

Y

Z